CW00972355

Oracle Job Scheduling

Creating robust task management v
Oracle 10g dbms_scheduler

Oracle In-Focus Series

Dr. Timothy S. Hall

This book is dedicated to every person I've met, every place I've been and every event I've experienced.

Dr. Timothy S. Hall

Oracle Job Scheduling
Creating robust task management with dbms_job and Oracle 10g dbms_scheduler

By Dr. Timothy S. Hall

Copyright © 2005 by Rampant TechPress. All rights reserved.

Printed in the United States of America.

Published in Kittrell, North Carolina, USA.

Oracle In-focus Series: Book #13

Series Editor: Donald K. Burleson

Editors: Janet Burleson, John Lavender, and Robin Haden

Production Editor: Teri Wade

Cover Design: Bryan Hoff

Printing History: April, 2005 for First Edition

Oracle, Oracle7, Oracle8, Oracle8i, Oracle9i and Oracle10g are trademarks of Oracle Corporation.

Many of the designations used by computer vendors to distinguish their products are claimed as Trademarks. All names known by Rampant TechPress to be trademark names appear in this text as initial caps.

Flame Warriors illustrations are copyright © by Mike Reed Illustrations Inc.

ISBN: 0-9744486-6-4

Library of Congress Control Number: 2005901259

Table of Contents

Using the Online Code Depot

Purchase of this book provides complete access to the online code depot that contains the sample code scripts. All of the code depot scripts in this book are available for download in zip format, ready to load and use and are located at the following URL:

rampant.cc/schedule.htm

If technical assistance is needed with downloading or accessing the scripts, please contact Rampant TechPress at info@rampant.cc.

Are you WISE?

Get the premier Oracle tuning tool. The Workload Interface Statistical Engine for Oracle provides unparallel capability for time-series Oracle tuning that is not available anywhere else.

WISE supplements Oracle Enterprise Manager and it can quickly plot and spot performance signatures to allow you to see hidden trends, fast. WISE interfaces with STATSPACK or AWR to provide unprecedented proactive tuning insights. Best of all, it is only $9.95 for the Standard Edition and $199.95 for the Enterprise Edition. Get WISE. Download now!

www.wise-oracle.com

Get the Oracle Script Collection

This is the complete Oracle script collection from Mike Ault and Donald Burleson, the world's best Oracle DBA's.

Packed with over 500 ready-to-use Oracle scripts, this is the definitive collection for every Oracle professional DBA. It would take many years to develop these scripts from scratch, making this download the best value in the Oracle industry.

It's only $39.95 (less than 7 cents per script!). For immediate download go to:

www.oracle-script.com

Conventions Used in this Book

It is critical for any technical publication to follow rigorous standards and employ consistent punctuation conventions to make the text easy to read.

However, this is not an easy task. Within Oracle there are many types of notation that can confuse a reader. Some Oracle utilities such as STATSPACK and TKPROF are always spelled in CAPITAL letters, while Oracle parameters and procedures have varying naming conventions in the Oracle documentation. It is also important to remember that many Oracle commands are case sensitive, and are always left in their original executable form, and never altered with italics or capitalization.

Parameters - All Oracle parameters will be *lowercase italics*. Exceptions to this rule are parameter arguments that are commonly capitalized (KEEP pool, TKPROF), these will be left in ALL CAPS.

Variables – All PL/SQL program variables and arguments will also remain in *lowercase italics* (*dbms_job, dbms_utility*).

Tables & dictionary objects – All data dictionary objects are referenced in lowercase italics (*dba_indexes, v$sql*). This includes all *v$* and *x$* views (*x$kcbcbh, v$parameter*) and dictionary views (*dba_tables, user_indexes*).

SQL – All SQL is formatted for easy use in the code depot, and all SQL is displayed in lowercase. The main SQL terms (select, from, where, group by, order by, having) will always appear on a separate line.

Programs & Products – All products and programs that are known to the author are capitalized according to the vendor specifications (IBM, DBXray, etc). All names known by Rampant TechPress to be trademark names appear in this text as initial caps. References to UNIX are always made in uppercase.

Acknowledgements

This type of highly technical reference book requires the dedicated efforts of many people. Even though we are the authors, our work ends when we deliver the content. After each chapter is delivered, several Oracle DBAs carefully review and correct the technical content. After the technical review, experienced copy editors polish the grammar and syntax.

The finished work is then reviewed as page proofs are turned over to the production manager, who arranges the creation of the online code depot and manages the cover art, printing distribution, and warehousing.

In short, the authors play a small role in the development of this book, and we need to thank and acknowledge everyone who helped bring this book to fruition:

Robert Tuttle, for the production management, including the coordination of the cover art, page proofing, printing, and distribution.

Teri Wade, for her help in the production of the page proofs.

Bryan Hoff, for his exceptional cover design and graphics.

Janet Burleson, for her assistance with the web site, and for creating the code depot and the online shopping cart for this book.

Many thanks to Don Burleson for starting the ball rolling.

Thanks to all the people at Rampant who were involved in the process of completing this book. It could never have happened this way without you.

Thanks to everyone who has influenced my journey.

Many thanks,

Jim

DR Timothy S. Hall

Preface

Job scheduling is a vital part of all databases regardless of the nature of the system they are designed to support. Some of the common tasks that require scheduling include:

- Database backups
- Batch operations such as data extracts and loads
- Archiving and/or cleanup of data
- Summarizing data to improve performance

This book starts by presenting an overview of the mechanisms available to schedule Oracle database tasks, including external operating system schedulers and the internal Oracle scheduler. Subsequent chapters focus on the usage of the internal Oracle scheduler.

The Oracle 10g scheduler is radically different to that of previous Oracle versions so explanations and examples are presented for Oracle 10g and previous versions where necessary.

Regards,

Tim

DR Timothy S. Hall

Overview of Oracle Job Scheduling

Ms. Post, would you please schedule some jobs for me?

Introduction

Job scheduling is an important but often overlooked part of every database environment. Even the simplest systems require scheduled jobs such as data loads, data extraction, report generation, backups and general cleanup. When scheduling these tasks, the DBA or developer has to make a choice whether to use an external scheduler provided by the operating system or an internal scheduler provided by the Oracle database.

This chapter introduces both external and internal schedulers, beginning with the external schedulers available in UNIX, Linux, and Windows systems.

External Oracle Job Scheduling

All popular operating systems have some form of job scheduler that can be used to schedule database specific tasks. In UNIX and Linux environments, the most established scheduler is CRON; while in Windows environments there are several schedulers available depending on the version of Windows being used. For this reason, each type of environment will be presented separately, starting with the CRON scheduler.

Using cron and crontab in UNIX and Linux

The CRON scheduler is available on both UNIX and Linux systems, allowing users to schedule operating system commands and shell scripts. The implementation of CRON varies slightly on each operating system, so it is worth checking the manual pages for *cron* and *crontab* to identify the specific files and paths used on the UNIX or Linux platform. The focus of the rest of this section will be on the implementation of CRON in the Red Hat Enterprise Linux AS distribution.

The CRON program is run as a daemon, typically with the name *cron* or *crond*. To identify if it is running, either of the following commands can be used:

```
ps -ef | grep crond | grep -v grep
root      2580      1  0 16:43 ?        00:00:00 crond

ps -ef | grep cron | grep -v grep
root      2580      1  0 16:43 ?        00:00:00 cron
```

Most UNIX and Linux implementations provide scripts that are located in an initialization directory and can be used to control daemon services. The specific location depends on the operating system, but several popular UNIX and Linux distributions use the */etc/init.d* directory. The following examples show how the CRON daemon can be controlled by calling its initialization script with the parameter relevant to the system, as indicated:

```
# Solaris and Red Hat Linux
/etc/init.d/crond start
/etc/init.d/crond restart
/etc/init.d/crond stop

# Tru64 and HP-UX
/sbin/init.d/cron start
/sbin/init.d/cron restart
/sbin/init.d/cron stop
```

Some operating systems provide command line tools for starting and stopping services. The following are available in Red Hat Linux:

```
service crond stop
Stopping crond:                                        [  OK  ]

service crond start
Starting crond:                                        [  OK  ]

service crond restart
Stopping crond:                                        [  OK  ]
Starting crond:                                        [  OK  ]
```

The simplest way to use *cron* in Red Hat Linux is to place the shell scripts into one of the following directories:

- */etc/cron.daily*

- */etc/cron.hourly*

- */etc/cron.monthly*

- */etc/cron.weekly*

The scripts will then be run at the time interval indicated by the directory name. The *cron* scheduler knows when to run these scripts due to the contents of the */etc/crontab* file. On Red Hat Linux, the default *crontab* script contains the following entries:

```
cat /etc/crontab

SHELL=/bin/bash
PATH=/sbin:/bin:/usr/sbin:/usr/bin
MAILTO=root
HOME=/

# run-parts
01 * * * * root run-parts /etc/cron.hourly
02 4 * * * root run-parts /etc/cron.daily
22 4 * * 0 root run-parts /etc/cron.weekly
42 4 1 * * root run-parts /etc/cron.monthly
```

The first part of the script sets up some environment variables, while the second part of the script schedules the jobs associated with the default directories. The *run-parts* script runs each of the scripts located in the specified directory.

With the exception of the environment setup, each line in the *crontab* file represents a scheduled task by using the following syntax:

```
field          allowed values
-----          --------------
minute         0-59
hour           0-23
day of month   1-31
month          1-12
day of week    0-7 (both 0 and 7 are Sunday)
user           Valid OS user
command        Valid command or script.
```

The date fields can contain a number of patterns to form complex schedules, as shown below.

```
*         - All available values or "first-last".
3-4       - A single range representing each possible from the start
to the end of the range inclusive.
1,2,5,6 - A specific list of values.
1-3,5-8 - A specific list of ranges.
0-23/2 - Every other value in the specified range.
```

In Red Hat Linux, the month and day names can be used to specify these fields. The following examples show a selection of possible schedules:

```
30 * * * * root echo "Runs at 30 minutes past the hour."
45 6 * * * root echo "Runs at 6:45 am every day."
45 18 * * * root echo "Runs at 6:45 pm every day."
00 1 * * 0 root echo "Runs at 1:00 am every Sunday."
00 1 * * 7 root echo "Runs at 1:00 am every Sunday."
00 1 * * Sun root echo "Runs at 1:00 am every Sunday."
30 8 1 * * root echo "Runs at 8:30 am on the first day of every month."
00 0-23/2 02 07 * root echo "Runs every other hour on the 2nd of July."
```

Comments must be on separate lines and must be preceded by a # character. The contents of the */etc/crontab* file should not be edited directly but via the *crontab* command, which has the following usage syntax:

```
usage:  crontab [-u user] file
        crontab [-u user] { -e | -l | -r }
                (default operation is replace, per 1003.2)
        -e      (edit user's crontab)
        -l      (list user's crontab)
        -r      (delete user's crontab)
```

As the usage indicates, only user-specific entries can be edited via the *crontab* command. There are essentially two ways of editing the contents of the */etc/crontab* file using this command. The *crontab -e* command opens the current user's *crontab* file in the default editor specified by the EDITOR environment variable. Any changes are applied to the *crontab* file when the editor saves the file. Alternatively, a text file can be produced containing the current users *crontab* entries by issuing the *crontab -l > filename* command.

Once this file is altered, the amendments can be applied by issuing the *crontab filename* command:

```
# Produce the file.
crontab -l > /tmp/mycrontab.txt

# Edit the file.
vi /tmp/mycrontab.txt

# Apply the modified file.
crontab /tmp/mycrontab.txt
```

The syntax of the entries is the same as that specified earlier with the exception of the *user* field. This is not specified, as it is defined on the command line or defaults to the current user. By default, all users can schedule their own jobs, but access can be controlled by creating or editing the contents of the */etc/cron.allow* and */etc/cron.deny* files. If these files are not present, all users can access schedule jobs. If only the *cron.deny* file is present, it is assumed that all users specified in this file are not allowed to schedule jobs. Likewise, if only the *cron.allow* file is present, it is assumed that only users specified in this file are allowed to schedule jobs. The absence of a file is the equivalent of the file being present containing the word ALL.

By default, the output from a job is electronically mailed to the owner of the job or the user specified by the *mailto* variable. If this is unacceptable, the output can be redirected in a number of ways including:

```
# Mail the output of the job to another user.
command | mail -s "Subject: Output of job" user

# Standard output redirected to a file.
command >> file.log

# Standard output and standard error redirected to a file.
command >> logfile 2>&1

# Throw all the output away.
command >> /dev/null 2>&1
```

Since the CRON scheduler has been explained, the focus will now shift to the schedulers available in Windows environments.

Using the Windows Job Schedulers

AT.EXE

The AT command can be used to schedule commands and programs on Windows NT, Windows 2000, Windows XP and Windows 2003. For the command to work, the scheduler service must be running. On Windows 2000, this can be done using the services dialog (Start → Programs → Administrative Tools → Services) or from the command line using the *net* command:

```
net stop "Task Scheduler"
net start "Task Scheduler"
```

The *at /?* command produces the following:

```
AT [\\computername] [ [id] [/DELETE] | /DELETE [/YES]]
AT [\\computername] time [/INTERACTIVE]
    [ /EVERY:date[,...] | /NEXT:date[,...]] "command"
```

\\computername scheduled on the	Specifies a remote computer. Commands are
	local computer if this parameter is omitted.
id scheduled	Is an identification number assigned to a
	command.
/delete all the	Cancels a scheduled command. If id is omitted,
	scheduled commands on the computer are canceled.
/yes	Used with cancel all jobs command when no further confirmation is desired.
time	Specifies the time when command is to run.
/interactive the user	Allows the job to interact with the desktop of
	who is logged on at the time the job runs.
/every:date[,...] week or	Runs the command on each specified day(s) of the
month	month. If date is omitted, the current day of the
	is assumed.
/next:date[,...] of the	Runs the specified command on the next occurrence
	day (for example, next Thursday). If date is
omitted, the	
	current day of the month is assumed.
"command" run.	Is the Windows NT command, or batch program to be

A couple of simple examples of its use include:

```
C:> at 21:00 /every:m,t,th,f "c:\jobs\MyJob.bat"
Added a new job with job ID = 1

C:> at 6:00 /next:20 "c:\jobs\MyJob.bat"
Added a new job with job ID = 2
```

The first example schedules a job which runs the *c:\jobs\MyJob.bat* script at 9:00 p.m. on Mondays, Tuesdays, Thursdays and Fridays. The second example schedules a job that runs the script at 6:00 a.m. on the next 20th of the month.

User ID = reader, Password = program

The current list of jobs can be displayed by issuing the *at* command with no parameters:

```
C:\>at
Status ID   Day                 Time       Command Line
-----------------------------------------------------------------
       1    Each M T Th F       21:00 PM   c:\jobs\MyJob.bat
       2    Next 20             06:00 AM   c:\jobs\MyJob.bat

C:\>
```

Jobs can be deleted using the */delete* option:

```
C:\>at 1 /delete

C:\>at 2 /delete

C:\>at
There are no entries in the list.

C:\>
```

The AT scheduler has been at the heart of Windows scheduling for some years, but recent Windows versions have introduced simpler and more flexible alternatives, which will be covered in the following section.

Scheduled Tasks Wizard

In Windows 2000, Windows XP, and Windows 2003 there is a GUI tool called the Scheduled Tasks Wizard, which is far more convenient than the AT command. It is available from the Control Panel or from the task bar (Start → Programs → Accessories → System Tools → Scheduled Tasks).

The resulting dialog lists the current scheduled tasks and an Add Scheduled Task icon, as seen in Figure 1.1.

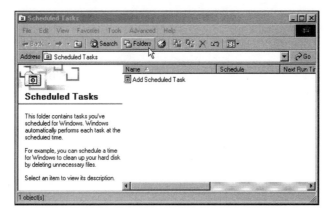

Figure 1.1 – *Scheduled Tasks dialog with no scheduled jobs*

To schedule a new task, simply double click on the *Add Scheduled Task* icon, which starts the Scheduled Tasks Wizard as shown in Figure 1.2.

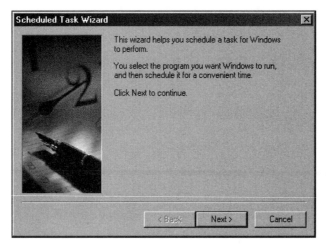

Figure 1.2 – *Scheduled Tasks Wizard*

Clicking the *Next* button produces a list of programs that can be scheduled as shown in Figure 1.3. If the program or script that is desired is not available in the list, the *Browse* button allows the user to select alternatives from the file system.

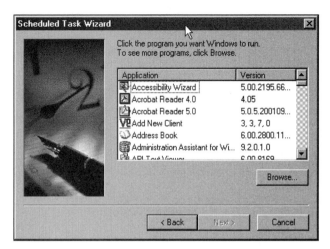

Figure 1.3 – *Scheduled Tasks Wizard: program list*

Once the relevant command or script is selected, clicking the *Next* button displays a screen that allows a name and basic schedule to be associated with the task as shown in Figure 1.4.

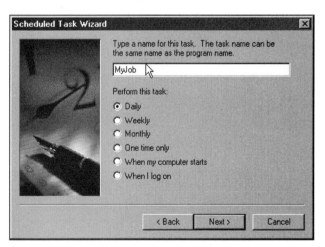

Figure 1.4 – *Scheduled Tasks Wizard: name and basic schedule*

The contents of the next screen vary depending on the type of basic schedule selected. Figure 1.5 shows the additional schedule information that can be defined for a daily task.

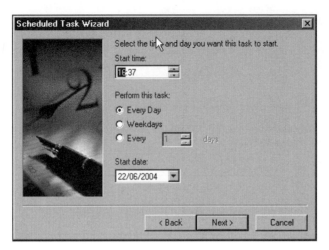

Figure 1.5 – *Scheduled Tasks Wizard: additional scheduling options*

The next screen, Figure 1.6, permits authorization credentials for the task to be assigned, allowing the task to run as any valid operating system user. It is important that tasks run with the correct credentials, as running tasks under privileged accounts can introduce potential security holes.

Figure 1.6 – *Scheduled Tasks Wizard: authorization details*

Finally, a summary page is displayed, as shown in Figure 1.7, which gives the option of displaying the advanced properties dialog once the job definition is complete. If this option is left unchecked, clicking the *Finish* button displays the original scheduled tasks list.

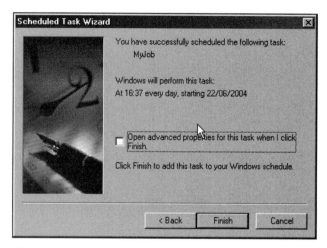

Figure 1.7 – *Scheduled Tasks Wizard: summary*

The newly scheduled task is now displayed in the scheduled tasks dialog as shown in Figure 1.8.

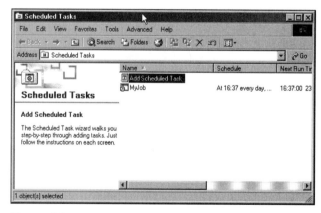

Figure 1.8 – *Scheduled Tasks dialog with newly scheduled job listed*

Right clicking on the job and selecting the *Properties* option from the pop-up menu in Figure 1.9, displays the advanced properties dialog. This dialog allows the task definition to be modified after it is created.

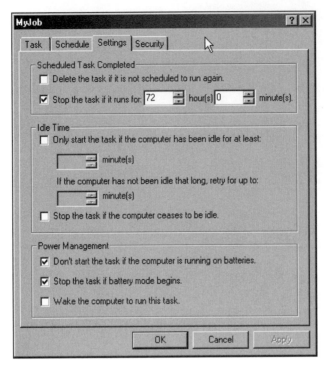

Figure 1.9 – *Scheduled job properties dialog*

The following section will present the SCHTASKS command which provides a more feature rich command line alternative to the AT command.

SCHTASKS.EXE

The SCHTASKS command was introduced in Windows XP and Windows 2003 as a more flexible and slightly more verbose replacement for the AT command. The AT command is still available for backwards compatibility, but it is no longer the preferred command line scheduling method.

As with Windows 2000, the simplest way to schedule jobs in Windows XP and Windows 2003 is via the Scheduled Tasks Wizard; however, the SCHTASKS command provides a command line API for situations in which a command line approach is preferable.

The usage notes for the SCHTASKS command are very comprehensive and include examples as well as basic syntax. The top level usage notes are displayed below, with examples indicating how more parameter specific usage notes can be obtained.

```
C:\>SCHTASKS /?

SCHTASKS /parameter [arguments]

Description:
    Enables an administrator to create, delete, query, change, run
and
    end scheduled tasks on a local or remote system. Replaces
AT.exe.

Parameter List:
    /Create        Creates a new scheduled task.

    /Delete        Deletes the scheduled task(s).

    /Query         Displays all scheduled tasks.

    /Change        Changes the properties of scheduled task.

    /Run           Runs the scheduled task immediately.

    /End           Stops the currently running scheduled task.

    /?             Displays this help/usage.

Examples:
    SCHTASKS
    SCHTASKS /?
    SCHTASKS /Run /?
    SCHTASKS /End /?
    SCHTASKS /Create /?
    SCHTASKS /Delete /?
    SCHTASKS /Query  /?
    SCHTASKS /Change /?
```

To schedule a job that runs the *c:\jobs\MyJob.bat* script at 9:00 p.m. on Mondays, Tuesdays, Thursdays and Fridays; do the following commands would be used:

```
SCHTASKS /Create /TN MyJob /TR C:\Jobs\MyJob.bat /ST 21:00:00 /SC
weekly /D MON,TUE,THU,FRI
The task will be created under current logged-on user name
("tim_hall").
Please enter the run as password for tim_hall: ******

SUCCESS: The scheduled task "MyJob" has successfully been created.
```

Once a task is created, it can be viewed by issuing the SCHTASKS command with no parameters:

```
C:\>SCHTASKS

TaskName                                  Next Run Time            Status
======================================= ========================
MyJob                                     21:00:00, 04/06/2004
```

Tasks that are no longer needed can be deleted using the /*delete* option:

```
C:\>SCHTASKS /delete /TN MyJob
WARNING: Are you sure you want to remove the task "MyJob" (Y/N )? y
SUCCESS: The scheduled task "MyJob" was successfully deleted.

C:\>SCHTASKS
INFO: There are no scheduled tasks present in the system.

C:\>
```

Since some of the external schedulers available on the most common operating systems have been presented, the following section will focus on the internal schedulers provided by the Oracle database.

Internal Oracle Job Scheduling

The Oracle scheduler allows jobs to be scheduled to run at a later date, or on a repeating cycle. Information about the scheduling session's environment is stored along with the scheduled job, allowing jobs to run in a consistent environment each time. Scheduled jobs are placed on a job queue that is managed by a coordinator process, which periodically scans the job queue looking for jobs to execute. When necessary, the coordinator process spawns job slaves to execute the jobs. The basic architecture of the Oracle scheduler is shown in Figure 1.10.

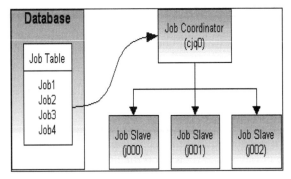

Figure 1.10 – *Oracle Scheduler Architecture*

The basic architecture of Oracle 9i and Oracle 10g schedulers may be similar, but the functionality and associated APIs are quite different. The Oracle 9i scheduler is extremely basic and a little clumsy, while the Oracle 10g scheduler is packed with features allowing job scheduling to be as simple or complicated as desired. The original scheduler API has been retained in Oracle 10g for backwards compatibility, and it is this scheduler that will be focused on first.

Oracle 9i Scheduler Overview

In Oracle9i, the *job_queue_processes* parameter sets an upper limit for the number of job slaves that can be spawned to execute jobs. The value assigned must be between 0-1000; with zero being the default. When the value is greater than zero, the job coordinator background process (cjq0) is started and remains active until the instance is shut down or the parameter is set to a value of zero. The *job_queue_processes* parameter is dynamic, so it can be set using the ALTER SYSTEM command, as shown in the following code.

```
SQL> alter system set job_queue_processes=10;

System altered.

SQL> show parameter job_queue_processes

NAME                                  TYPE         VALUE
------------------------------------- ------------ --------------------
job_queue_processes                   integer      10
```

Each node in a Real Application Cluster (RAC) installation can have different settings for the *job_queue_processes* parameter.

The job coordinator periodically scans the *job$* table looking for jobs to execute. When it finds a job to execute, it spawns a job queue slave process (j000 to j999) and passes the job to it. Once the job slave has completed executing a job, it requests another job from the job coordinator. If a job is not available, the job slave switches to an idle state, periodically requesting more work. If the job slave remains idle for too long, it terminates and is re-spawned as needed.

For a long time, the *dbms_job* package has been the focus of Oracle's internal job scheduling, providing a simple API that allows jobs to be created, modified and deleted. The usage of the *dbms_job* package is included in more detail in Chapter 2; however, the following example gives an indication of how a simple job can be scheduled using it:

```
VARIABLE l_job NUMBER;

BEGIN
  DBMS_JOB.submit (
    job       => :l_job,
    what      => 'BEGIN NULL; /* Do Nothing */ END;',
    next_date => SYSDATE,
    interval  => 'SYSDATE + 1 /* 1 Day */');

  COMMIT;
END;
/

PRINT l_job
```

In the above example, an anonymous PL/SQL block is scheduled to run instantly, then rerun every 24 hours indefinitely. A quick look at the contents of the anonymous block reveals that it doesn't actually do anything, but it could easily contain DML or a database procedure call.

If the *dbms_job* package was the past, the *dbms_scheduler* package is the future and is the focus of the next section.

Oracle 10g Scheduler Overview

By default the Oracle 10g job coordinator is not permanently running. It is started and stopped, as required. If the database detects any jobs that must be executed or windows opened in the near future, the job coordinator process (cjq0) is started. If there is no current job activity and no open windows, the job coordinator is stopped.

The job coordinator spawns as many job slaves (j000 to j999) as are needed to execute the outstanding jobs, making the *job_queue_processes* parameter redundant in Oracle 10g. A job slave gathers metadata from the scheduler tables to enable it to execute a job. Upon completion of a job, the slave process updates any relevant information in the job table, inserts data into the job run history and requests another job from the job coordinator. If a job is not available, the job slave sleeps until there is work to do. The job coordinator periodically terminates idle job slaves to reduce the slave pool.

The job table used by the scheduler is implemented using Oracle Advanced Queuing (AQ) and the supporting tables listed below.

```
select
   table_name
from
   user_tables
where
   table_name like '%SCHEDULER$_JOB%'
;

TABLE_NAME
------------------------------
SCHEDULER$_JOB_RUN_DETAILS
SCHEDULER$_JOB_STEP_STATE
AQ$_SCHEDULER$_JOBQTAB_S
SCHEDULER$_JOB
SCHEDULER$_JOBQTAB
SCHEDULER$_JOB_ARGUMENT
SCHEDULER$_JOB_CHAIN
SCHEDULER$_JOB_STEP
AQ$_SCHEDULER$_JOBQTAB_G
AQ$_SCHEDULER$_JOBQTAB_H
AQ$_SCHEDULER$_JOBQTAB_I
AQ$_SCHEDULER$_JOBQTAB_T

12 rows selected.
```

In addition to the conceptual job table, the scheduler uses several other tables to store metadata about scheduler objects.

```
select
   table_name
from
   user_tables
where
   table_name like '%SCHEDULER$%'
and
   table_name not like '%SCHEDULER$_JOB%'
;

TABLE_NAME
------------------------------
SCHEDULER$_EVENT_LOG
SCHEDULER$_WINDOW_DETAILS
SCHEDULER$_CHAIN_VARLIST
SCHEDULER$_CLASS
SCHEDULER$_GLOBAL_ATTRIBUTE
SCHEDULER$_OLDOIDS
SCHEDULER$_PROGRAM
SCHEDULER$_PROGRAM_ARGUMENT
SCHEDULER$_SCHEDULE
```

```
SCHEDULER$_WINDOW
SCHEDULER$_WINDOW_GROUP
SCHEDULER$_WINGRP_MEMBER

12 rows selected.
```

Under normal circumstances, one would not expect to interact with any of the scheduler tables directly. Information about the scheduler is displayed using the *dba_scheduler_%* views, and the *dbms_scheduler* package is used for the creation and manipulation of several scheduler objects including:

- Schedules - Components that define repeat intervals, allowing several jobs and windows to share a single schedule definition.

- Programs - Components that define the work done by a job, allowing multiple jobs to share a single definition.

- Jobs - Scheduled jobs that can be defined as individual entities or defined using existing schedules and programs.

- Job Classes - Logical groupings of jobs that have similar resource and administration requirements. Job classes provide a link between the scheduler and the resource manager.

- Windows - Components that define a period of time and link it to a specific resource plan, allowing the automatic control of system resources allocated to scheduled jobs.

- Window Groups - Logical grouping of windows.

These scheduler objects and the usage of the *dbms_scheduler* package are presented in greater detail in subsequent chapters. However, the following example demonstrates how a simple job can be scheduled in Oracle 10g.

```
BEGIN
  DBMS_SCHEDULER.create_job (
    job_name        => 'dummy_job',
    job_type        => 'PLSQL_BLOCK',
    job_action      => 'BEGIN NULL; /* Do Nothing */ END;',
    start_date      => SYSTIMESTAMP,
    repeat_interval => 'SYSTIMESTAMP + 1 /* 1 Day */');
END;
/
```

The above example is the Oracle 10g equivalent of the job defined in the previous Oracle 9i section. From a quick look at this example, one might conclude that there is little difference between the old and the new schedulers; however, that would be an incorrect assumption.

For backwards compatibility, it is possible to schedule jobs using both the *dbms_job* and *dbms_scheduler* packages in Oracle 10g. When jobs are scheduled using the *dbms_job* package, they are still dependant on the *job_queue_processes* parameter. When this parameter is set to zero, jobs scheduled using the *dbms_job* package will not run, but those scheduled using the *dbms_scheduler* package will still run normally.

If the parameter is set to a non-zero value, the job coordinator will run permanently, but the value will only constrain the number of job slaves that can be started to run jobs scheduled using the *dbms_job* package. The value has no affect on the number of job slave processes that are allocated to jobs scheduled using the *dbms_scheduler* package.

The next section will provide a brief comparison of the features available in the old and in the new style Oracle schedulers.

Features Comparison between *dbms_job* and *dbms_scheduler*

The Oracle 10g scheduler has significantly more functionality than its predecessor, which invariably results in it having a significantly more feature rich API. The following table, Table 1.1, provides a brief feature comparison between the *dbms_job* and *dbms_scheduler* packages.

Feature	dbms_job	dbms_scheduler
Schedule jobs based on anonymous PL/SQL blocks.	Yes	Yes
Schedule jobs based on PL/SQL procedures.	Yes	Yes
Schedule jobs based on operating system command and executable scripts.	No	Yes
Schedule reoccurring jobs with a repeat interval based on a PL/SQL expression that equates to a DATE or TIMESTAMP.	Yes	Yes
Schedule reoccurring jobs with a repeat interval based on an INTERVAL.	Yes	Yes

Feature	dbms_job	dbms_scheduler
Schedule reoccurring jobs with a repeat interval based on a calendar syntax expression.	No	Yes
Schedule reoccurring jobs with a repeat interval based on predefined Schedule object.	No	Yes
Schedule reoccurring jobs with a repeat interval based on predefined Window object.	No	Yes
Modify attributes of jobs that are already scheduled.	Yes	Yes
Assign priorities to jobs.	No	Yes
Provide extensive and configurable job run history.	No	Yes
Group related jobs into a Job Class to simplify job administration.	No	Yes
Allow multiple jobs to share a single schedule definition.	No	Yes
Allow multiple jobs to share a single program, or action, definition.	No	Yes
Link groups of jobs directly to resource manager consumer groups.	No	Yes
Define complex timetables for automatic resource plan switches using Windows.	No	Yes
Limit jobs to a single instance in a RAC configuration.	Yes	Yes
Limit jobs to a group of instances within a RAC configuration using Service definitions.	No	Yes
Allow jobs to run on several nodes in a RAC configuration, but define a basic preference list.	No	Yes
Provide full integration of job creation and modification in Oracle Enterprise Manager.	Yes	Yes
Provide full integration of job creation and modification in Oracle Enterprise Manager.	Yes	Yes

Feature	dbms_job	dbms_scheduler
Provide privileges and roles specifically for the scheduler to increase control over the scheduling of jobs.	No	Yes

Table 1.1 - *Features comparison between the dbms_job and dbms_scheduler packages*

The next section presents an overview of the approach that can be taken during the migration of jobs from the old to the new scheduler.

Migrating from *dbms_job* to *dbms_scheduler*

This section will introduce options available for migrating jobs from the *dbms_job* package to the *dbms_scheduler* package. Depending on how simple or complex the process is, it is a matter of personal preference how far through this migration process to go.

Since Oracle 10g supports both the *dbms_job* and *dbms_scheduler* packages, it may be wise to continue running existing jobs until familiar with all the features of the new scheduler. This "do nothing" approach is only a temporary option as the original scheduler is retained for backwards compatibility only. There is no guarantee that it will be present in future versions of the database, so take steps now to future-proof the system.

When deciding to start converting jobs, the easiest option is to use the new scheduler the same way the old one was used. In previous sections, a simple example of each scheduling mechanism was presented.

```
-- Old scheduler.
VARIABLE l_job NUMBER;
BEGIN
  DBMS_JOB.submit (
    job       => :l_job,
    what      => 'BEGIN NULL; /* Do Nothing */ END;',
    next_date => SYSDATE,
    interval  => 'SYSDATE + 1 /* 1 Day */');

  COMMIT;
END;
/
PRINT l_job
```

```
-- New scheduler.
BEGIN
  DBMS_SCHEDULER.create_job (
    job_name        => 'dummy_job',
    job_type        => 'PLSQL_BLOCK',
    job_action      => 'BEGIN NULL; /* Do Nothing */ END;',
    start_date      => SYSTIMESTAMP,
    repeat_interval => 'SYSTIMESTAMP + 1 /* 1 Day */');
END;
/
```

By comparing these examples, it is noted that conversion of basic jobs is quite simple, involving the following steps:

- Define a meaningful *job_name* for the new job.

- Assign a *job_action* of PLSQL_BLOCK.

- Use the *what* value from the old job as the *job_action* value in the new job.

- Use SYSTIMESTAMP for the *start_date* value.

- Use the *interval* value from the old job as the *repeat_interval* value in the new job, making sure the result of the expression is a TIMESTAMP not a DATE.

Once this conversion has been completed for all jobs, there is freedom from using the old scheduler, so the *job_queue_processes* parameter can now be set to zero.

```
alter system set job_queue_processes=0;
```

Next, the use of the calendar syntax to replace the PL/SQL expressions used in the *repeat_interval* should be investigated. The calendar syntax is easier to read than a PL/SQL expression and always results in a specific run time, rather than a drifting interval. The previous *repeat_interval* value could be altered as shown below, scheduling the job to run every day at 6:00 a.m.

```
repeat_interval => 'freq=daily; byhour=6; byminute=0; bysecond=0'
```

Once the basic jobs are converted, the next step might be to identify common *job_action* and *repeat_interval* values that can be used to create programs and schedules, respectively. The job definitions can then be revised to use these sharable components, allowing a single point for management of job definitions.

If control of the resources allocated to jobs is desired, related jobs can be grouped into job classes which are linked to specific resource consumer groups. In addition, window definitions permit automatic switching of the server's active resource plan, which allows the automatic process of altering resource usage over time.

Conclusion

This chapter has outlined the various scheduling mechanisms available, both external and internal to the database including:

- The use of the CRON scheduler in UNIX and Linux environments.

- The use of several Windows schedulers including AT, SCHTASKS and the Scheduled Tasks Wizard.

- An overview of the functionality of the Oracle scheduler prior to Oracle 10g.

- An overview of the functionality of the Oracle 10g scheduler.

- A feature comparison between the new and the old Oracle schedulers.

- An overview of the process of migrating jobs from the old to the new scheduler.

The next chapter will reveal the syntax for creating scheduled jobs using both the old and the new Oracle scheduler.

Configuring Oracle Job Scheduling

Taming the Job Scheduling beast

Introduction

This chapter will present information on how to schedule Oracle jobs using the *dbms_job* and *dbms_scheduler* packages supplied by Oracle. The *dbms_scheduler* package was introduced in Oracle 10g, so the example code associated with these sections will not work on previous versions. Where appropriate, Enterprise Manager (EM) screen shots will be used to illustrate the GUI/Web alternative to using the PL/SQL API.

The example code shows how objects can be created, manipulated and dropped. In a number of cases, code examples rely on previously created objects, which may have already been dropped, so they will have to be recreated before it will be possible to move on.

The following section will detail how to set up a test environment to enable the running of any example code.

Setting up a Test Environment

In order to use the examples in this chapter, it is necessary to create a user to work with and define a task to schedule. The following code creates a user called *"job_user"* and grants it the necessary privileges. Some privileges used are specific for Oracle 10g and should be ignored if a prior version is used.

```
conn sys/password as sysdba

-- Create user.
create user job_user identified by job_user default tablespace users
quota unlimited on users;
grant connect to job_user;
grant select_catalog_role to job_user;

-- Privileges for task, not for dbms_job.
grant create procedure to job_user;
grant execute on dbms_lock to job_user;
grant execute on dbms_system to job_user;

-- Oracle 10g only.
grant create job to job_user;
grant manage scheduler to job_user;

conn job_user/job_user
```

The MANAGE SCHEDULER privilege should only be granted when a user must administer job classes, windows and window groups. These objects provide a link between the scheduler and the resource manager, a feature which had traditionally required the DBA role. The roles and privileges associated with the 10g scheduler will be presented in the following text.

In the previous script, a system privilege and an object privilege were granted to *job_user* to allow the creation of a task to schedule. The following script creates a database procedure that will be used throughout this book when creating jobs. This procedure uses the *dbms_system* package to write a user defined string to the alert log at the start and end of the job. The body of the procedure loops 100 times with a sleep of one second in each loop. It also uses the *dbms_application_info* package to write information to the *v$session* and *v$session_longops* views. The use of the *dbms_system* and *dbms_application_info* packages will be covered in more detail in Chapter 5 of this text.

```
-- ***************************************************
-- Copyright © 2005 by Rampant TechPress
-- This script is free for non-commercial purposes
-- with no warranties.  Use at your own risk.
--
-- To license this script for a commercial purpose,
-- contact info@rampant.cc
-- ***************************************************
-- Parameters:
--    1) Text to identify this test job.
-- *********************************************************************

CREATE OR REPLACE PROCEDURE my_job_proc (p_text  IN  VARCHAR2) AS
   l_rindex   PLS_INTEGER;
   l_slno     PLS_INTEGER;
   l_total    NUMBER;
   l_obj      PLS_INTEGER;
BEGIN
   SYS.DBMS_SYSTEM.ksdwrt(2, 'MY_JOB_PROC Start: ' || p_text);

   DBMS_APPLICATION_INFO.set_module(
     module_name => 'my_job_proc',
     action_name => p_text || ': Start.');

   l_rindex    := Dbms_Application_Info.Set_Session_Longops_Nohint;
   l_total := 100;

   FOR i IN 1 .. l_total LOOP
     DBMS_APPLICATION_INFO.set_action(
       action_name => p_text || ': Sleep ' || i || ' of ' || l_total
|| '.');

     DBMS_APPLICATION_INFO.set_session_longops(
       rindex       => l_rindex,
       slno         => l_slno,
       op_name      => 'MY_JOB_PROC',
       target       => l_obj,
       context      => 0,
       sofar        => i,
       totalwork    => l_total,
       target_desc  => 'MY_JOB_PROC',
       units        => 'loops');

     DBMS_LOCK.sleep(1);
   END LOOP;

   DBMS_APPLICATION_INFO.set_action(
     action_name => p_text || ': End.');

   SYS.DBMS_SYSTEM.ksdwrt(2, 'MY_JOB_PROC End: ' || p_text);
END;
/
SHOW ERRORS
```

The procedure can be tested by calling it from SQL*Plus as follows:

```
SQL> exec my_job_proc('Test It!');
```

Once the procedure has completed, the alert log should contain an entry that looks similar to the following:

```
Sat Jun 19 12:29:16 2004
MY_JOB_PROC Start: Test It!
Sat Jun 19 12:30:59 2004
MY_JOB_PROC End: Test It!
```

Obviously, these entries may be separated by other messages, depending on what else has happened on the instance during the time it took for the job to run.

Now that the user named *job_user* has been created and granted privileges, it is time to schedule jobs. The first step is the examination of the *dbms_job* package.

Overview and Examples of *dbms_job* Functions

Prior to Oracle 10g, the *dbms_job* package was the preferred method for scheduling Oracle jobs. With this package, jobs are created using either the submit or isubmit procedures, whose call specifications are displayed below:

```
PROCEDURE isubmit (
  job       IN  BINARY_INTEGER,
  what      IN  VARCHAR2,
  next_date IN  DATE,
  interval  IN  VARCHAR2 DEFAULT 'null',
  no_parse  IN  BOOLEAN DEFAULT FALSE)

PROCEDURE submit (
  job       OUT BINARY_INTEGER,
  what      IN  VARCHAR2,
  next_date IN  DATE DEFAULT sysdate,
  interval  IN  VARCHAR2 DEFAULT 'null',
  no_parse  IN  BOOLEAN DEFAULT FALSE,
  instance  IN  BINARY_INTEGER DEFAULT 0,
  force     IN  BOOLEAN DEFAULT FALSE)
```

The parameters associated with these procedures and their usage are as follows:

- *job* - A number that uniquely identifies the job.

- *what* - A string that specifies the actual work that should be executed by the job.

- *next_date* - A date that specifies the next time the job will run.

- *interval* - A string that is evaluated when the job is executed to determine the next time the job should run. The value NULL means the job should not run again.

- *no_parse* - A boolean that indicates if the validity of the job specified in the what parameter should be checked.

- *instance* - The instance number that is allowed to run this job, allowing the job queue affinity to be set. By default, any instance can run the job.

- *force* - If TRUE, this parameter prevents errors when the job is defined against an instance that is not running.

The *isubmit* procedure allows the user to create a job and specify their own job number for it; whereas, the submit procedure allocates a job number for the user. The following examples show how to use these procedures to schedule the *my_job_proc* procedure to run immediately, then once every hour after that.

```
BEGIN
  DBMS_JOB.isubmit (
    job       => 99,
    what      => 'my_job_proc(''DBMS_JOB.ISUBMIT Example.'');',
    next_date => SYSDATE,
    interval  => 'SYSDATE + 1/24 /* 1 Hour */');

  COMMIT;
END;
/

VARIABLE l_job NUMBER;

BEGIN
  DBMS_JOB.submit (
    job       => :l_job,
    what      => 'my_job_proc(''DBMS_JOB.SUBMIT Example.'');',
    next_date => SYSDATE,
    interval  => 'SYSDATE + 1/24 /* 1 Hour */');

  COMMIT;
END;
/

PRINT l_job
```

The contents of the alert log show that both jobs executed correctly.

```
Tue Jun 22 10:09:02 2004
MY_JOB_PROC Start: DBMS_JOB.SUBMIT Example.
Tue Jun 22 10:11:25 2004
MY_JOB_PROC Start: DBMS_JOB.ISUBMIT Example.
Tue Jun 22 10:13:08 2004
MY_JOB_PROC End: DBMS_JOB.SUBMIT Example.
Tue Jun 22 10:13:09 2004
MY_JOB_PROC End: DBMS_JOB.ISUBMIT Example.
```

Information about the jobs can be shown using the *dba_jobs* view. The following script displays basic information about scheduled jobs for a specified user or all users.

🖫 jobs.sql

```
-- ***************************************************
-- Copyright © 2005 by Rampant TechPress
-- This script is free for non-commercial purposes
-- with no warranties.  Use at your own risk.
--
-- To license this script for a commercial purpose,
-- contact info@rampant.cc
-- ***************************************************

-- ***********************************************************************
-- Parameters:
--    1) Specific USERNAME or ALL which doesn't limit output.
-- ***********************************************************************

set verify off
set linesize 120
set feedback off
alter session set nls_date_format='DD-MON-YYYY HH24:MI:SS';
set feedback on

COLUMN job FORMAT 999
COLUMN what FORMAT A55
COLUMN interval FORMAT A30

select
   job,
   what,
   next_date,
   interval
from
   user_jobs
where
   schema_user = decode(upper('&1'), 'ALL', schema_user,
upper('&1'))
order by
   next_date
;
```

The output generated by the jobs.sql script is displayed below.

```
SQL> @jobs job_user

JOB WHAT
NEXT_DATE        INTERVAL
---- --------------------------------------------------------- -------
------------ -------------------------------
  99 my_job_proc('DBMS_JOB.ISUBMIT Example.');               22-JUN-
2004 10:11:20 SYSDATE + 1/24 /* 1 Hour */
   3 my_job_proc('DBMS_JOB.SUBMIT Example.');                22-JUN-
2004 10:11:20 SYSDATE + 1/24 /* 1 Hour */

2 rows selected.
```

Job information is also available from the Oracle Enterprise Manager (OEM) (Network → Databases → Your-Instance → Distributed → Advanced Replication → Administration → DBMS Job Tab). Figure 2.1 shows the typical information displayed on this screen.

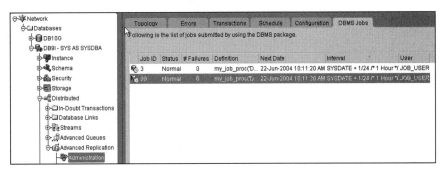

Figure 2.1 – *OEM: DBMS Jobs*

Once a job is scheduled, a change to some of its attributes may be desired. This can be achieved using the what, *next_date*, instance, interval and change procedures whose call specifications are displayed below.

```
PROCEDURE what (
   job        IN  BINARY_INTEGER,
   what       IN  VARCHAR2)

PROCEDURE next_date (
   job        IN  BINARY_INTEGER,
   next_date IN  DATE)

PROCEDURE instance (
   job        IN  BINARY_INTEGER,
```

```
  instance  IN  BINARY_INTEGER,
  force     IN  BOOLEAN DEFAULT FALSE)

PROCEDURE interval (
  job       IN  BINARY_INTEGER,
  interval  IN  VARCHAR2)

PROCEDURE change (
  job       IN  BINARY_INTEGER,
  what      IN  VARCHAR2,
  next_date IN  DATE,
  interval  IN  VARCHAR2,
  instance  IN  BINARY_INTEGER DEFAULT NULL,
  force     IN  BOOLEAN DEFAULT FALSE)
```

The what, *next_date*, *instance* and *interval* procedures allows the individual attributes of the same name to be altered, while the change procedure allows all of them to be altered in one go, effectively replacing the existing job. The examples below show how the procedures can be used:

```
BEGIN
  DBMS_JOB.what (
    job  => 99,
    what => 'my_job_proc(''DBMS_JOB.ISUBMIT Example (WHAT).'');');

  DBMS_JOB.next_date (
    job       => 99,
    next_date => SYSDATE + 1/12);

  DBMS_JOB.interval (
    job      => 99,
    interval => 'SYSDATE + 1/12 /* 2 Hours */');

  COMMIT;
END;
/
```

The output generated by the *user_jobs.sql* shows that the changes have been applied.

```
SQL> @jobs job_user

JOB WHAT                                                      NEXT_DATE            INTERVAL
---- -------------------------------------------------------- -------------------- ---------
--------------------
   3 my_job_proc('DBMS_JOB.SUBMIT Example.');                 22-JUN-2004 11:11:25 SYSDATE +
1/24 /* 1 Hour */
  99 my_job_proc('DBMS_JOB.ISUBMIT Example (WHAT).');         22-JUN-2004 12:24:13 SYSDATE +
1/12 /* 2 Hours */

2 rows selected.
```

The entire job definition can also be changed back using the change procedure. If the *what*, *next_date* or *interval* parameters are NULL, the existing value is unchanged.

```
BEGIN
  DBMS_JOB.change (
    job       => 99,
    what      => 'my_job_proc(''DBMS_JOB.ISUBMIT Example.'');',
    next_date => TO_DATE('22-JUN-2004 10:11:20', 'DD-MON-YYYY
HH24:MI:SS'),
    interval  => 'SYSDATE + 1/24 /* 1 Hour */');
  COMMIT;
END;
/
```

The output generated by the *user_jobs.sql* shows that the changes have been applied.

```
SQL> @jobs job_user

JOB WHAT                                     NEXT_DATE            INTERVAL
--- ---------------------------------------- -------------------- -------------------------
 99 my_job_proc('DBMS_JOB.ISUBMIT Example.'); 22-JUN-2004 11:36:23 SYSDATE + 1/24 /* 1 Hour */
  3 my_job_proc('DBMS_JOB.SUBMIT Example.');  22-JUN-2004 11:11:17 SYSDATE + 1/24 /* 1 Hour */

2 rows selected.
```

The broken procedure allows the broken flag associated with the job to be altered, as shown below.

```
PROCEDURE broken (
   job       IN  BINARY_INTEGER,
   broken    IN  BOOLEAN,
   next_date IN  DATE DEFAULT SYSDATE)
```

Jobs that are set as broken are not run, so this is a convenient way to temporarily stop them. The following example shows how the broken procedure is used:

```
BEGIN
  DBMS_JOB.broken (
    job    => 99,
    broken => TRUE);

  DBMS_JOB.broken (
    job    => 99,
    broken => FALSE);

  COMMIT;
END;
/
```

The job details, including the schedule, job definition and the broken flag, can be edited within the OEM by double clicking on the job of interest. Figure 2.2 shows the edit job dialog screen.

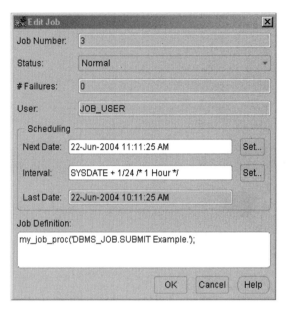

Figure 2.2 – *OEM: Edit job*

The run procedure allows a specified job to run immediately with the *next_date* recalculated from that point. The *force* parameter indicates that the job queue affinity can be ignored allowing any instance to run the job.

```
PROCEDURE run (
   job      IN  BINARY_INTEGER,
   force    IN  BOOLEAN DEFAULT FALSE)
```

The following example shows how to run a specific job:

```
BEGIN
  DBMS_JOB.run (
    job => 99);

  COMMIT;
END;
/
```

The *user_export* procedures allow the creation text for a specific job to be recreated. Their call specifications are listed below.

```
PROCEDURE user_export (
  job    IN    BINARY_INTEGER,
  mycall IN OUT VARCHAR2)

PROCEDURE user_export (
  job    IN    BINARY_INTEGER,
  mycall IN OUT VARCHAR2,
  myinst IN OUT VARCHAR2)
```

The *myinst* parameter allows the job queue affinity to be set in the resulting statement.

To recreate the job creation script for job 99, do the following:

```
VARIABLE l_my_call  VARCHAR2(1000);

BEGIN
  DBMS_JOB.user_export (
    job    => 99,
    mycall => :l_my_call);
END;
/

PRINT l_my_call

L_MY_CALL
-----------------------------------------------------------------
-------------------------------------------------
dbms_job.isubmit (job=>99,what=>'my_job_proc(''DBMS_JOB.ISUBMIT
Example.'');',next_date=>to_date('2004-06-22:11:36:23','Y
YYY-MM-DD:HH24:MI:SS'),interval=>'SYSDATE + 1/24 /* 1 Hour
*/',no_parse=>TRUE);
```

When a job is no longer needed, it can be permanently removed from the queue using the remove procedure.

```
PROCEDURE remove (
  job  IN  BINARY_INTEGER)
```

The jobs created thus far can be removed using the following code. Removing a job that is currently running does not stop it.

```
BEGIN
  DBMS_JOB.remove (
    job => 99);

  DBMS_JOB.remove (
```

```
    job => 48);

  COMMIT;
END;
/
```

Now that the basic functions of *dbms_job* have been presented, the data dictionary views that allow authorized users to view information about scheduled jobs will be examined.

Data Dictionary Views Related to *dbms_job*

There are two main *dba_%* views that relate directly to jobs scheduled via the *dba_jobs* package. The following script lists them and their dictionary comments:

🖫 **table_comments.sql**

```
-- ***************************************************
-- Copyright © 2005 by Rampant TechPress
-- This script is free for non-commercial purposes
-- with no warranties.  Use at your own risk.
--
-- To license this script for a commercial purpose,
-- contact info@rampant.cc
-- ***************************************************

-- Parameters:
--     1) Specific USERNAME or ALL which doesn't limit output.
--     2) Table or view name. Partial matches are allowed.
-- *********************************************************************

set verify off
column table_name format a20
column comments    format a50

select
   table_name,
   comments
from
   dba_tab_comments
where
   owner = upper('&1')
and
   table_name like upper('&2%')
order by
   table_name
;
```

The output displayed by the *table_comments.sql* script is listed below.

```
SQL> @table_comments.sql sys dba_jobs

TABLE_NAME            COMMENTS
-------------------   ------------------------------------------------
DBA_JOBS             All jobs in the database
DBA_JOBS_RUNNING     All jobs in the database which are currently
  runni
                     ng, join v$lock and job

2 rows selected.
```

As with the majority of *dba_%* views, there are equivalent *all_%* and *user_%* views. The *all_%* views display all objects the user owns or has privileges on, while the *user_%* views display only those objects the user owns. For the remainder of this topic, the focus will only be on the *dba_%* views as these views display the full list of objects, regardless of ownership or privileges.

For detailed examples of the proper usage of views, refer to Chapter 5 *Monitoring Oracle Job Execution.*

dba_jobs

The *dba_jobs* view is used to display all information related to the database jobs. This view is described below.

```
SQL> describe dba_jobs
 Name                            Null?     Type
 -----------------------------   --------  ----------------
 JOB                             NOT NULL  NUMBER
 LOG_USER                        NOT NULL  VARCHAR2(30)
 PRIV_USER                       NOT NULL  VARCHAR2(30)
 SCHEMA_USER                     NOT NULL  VARCHAR2(30)
 LAST_DATE                                 DATE
 LAST_SEC                                  VARCHAR2(8)
 THIS_DATE                                 DATE
 THIS_SEC                                  VARCHAR2(8)
 NEXT_DATE                       NOT NULL  DATE
 NEXT_SEC                                  VARCHAR2(8)
 TOTAL_TIME                                NUMBER
 BROKEN                                    VARCHAR2(1)
 INTERVAL                        NOT NULL  VARCHAR2(200)
 FAILURES                                  NUMBER
 WHAT                                      VARCHAR2(4000)
 NLS_ENV                                   VARCHAR2(4000)
 MISC_ENV                                  RAW(32)
 INSTANCE                                  NUMBER
```

The usage of the individual columns is explained by their dictionary comments. The following script can be used to display the column comments.

💾 **column_comments.sql**

```
-- ****************************************************
-- Copyright © 2005 by Rampant TechPress
-- This script is free for non-commercial purposes
-- with no warranties.  Use at your own risk.
--
-- To license this script for a commercial purpose,
-- contact info@rampant.cc
-- ****************************************************

-- Parameters:
--    1) Specific USERNAME or ALL which doesn't limit output.
--    2) Table or view name.
-- ****************************************************************

set verify off
set pagesize 100
column column_name format a20
column comments     format a50

select
   column_name,
   comments
from
   dba_col_comments
where
   owner = upper('&1')
and
   table_name like upper('&2')
order by
   column_name
;
```

The output generated from the *column_comments.sql* script is displayed below.

```
SQL> @column_comments sys dba_jobs

COLUMN_NAME    COMMENTS
------------   ------------------------------------------------
BROKEN         If Y, no attempt is being made to run this job.
               See dbms_jobq.broken(job).

FAILURES       How many times has this job started and failed sin
               ce its last success?

INSTANCE       Instance number restricted to run the job
INTERVAL       A date function, evaluated at the start of executi
               on, becomes next NEXT_DATE
```

JOB	Identifier of job. Neither import/export nor repeated executions change it.
LAST_DATE	Date that this job last successfully executed
LAST_SEC	Same as LAST_DATE. This is when the last successful execution started.
LOG_USER	USER who was logged in when the job was submitted
MISC_ENV	a versioned raw maintained by the kernel, for other session parameters
NEXT_DATE	Date that this job will next be executed
NEXT_SEC	Same as NEXT_DATE. The job becomes due for execution at this time.
NLS_ENV	alter session parameters describing the NLS environment of the job
PRIV_USER	USER whose default privileges apply to this job
SCHEMA_USER	select * from bar means select * from schema_user.bar
THIS_DATE	Date that this job started executing (usually null if not executing)
THIS_SEC	Same as THIS_DATE. This is when the last successful execution started.
TOTAL_TIME	Total wallclock time spent by the system on this job, in seconds
WHAT	Body of the anonymous PL/SQL block that this job executes

18 rows selected.

dba_jobs_running

The *dba_jobs_running* view lists information about all currently running jobs. This view is described below.

```
SQL> describe dba_jobs_running
 Name                     Null?    Type
 ----------------------- -------- ----
 SID                               NUMBER
 JOB                               NUMBER
 FAILURES                          NUMBER
 LAST_DATE                         DATE
 LAST_SEC                          VARCHAR2(8)
 THIS_DATE                         DATE
 THIS_SEC                          VARCHAR2(8)
 INSTANCE                          NUMBER
```

The usage of the individual columns is explained by their dictionary comments, which can be displayed using the *column_comments.sql* script.

```
SQL> @ column_comments sys dba_jobs_running

COLUMN_NAME          COMMENTS
-------------------- -------------------------------------------
FAILURES             How many times has this job started and failed
                     since its last success?

INSTANCE             The instance number restricted to run the job
JOB                  Identifier of job.  This job is currently
                     executin g.

LAST_DATE            Date that this job last successfully executed
LAST_SEC             Same as LAST_DATE.  This is when the last
                     successful execution started.

SID                  Identifier of process which is executing the.
                     job See v$lock.

THIS_DATE            Date that this job started executing (usually
                     null if not executing)

THIS_SEC             Same as THIS_DATE.  This is when the last
                     successf ul execution started.

8 rows selected.
```

Now that two data dictionary views have been explained, it is appropriate to review the new scheduling functionality available in Oracle 10g.

Overview of *dbms_scheduler* Functions

It quickly becomes apparent why the *dbms_scheduler* package is the recommended way to schedule jobs in Oracle10g. The *dbms_job* package is still present in 10g, but only for backward compatibility. The jobs created using the *dbms_job* package were very much stand-alone in nature in that they were defined with their own schedules and actions. In addition, the *dbms_scheduler* package allows the user to define standard programs and schedules, which can be used by many jobs.

Support for the scheduler is built into the Oracle Enterprise Manager 10g Database Control (OEM 10g DB Control). The majority of the scheduler objects can be managed via links from the administration page. Figure 2.3 shows the administration page with the scheduler links on the right hand side towards the bottom of the screen.

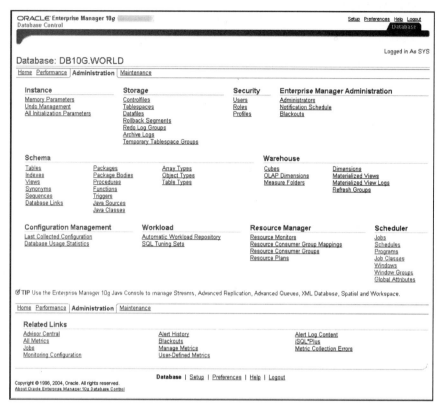

Figure 2.3 – *OEM 10g DB Control: Administration*

Job classes, windows and window groups provide a link between the scheduler and the resource manager, allowing jobs to run with a variety of resource profiles. They are considered part of the scheduler administration and require the MANAGE SCHEDULER privilege. Specific details about the resource manager is beyond the scope of this chapter, so the sections that deal with administration objects will focus on how to create each type of object, rather than how they should be used.

Before defining objects, it is worth taking a closer look at the privileges necessary to access the scheduler.

Scheduler Privileges

Table 2.1 shows the system privileges associated with the scheduler.

SYSTEM PRIVILEGE	PURPOSE
CREATE JOB	Enables the user to create jobs, schedules and programs in their own schema. The user can always alter and drop jobs, schedules and programs which they own, even when they do not have the CREATE JOB privilege.
CREATE ANY JOB	Enables the user to create jobs, schedules, and programs in any schema. This effectively gives the grantee the ability to run code as any user so it must be issued with care.
EXECUTE ANY PROGRAM	Enables jobs the ability to use programs from any schema.
EXECUTE ANY CLASS	Enables jobs to run under any job class.
MANAGE SCHEDULER	Enables the user to create, alter and drop job classes, windows and window groups. It also enables the user to purge scheduler logs and modify scheduler attributes.

Table 2.1 - *System privileges associated with the scheduler.*

Table 2.2 shows the object privileges associated with the scheduler.

OBJECT PRIVILEGE	PURPOSE
EXECUTE	This can only be granted for programs and job classes, enabling jobs to use the granted objects.
ALTER	Enables the user to alter or drop the object it is granted on. The alter operations vary depending on the object.
ALL	The can be granted on jobs, programs, schedules and job classes. It enables the user to perform all possible operations on the object it is granted on.

Table 2.2 - *The object privileges associated with the scheduler.*

The SCHEDULER_ADMIN role has all the above privileges granted to it with the ADMIN option, making it extremely powerful. This role is granted in turn to the DBA with the ADMIN option.

Programs

The create_program procedure is used to store metadata about a task, but it stores no schedule information.

```
PROCEDURE create_program(
  program_name          IN VARCHAR2,
  program_type          IN VARCHAR2,
  program_action        IN VARCHAR2,
  number_of_arguments   IN PLS_INTEGER DEFAULT 0,
  enabled               IN BOOLEAN DEFAULT FALSE,
  comments              IN VARCHAR2 DEFAULT NULL)
```

The parameters associated with this procedure and their usage are as follows:

- *program_name* - A name that uniquely identifies the program. The program name can include a schema qualifier.

- *program_type* - The type of action associated with this program (PLSQL_BLOCK, STORED_PROCEDURE or EXECUTABLE).

- *program_action* - The actual work that is done by the program.

- *number_of_arguments* - The number of arguments required by this program. Programs using arguments must have their arguments defined before they can be enabled.

- *enabled* - A flag which indicates if the program is enabled or not. If the program accepts arguments, it cannot be enabled until the arguments are defined.

- *comments* - Free text, allowing the user to record additional information.

The action of a program may be a PL/SQL block, a stored procedure or an OS executable file. The following examples show how each type of program is defined.

```
BEGIN
  -- PL/SQL Block.
  DBMS_SCHEDULER.create_program (
    program_name    => 'test_plsql_block_prog',
    program_type    => 'PLSQL_BLOCK',
    program_action  => 'BEGIN my_job_proc(''CREATE_PROGRAM
(BLOCK)''); END;',
    enabled         => TRUE,
    comments        => 'CREATE_PROGRAM test using a PL/SQL block.');
END;
/
```

```
BEGIN
  -- Stored Procedure with Arguments.
  DBMS_SCHEDULER.create_program (
    program_name        => 'test_stored_procedure_prog',
    program_type        => 'STORED_PROCEDURE',
    program_action      => 'my_job_proc',
    number_of_arguments => 1,
    enabled             => FALSE,
    comments            => 'CREATE_PROGRAM test using a
procedure.');

  DBMS_SCHEDULER.define_program_argument (
    program_name        => 'test_stored_procedure_prog',
    argument_name       => 'p_text',
    argument_position   => 1,
    argument_type       => 'VARCHAR2',
    default_value       => 'This is a default value.');

  DBMS_SCHEDULER.enable (name => 'test_stored_procedure_prog');
END;
/

BEGIN
  -- Shell Script (OS executable file).
  DBMS_SCHEDULER.create_program (
    program_name        => 'test_executable_prog',
    program_type        => 'EXECUTABLE',
    program_action      => '/u01/app/oracle/dba/MyJob.ksh',
    number_of_arguments => 0,
    enabled             => TRUE,
    comments            => 'CREATE_PROGRAM test using a schell
script.');
END;
/
```

Programs that accept arguments must have their arguments defined before
they can be enabled. Arguments are defined, manipulated and dropped using
the *define_program_argument*, *define_metadata_argument*, and *drop_program_argument*
procedures, whose call specifications are listed below.

```
PROCEDURE define_program_argument (
  program_name          IN VARCHAR2,
  argument_position     IN PLS_INTEGER,
  argument_name         IN VARCHAR2 DEFAULT NULL,
  argument_type         IN VARCHAR2,
  out_argument          IN BOOLEAN DEFAULT FALSE)

PROCEDURE define_anydata_argument(
  program_name          IN VARCHAR2,
  argument_position     IN PLS_INTEGER,
  argument_name         IN VARCHAR2 DEFAULT NULL,
  argument_type         IN VARCHAR2,
  default_value         IN SYS.ANYDATA,
  out_argument          IN BOOLEAN DEFAULT FALSE)
```

```
PROCEDURE define_metadata_argument(
  program_name              IN VARCHAR2,
  metadata_attribute        IN VARCHAR2,
  argument_position         IN PLS_INTEGER,
  argument_name             IN VARCHAR2 DEFAULT NULL)

PROCEDURE drop_program_argument (
  program_name              IN VARCHAR2,
  argument_position         IN PLS_INTEGER)

PROCEDURE drop_program_argument (
  program_name              IN VARCHAR2,
  argument_name             IN VARCHAR2)
```

The important parameters associated with these procedures and their usage are noted as follows:

- *program_name* - A name that uniquely identifies the program.

- *argument_position* - The position of the argument in the call specification.

- *argument_name* - The name of the argument.

- *argument_type* - The datatype of the argument.

- *default_value* - The argument value used if no specific value is assigned via the job.

- *out_argument* - A flag that indicates the direction of the argument.

Programs can be created using the Create Program screen of the OEM 10g DB Control as shown in Figure 2.4.

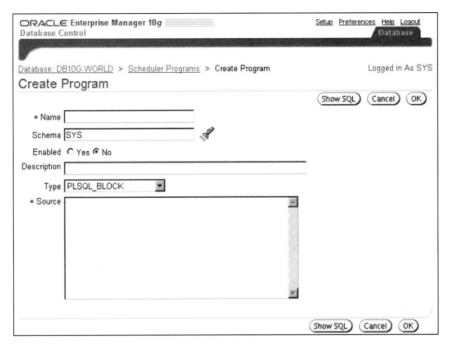

Figure 2.4 – *OEM DB Control: Create Program*

Information about programs can be displayed using the *dba_scheduler_programs* view. The following script uses this view to display basic information about the currently defined programs.

💾 **programs.sql**

```
-- **************************************************
-- Copyright © 2005 by Rampant TechPress
-- This script is free for non-commercial purposes
-- with no warranties.  Use at your own risk.
--
-- To license this script for a commercial purpose,
-- contact info@rampant.cc
-- **************************************************

set verify off

select
   owner,
   program_name,
   enabled
from
```

```
    dba_scheduler_programs
where
    owner = decode(upper('&1'), 'ALL', owner, upper('&1'))
;
```

The *programs.sql* script can display all programs or only those programs of a specified user.

```
SQL> @programs all

OWNER                          PROGRAM_NAME                   ENABL
------------------------------ ------------------------------ -----
SYS                            PURGE_LOG_PROG                 TRUE
SYS                            GATHER_STATS_PROG              TRUE
JOB_USER                       TEST_PLSQL_BLOCK_PROG          TRUE
JOB_USER                       TEST_STORED_PROCEDURE_PROG     TRUE
JOB_USER                       TEST_EXECUTABLE_PROG           TRUE

5 rows selected.

SQL> @programs job_user

OWNER                          PROGRAM_NAME                   ENABL
------------------------------ ------------------------------ -----
JOB_USER                       TEST_PLSQL_BLOCK_PROG          TRUE
JOB_USER                       TEST_STORED_PROCEDURE_PROG     TRUE
JOB_USER                       TEST_EXECUTABLE_PROG           TRUE

3 rows selected.
```

Information about program arguments can be displayed using the *dba_scheduler_program_args* view. The following script uses this view to display information about the arguments of currently defined programs.

🖫 program_args.sql

```
-- ************************************************
-- Copyright © 2005 by Rampant TechPress
-- This script is free for non-commercial purposes
-- with no warranties.  Use at your own risk.
--
-- To license this script for a commercial purpose,
-- contact info@rampant.cc
-- ************************************************
-- Parameters:
--    1) Specific USERNAME or ALL which doesn't limit output.
--    2) Program name.
-- ************************************************************

set verify off
column argument_name format a20
```

```
column default_value format a30

select
   argument_position,
   argument_name,
   default_value
from
   dba_scheduler_program_args
where
   owner = decode(upper('&1'), 'ALL', owner, upper('&1'))
and
   program_name = upper('&2')
;
```

The output from the *program_args.sql* script is displayed below.

```
SQL> @program_args job_user test_stored_procedure_prog

ARGUMENT_POSITION ARGUMENT_NAME        DEFAULT_VALUE
----------------- -------------------- ----------------------------
                1 P_TEXT               This is a default value.

1 row selected.
```

Programs that are no longer used can be removed using the *drop_program* procedure, whose call specification is listed below.

```
PROCEDURE drop_program (
  program_name              IN VARCHAR2,
  force                     IN BOOLEAN DEFAULT FALSE)
```

The parameters associated with this procedure and their usage are as follows.

- *program_name* - A name that uniquely identifies the program.

- *force* - When set to TRUE, all jobs which reference the program are disabled prior to the program being dropped. If set to FALSE and jobs reference the program, an error is produced. In addition, all program arguments information is dropped.

The following examples show how the *drop_program* procedure is used.

```
BEGIN
  DBMS_SCHEDULER.drop_program (program_name =>
'test_plsql_block_prog');
  DBMS_SCHEDULER.drop_program (program_name =>
'test_stored_procedure_prog');
  DBMS_SCHEDULER.drop_program (program_name =>
'test_executable_prog');
END;
/
```

One can determine that the programs have been removed by checking the output of the *programs.sql* script.

```
SQL> @programs all

OWNER                         PROGRAM_NAME                      ENABL
----------------------------- --------------------------------- -----
SYS                           PURGE_LOG_PROG                    TRUE
SYS                           GATHER_STATS_PROG                 TRUE

2 rows selected.
```

Program information is also available from the OEM 10g DB Control via the Scheduler Programs screen shown in Figure 2.5.

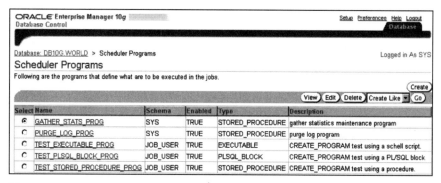

Figure 2.5 – *OEM 10g DB Control: Sheduler Programs*

Now that defining reusable programs has been explained, the next section will explain the defining of reusable schedules.

Schedules

The *create_schedule* procedure defines the start time, end time and interval that can be applied to a job.

```
PROCEDURE create_schedule (
   schedule_name        IN VARCHAR2,
   start_date           IN TIMESTAMP WITH TIME ZONE   DEFAULT NULL,
   repeat_interval      IN VARCHAR2,
   end_date             IN TIMESTAMP WITH TIME ZONE   DEFAULT NULL,
   comments             IN VARCHAR2                   DEFAULT NULL)
```

The parameters associated with this procedure and their usage are as follows:

- *schedule_name* - A name that uniquely identifies the schedule.

- *start_date* - The date when this schedule will take effect. This date may be in the future if scheduled jobs are set up in advance.

- *repeat_interval* - The definition of how often the job should execute. A value of NULL indicates that the job should only run once. The repeat interval is defined using a calendaring syntax, which is new to Oracle 10g. This will be explained in more detail in a later chapter.

- *end_date* - The date when this schedule will stop. This combined with the *start_date* parameter enables a job to be scheduled for a finite period of time.

- *comments* - Free text, allowing the user to record additional information.

The following code segment defines a new schedule that runs every hour on minute "0". The lack of an *end_date* parameter value means that the job will repeat forever based on the interval.

```
BEGIN
  DBMS_SCHEDULER.create_schedule (
    schedule_name   => 'test_hourly_schedule',
    start_date      => SYSTIMESTAMP,
    repeat_interval => 'freq=hourly; byminute=0',
    end_date        => NULL,
    comments        => 'Repeats hourly, on the hour, for ever.');
END;
/
```

Schedules are created in the OEM 10g DB Control via the Create Schedule screen shown in Figure 2.6.

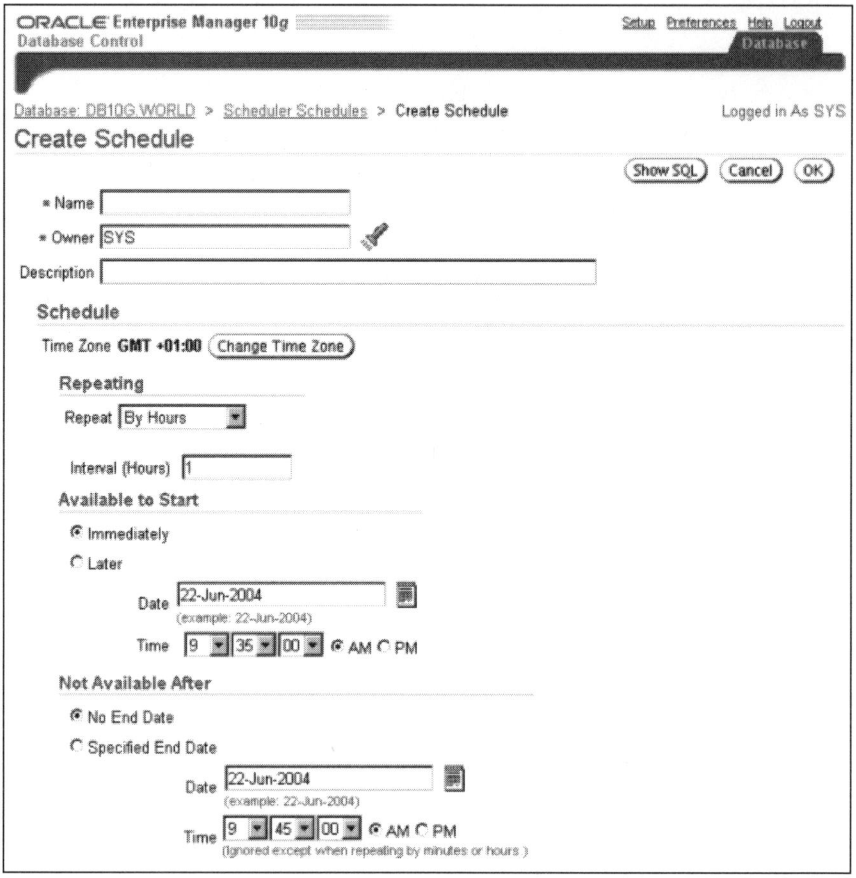

Figure 2.6 – *OEM 10g DB Control: Create Schedule*

Information about schedules can be displayed using the *dba_scheduler_schedules* view. The following script uses this view to display information about schedules for a specified user or all users.

💾 **schedules.sql**

```
-- ***************************************************
-- Copyright © 2005 by Rampant TechPress
-- This script is free for non-commercial purposes
-- with no warranties.  Use at your own risk.
-- To license this script for a commercial purpose,
-- contact info@rampant.cc
-- ***************************************************
-- Parameters:
```

```
--      1) Specific USERNAME or ALL which doesn't limit output.
-- *********************************************************************

set verify off

select
   owner,
   schedule_name,
   repeat_interval
from
   dba_scheduler_schedules
where
   owner = decode(upper('&1'), 'ALL', owner, upper('&1'))
;
```

The following is an example of output from the *schedules.sql* script.

```
SQL> @schedules job_user

OWNER                          SCHEDULE_NAME
------------------------------ ------------------------------
REPEAT_INTERVAL
-----------------------------------------------------------
JOB_USER                       TEST_HOURLY_SCHEDULE
freq=hourly; byminute=0

1 row selected.
```

Alternately, the Scheduler Schedules screen of the OEM 10g DB Control, shown in Figure 2.7, can be used to display schedule information.

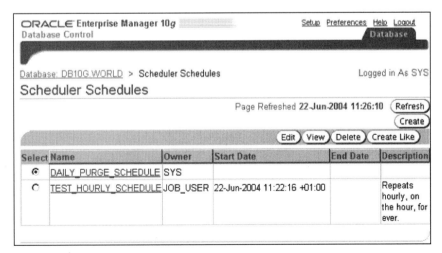

Figure 2.7 – *OEM 10g DB Control: Scheduler Schedules*

Schedules can be dropped using the *drop_schedule* procedure, whose call specification is listed below.

```
PROCEDURE drop_schedule (
  schedule_name           IN VARCHAR2,
  force                   IN BOOLEAN    DEFAULT FALSE)
```

The parameters associated with this procedure and their usage are as follows:

- *schedule_name* - A name that identifies a single schedule or a comma separated list of schedule names.

- *force* - If set to TRUE, all jobs and windows which reference this schedule are disabled prior to the schedule being dropped. If set to FALSE, the presence of dependants will produce errors.

The following examples show how the *drop_schedule* procedure is used:

```
BEGIN
  DBMS_SCHEDULER.drop_schedule (schedule_name =>
'TEST_HOURLY_SCHEDULE');
END;
/
```

The output from the schedules.sql script shows that the schedule has been removed.

```
SQL> @schedules job_user

no rows selected
```

Now that details on how to define reusable objects such as programs and schedules have been presented, the following section will show how they are used to schedule jobs.

Jobs

Jobs are what the scheduler is all about. They are created using the *create_job* procedure, which is overloaded allowing a job to be defined in one of four ways:

- Completely self-contained, with the program and schedule defined inline.

- Referencing both a predefined program and schedule.

- Referencing a predefined program, but with an inline schedule.

- Referencing a predefined schedule, but with an inline program.

The overloaded call specifications are listed below.

```
PROCEDURE create_job (
    job_name                IN VARCHAR2,
    job_type                IN VARCHAR2,
    job_action              IN VARCHAR2,
    number_of_arguments     IN PLS_INTEGER              DEFAULT 0,
    start_date              IN TIMESTAMP WITH TIME ZONE DEFAULT NULL,
    repeat_interval         IN VARCHAR2                 DEFAULT NULL,
    end_date                IN TIMESTAMP WITH TIME ZONE DEFAULT NULL,
    job_class               IN VARCHAR2                 DEFAULT
'DEFAULT_JOB_CLASS',
    enabled                 IN BOOLEAN                  DEFAULT FALSE,
    auto_drop               IN BOOLEAN                  DEFAULT TRUE,
    comments                IN VARCHAR2                 DEFAULT NULL)

PROCEDURE create_job (
    job_name                IN VARCHAR2,
    program_name            IN VARCHAR2,
    schedule_name           IN VARCHAR2,
    job_class               IN VARCHAR2                 DEFAULT
'DEFAULT_JOB_CLASS',
    enabled                 IN BOOLEAN                  DEFAULT FALSE,
    auto_drop               IN BOOLEAN                  DEFAULT TRUE,
    comments                IN VARCHAR2                 DEFAULT NULL)

PROCEDURE create_job (
    job_name                IN VARCHAR2,
    program_name            IN VARCHAR2,
    start_date              IN TIMESTAMP WITH TIME ZONE DEFAULT NULL,
    repeat_interval         IN VARCHAR2                 DEFAULT NULL,
    end_date                IN TIMESTAMP WITH TIME ZONE DEFAULT NULL,
    job_class               IN VARCHAR2                 DEFAULT
'DEFAULT_JOB_CLASS',
    enabled                 IN BOOLEAN                  DEFAULT FALSE,
    auto_drop               IN BOOLEAN                  DEFAULT TRUE,
    comments                IN VARCHAR2                 DEFAULT NULL)

PROCEDURE create_job (
    job_name                IN VARCHAR2,
    schedule_name           IN VARCHAR2,
    job_type                IN VARCHAR2,
    job_action              IN VARCHAR2,
    number_of_arguments     IN PLS_INTEGER              DEFAULT 0,
    job_class               IN VARCHAR2                 DEFAULT
'DEFAULT_JOB_CLASS',
    enabled                 IN BOOLEAN                  DEFAULT FALSE,
    auto_drop               IN BOOLEAN                  DEFAULT TRUE,
    comments                IN VARCHAR2                 DEFAULT NULL)
```

The parameters associated these procedures and their usage are as follows:

- *job_name* - A name that uniquely identifies the job.

- *job_type* - The type of action associated with this job (PLSQL_BLOCK, STORED_PROCEDURE or EXECUTABLE).

- *job_action* - The actual work that is done by the job.

- *number_of_arguments* - The number of arguments required by this job. Programs which use arguments must have their arguments defines before they can be enabled.

- *start_date* - The date when this schedule will take effect. This may be in the future if scheduled jobs are setup in advance.

- *repeat_interval* - The definition of how often the job should execute. A value of NULL indicates that the job should only run once. The repeat interval is defined using a PL/SQL expression or the calendaring syntax, which is new to Oracle 10g. This will be explained in more detail in a later chapter.

- *end_date* - The date when this schedule will stop. This combined with the *start_date* parameter enables a job to be scheduled for a finite period of time.

- *job_class* - The job class associated with this job. If no *job_class* is defined, the DEFAULT_JOB_CLASS is assigned.

- *enabled* - A flag which indicates if the job is enabled or not. If the job accepts arguments, it cannot be enabled until the arguments are defined.

- *auto_drop* - Indicates if the job should be dropped once it has run for the last time.

- *comments* - Free text, allowing the user to record additional information.

- *schedule_name* - The name of the schedule, window or window group used to define the job schedule.

- *program_name* - The name of the program which defines the action of the job.

The following code examples rely on the previously defined programs and schedules to show how the overloads of the *create_job* procedure are used.

```
BEGIN
  -- Job defined entirely by the CREATE JOB procedure.
  DBMS_SCHEDULER.create_job (
    job_name          => 'test_full_job_definition',
    job_type          => 'PLSQL_BLOCK',
    job_action        => 'BEGIN my_job_proc(''CREATE_PROGRAM
(BLOCK)''); END;',
    start_date        => SYSTIMESTAMP,
```

```
    repeat_interval => 'freq=hourly; byminute=0',
    end_date        => NULL,
    enabled         => TRUE,
    comments        => 'Job defined entirely by the CREATE JOB
procedure.');
END;
/
BEGIN
  -- Job defined by an existing program and schedule.
  DBMS_SCHEDULER.create_job (
    job_name      => 'test_prog_sched_job_definition',
    program_name  => 'test_plsql_block_prog',
    schedule_name => 'test_hourly_schedule',
    enabled       => TRUE,
    comments      => 'Job defined by an existing program and
schedule.');
END;
/
BEGIN
  -- Job defined by an existing program and inline schedule.
  DBMS_SCHEDULER.create_job (
    job_name        => 'test_prog_job_definition',
    program_name    => 'test_plsql_block_prog',
    start_date      => SYSTIMESTAMP,
    repeat_interval => 'freq=hourly; byminute=0',
    end_date        => NULL,
    enabled         => TRUE,
    comments        => 'Job defined by existing program and inline
schedule.');
END;
/
BEGIN
  -- Job defined by existing schedule and inline program.
  DBMS_SCHEDULER.create_job (
    job_name      => 'test_sched_job_definition',
    schedule_name => 'test_hourly_schedule',
    job_type      => 'PLSQL_BLOCK',
    job_action    => 'BEGIN my_job_proc(''CREATE_PROGRAM
(BLOCK)''); END;',
    enabled       => TRUE,
    comments      => 'Job defined by existing schedule and inline
program.');
END;
/
```

The *generate_job_name* function can be used to generate a unique name for a job.

```
FUNCTION generate_job_name (
    prefix        IN VARCHAR2 DEFAULT 'JOB$_') RETURN VARCHAR2
```

A sequence number is appended to the specified job name prefix to guarantee uniqueness. If the prefix is not specified, a standard prefix is used. The query below shows how it can be used:

```
column job_name_1 format a20
column job_name_2 format a20

select
    DBMS_SCHEDULER.generate_job_name ('test_job') as job_name_1,
    DBMS_SCHEDULER.generate_job_name as job_name_2
from
    dual;

JOB_NAME_1            JOB_NAME_2
-------------------- --------------------
TEST_JOB6            JOB$_7

1 row selected.
```

Figures 2.8 and 2.9 show the Create Job (General) and Create Job (Schedule) screens respectively. These provide a web-based alternative to the *create_job* procedure.

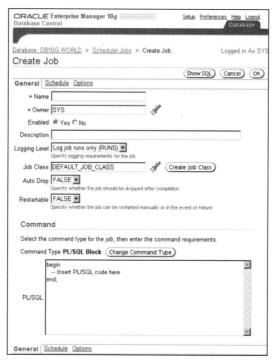

Figure 2.8 – *OEM 10g DB Control: Create Job (General)*

Figure 2.9 – *OEM 10g DB Control: Create Job (Schedule)*

Information about jobs can be displayed using the *dba_scheduler_jobs* view. The following script uses this view to display information about currently defined jobs.

🖫 jobs_10g.sql

```
-- *************************************************
-- Copyright © 2005 by Rampant TechPress
-- This script is free for non-commercial purposes
-- with no warranties.  Use at your own risk.
--
-- To license this script for a commercial purpose,
-- contact info@rampant.cc
-- *************************************************

-- Parameters:
--    1) Specific USERNAME or ALL which doesn't limit output.
-- *****************************************************************

set verify off

select
   owner,
   job_name,
   job_class,
   enabled,
```

```
   next_run_date,
   repeat_interval
from
   dba_scheduler_jobs
where
   owner = decode(upper('&1'), 'ALL', owner, upper('&1'))
;
```

The output of the *jobs_10g.sql* script for the current user is displayed below.

```
SQL> @jobs_10g job_user

OWNER                          JOB_NAME                      JOB_CLASS
ENABL
---------------------------- ---------------------------- ----------------------------
- -----
NEXT_RUN_DATE
--------------------------------------------------------------------------------
REPEAT_INTERVAL
-----------------------------------------------------------------
------------------------------
JOB_USER                       TEST_FULL_JOB_DEFINITION      DEFAULT_JOB_CLASS
TRUE
22-JUN-04 15.00.08.900000 +01:00
freq=hourly; byminute=0

JOB_USER                       TEST_PROG_SCHED_JOB_DEFINITION DEFAULT_JOB_CLASS
TRUE
22-JUN-04 15.00.16.200000 +01:00

JOB_USER                       TEST_PROG_JOB_DEFINITION      DEFAULT_JOB_CLASS
TRUE
22-JUN-04 15.00.09.600000 +01:00
freq=hourly; byminute=0

JOB_USER                       TEST_SCHED_JOB_DEFINITION     DEFAULT_JOB_CLASS
TRUE
22-JUN-04 15.00.16.200000 +01:00

4 rows selected.
```

When the *test_stored_procedure_prog* program is defined, a default argument value is specified. The argument values of jobs that access predefined programs can be manipulated using the following procedures:

```
PROCEDURE set_job_argument_value (
   job_name               IN VARCHAR2,
   argument_position      IN PLS_INTEGER,
   argument_value         IN VARCHAR2)

PROCEDURE set_job_argument_value (
   job_name               IN VARCHAR2,
   argument_name          IN VARCHAR2,
   argument_value         IN VARCHAR2)

PROCEDURE set_job_anydata_value(
   job_name               IN VARCHAR2,
   argument_position      IN PLS_INTEGER,
   argument_value         IN SYS.ANYDATA)
```

```
PROCEDURE set_job_anydata_value(
  job_name                IN VARCHAR2,
  argument_name           IN VARCHAR2,
  argument_value          IN SYS.ANYDATA)

PROCEDURE reset_job_argument_value (
  job_name                IN VARCHAR2,
  argument_position       IN PLS_INTEGER)

PROCEDURE reset_job_argument_value (
  job_name                IN VARCHAR2,
  argument_name           IN VARCHAR2)
```

The parameters associated with these procedures and their usage are as follows:

- *job_name* - A name that uniquely identifies the job.

- *argument_position* - The position of the argument in the call specification.

- *argument_name* - The name of the argument.

- *argument_value* - The value assigned to the argument.

Arguments can be referenced by name or by position, and their values can be set or reset to the default value. The example below shows how the argument values for a job can be reset:

```
BEGIN
  DBMS_SCHEDULER.create_job (
    job_name        => 'argument_job_definition',
    program_name    => 'test_stored_procedure_prog',
    schedule_name   => 'test_hourly_schedule',
    enabled         => FALSE,
    comments        => 'Job defined by an existing program and
schedule.');

  DBMS_SCHEDULER.set_job_argument_value (
    job_name        => 'argument_job_definition',
    argument_name   => 'p_text',
    argument_value  => 'A different argument value.');

  DBMS_SCHEDULER.enable (
    name            => 'argument_job_definition');
END;
/
```

Information about job arguments can be displayed using the *dba_scheduler_job_args* view. The following script uses this view to display argument information about a specified job.

🖫 job_arguments.sql

```
-- **************************************************
-- Copyright © 2005 by Rampant TechPress
-- This script is free for non-commercial purposes
-- with no warranties.  Use at your own risk.
--
-- To license this script for a commercial purpose,
-- contact info@rampant.cc
-- **************************************************

-- Parameters:
--    1) Specific USERNAME or ALL which doesn't limit output.
--    2) Job name.
-- *********************************************************************

set verify off
column argument_name format a20
column value format a30

select
   argument_position,
   argument_name,
   value
from
   dba_scheduler_job_args
where
   owner = decode(upper('&1'), 'ALL', owner, upper('&1'))
and
   job_name = upper('&2')
;
```

Using this script, one can see that the value of the job argument no longer matches the default value of the program argument.

```
SQL> @job_arguments job_user argument_job_definition


ARGUMENT_POSITION ARGUMENT_NAME        VALUE
----------------- -------------------- ----------------------------
                1 P_TEXT               A different argument value.

1 row selected.
```

Figure 2.10 shows the information displayed on the Scheduler Jobs screen in the OEM 10g DB Control.

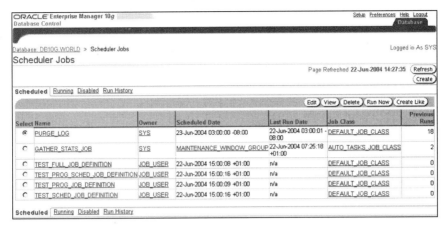

Figure 2.10 – *OEM 10g DB Control: Scheduler Jobs*

Jobs are normally run asynchronously under the control of the job coordinator, but they can also be controlled manually using the *run_job* and *stop_job* procedures.

```
PROCEDURE run_job (
    job_name            IN VARCHAR2,
    use_current_session IN BOOLEAN DEFAULT TRUE)

PROCEDURE stop_job (
    job_name            IN VARCHAR2,
    force               IN BOOLEAN DEFAULT FALSE)
```

The parameters associated with these procedures and their usage are as follows:

- *job_name* - A name that identifies a single job, a job class or a comma separated list of job names.

- *use_current_session* - When set to TRUE, the job is run in the user's current session; otherwise, a job slave runs it in the background.

- *force* - When set to FALSE, a job is stopped using the equivalent of sending a ctrl-c to the job. When TRUE, a graceful shutdown is attempted, but if this fails, the slave process is killed. Using the *force* parameter requires the user to have the MANAGE SCHEDULER system privilege.

The following code shows how the procedures can be used:

```
BEGIN
  -- Run job synchronously.
  DBMS_SCHEDULER.run_job (
    job_name             => 'test_full_job_definition',
    use_current_session => FALSE);

  -- Stop jobs.
  DBMS_SCHEDULER.stop_job (
    job_name => 'test_full_job_definition,
test_prog_sched_job_definition');
END;
/
```

A new job can be created as a replica of an existing job using the *copy_job* procedure. The new job is created in the disabled state, with the old job remaining unchanged.

```
PROCEDURE copy_job (
  old_job               IN VARCHAR2,
  new_job               IN VARCHAR2)
```

The parameters associated with this procedure and their usage are as follows:

- *old_job* - The name of the job whose attribute will be duplicated to create the new job.

- *new_job* - The name of the duplicate job to be created.

An example of its usage might be as follows:

```
BEGIN
  DBMS_SCHEDULER.copy_job (
    old_job => 'test_full_job_definition',
    new_job => 'new_test_full_job_definition');
END;
/
```

Jobs can be deleted using the *drop_job* procedure listed blow.

```
PROCEDURE drop_job (
  job_name              IN VARCHAR2,
  force                 IN BOOLEAN       DEFAULT FALSE)
```

The parameters associated with this procedure and their usage are as follows:

- *job_name* - A name that identifies a single job, a job class name or a comma separated list.

- *force* - TRUE running jobs are stopped before the job is dropped. When FALSE, dropping a job that is running will fail.

The following code shows how the *drop_job* procedure can be used:

```
BEGIN
  DBMS_SCHEDULER.drop_job (
    job_name => 'test_full_job_definition,
test_prog_sched_job_definition,
               test_prog_job_definition, test_sched_job_definition,
               argument_job_definition',
    force    => TRUE);
END;
/
```

The output from the *jobs_10g.sql* script shows that the jobs have been removed.

```
SQL> @jobs_10g job_user

no rows selected
```

The following section will focus on job classes, which are the first of the scheduler administration objects.

Job Classes

Job classes allow the grouping of jobs with similar characteristics and resource requirements to ease administration. If the *job_class* parameter of the *create_job* procedure is undefined, the job is assigned to a job class called DEFAULT_JOB_CLASS.

Job classes are created using the *create_job_class* procedure listed below.

```
PROCEDURE create_job_class(
  job_class_name          IN VARCHAR2,
  resource_consumer_group IN VARCHAR2   DEFAULT NULL,
  service                 IN VARCHAR2   DEFAULT NULL,
  logging_level           IN PLS_INTEGER DEFAULT
DBMS_SCHEDULER.LOGGING_RUNS,
  log_history             IN PLS_INTEGER DEFAULT NULL,
  comments                IN VARCHAR2   DEFAULT NULL)
```

The parameters associated with this procedure and their usage are as follows.

- *job_class_name* - A name that uniquely identifies the job class.

- *resource_consumer_group* - The resource consumer group associated with the job class.

- *service* - The service database object the job belongs to, not the tnsnames.ora service.

- *logging_level* - The amount of logging that should be done for this job, specified by the constants *logging_off*, *logging_runs*, and *logging_full*.

- *log_history* - The number of days the logging information is kept before purging.

- *comments* - Free text allowing the user to record additional information.

Suffice it to say that it must be decided with which resource consumer group the job class should be associated. Information about resource consumer groups can be displayed using the *dba_rsrc_consumer_groups* view.

```
select
   consumer_group
from
   dba_rsrc_consumer_groups
;

CONSUMER_GROUP
------------------------------
OTHER_GROUPS
DEFAULT_CONSUMER_GROUP
SYS_GROUP
LOW_GROUP
AUTO_TASK_CONSUMER_GROUP

5 rows selected.
```

With this information a new job class can be defined as follows:

```
BEGIN
  DBMS_SCHEDULER.create_job_class (
    job_class_name          => 'test_job_class',
    resource_consumer_group => 'default_consumer_group');
END;
/
```

Figure 2.11 shows the Create Job Class screen in the OEM 10g DB Control.

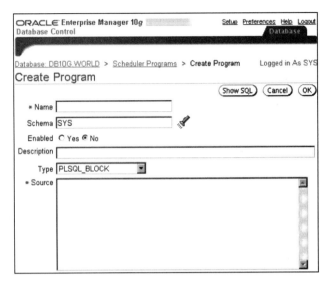

Figure 2.11 – *OEM 10g DB Control: Create Job Class*

Information about job classes can be displayed using the *dba_scheduler_job_classes* view. The following script uses this view:

💾 job_classes.sql

```
--   ****************************************************
--   Copyright © 2005 by Rampant TechPress
--   This script is free for non-commercial purposes
--   with no warranties.  Use at your own risk.
--
--   To license this script for a commercial purpose,
--   contact info@rampant.cc
--   ****************************************************

select
    job_class_name,
    resource_consumer_group
from
    dba_scheduler_job_classes
;
```

The output from the job_classes.sql script is displayed below.

```
SQL> @job_classes
JOB_CLASS_NAME                          RESOURCE_CONSUMER_GROUP
------------------------------          ------------------------------
DEFAULT_JOB_CLASS
AUTO_TASKS_JOB_CLASS                    AUTO_TASK_CONSUMER_GROUP
TEST_JOB_CLASS                          DEFAULT_CONSUMER_GROUP

3 rows selected.
```

Figure 2.12 shows the Scheduler Job Classes screen in the OEM 10g DB Control.

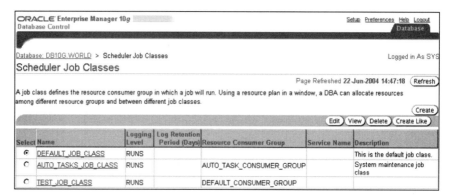

Figure 2.12 – *OEM 10g DB Control: Scheduler Job Classes*

Jobs can be assigned to a job class during creation. It is also possible to assign a job to an alternative job class after creation using one of the *set_attribute* procedure overloads.

```
BEGIN
  -- Job defined and assigned to a job class.
  DBMS_SCHEDULER.create_job (
    job_name      => 'test_prog_sched_class_job_def',
    program_name  => 'test_plsql_block_prog',
    schedule_name => 'test_hourly_schedule',
    job_class     => 'test_job_class',
    enabled       => TRUE,
    comments      => 'Job defined and assigned to a job class ');
END;
/
BEGIN
  -- Assign an existing job to a job class.
  DBMS_SCHEDULER.set_attribute (
    name      => 'test_prog_sched_job_definition',
    attribute => 'job_class',
    value     => 'test_job_class');
END;
/
```

The output from the *jobs_10g.sql* script shows that the job classes associated with these jobs has been set correctly.

```
SQL> @jobs_10g job_user

OWNER       JOB_NAME                             JOB_CLASS         ENABLE
----------  ------------------------------------ ----------------- ------
NEXT_RUN_DATE
--------------------------------------------------------------------------
REPEAT_INTERVAL
--------------------------------------------------------------------------
JOB_USER    TEST_FULL_JOB_DEFINITION             DEFAULT_JOB_CLASS TRUE
22-JUN-04 15.00.08.900000 +01:00
freq=hourly; byminute=0

JOB_USER    TEST_PROG_SCHED_JOB_DEFINITION TEST_JOB_CLASS           TRUE
22-JUN-04 15.00.16.200000 +01:00

JOB_USER    TEST_PROG_JOB_DEFINITION             DEFAULT_JOB_CLASS TRUE
22-JUN-04 15.00.09.600000 +01:00
freq=hourly; byminute=0

JOB_USER    TEST_SCHED_JOB_DEFINITION            DEFAULT_JOB_CLASS TRUE
22-JUN-04 15.00.16.200000 +01:00

JOB_USER    ARGUMENT_JOB_DEFINITION              DEFAULT_JOB_CLASS TRUE
22-JUN-04 15.00.16.200000 +01:00

JOB_USER    TEST_PROG_SCHED_CLASS_JOB_DEF TEST_JOB_CLASS            TRUE
22-JUN-04 15.00.16.200000 +01:00

6 rows selected.
```

Job classes can be removed using the *drop_job_class* procedure listed below:

```
PROCEDURE drop_job_class (
  job_class_name          IN VARCHAR2,
  force                   IN BOOLEAN DEFAULT FALSE)
```

The parameters associated with this procedure and their usage are as follows:

- *job_class_name* - A name that specifies a single or comma separated list of job class names.

- *force* - When set to TRUE, all jobs that are assigned to the job class are disabled and have their job class set to the default. When set to FALSE, attempting to drop a job class that has dependant jobs will cause an error.

The following code example shows how a job class can be removed.

```
BEGIN
  DBMS_SCHEDULER.drop_job_class (
    job_class_name => 'test_job_class',
    force          => TRUE);
END;
/
```

The output of the *job_classes.sql* script shows that the job class has been removed successfully.

```
SQL> @job_classes

JOB_CLASS_NAME                   RESOURCE_CONSUMER_GROUP
------------------------------   ------------------------------
DEFAULT_JOB_CLASS
AUTO_TASKS_JOB_CLASS             AUTO_TASK_CONSUMER_GROUP

2 rows selected.
```

Now that to the creation of job classes has been presented, the next section will cover windows, another type of scheduler administration object.

Windows

Windows define the times when resource plans are active. Since job classes point to resource consumer groups, and therefore resource plans, this mechanism allows control over the resources allocated to job classes and their associated jobs during specific time periods. A window can be assigned to the *schedule_name* parameter of a job instead of a schedule object.

Only one window can be active at any time, with one resource plan assigned to the window. The effects of resource plan switches are instantly visible to running jobs that are assigned to job classes.

A window can be created using the *create_window* procedure with a predefined or an inline schedule.

```
PROCEDURE create_window (
  window_name            IN VARCHAR2,
  resource_plan          IN VARCHAR2,
  schedule_name          IN VARCHAR2,
  duration               IN INTERVAL DAY TO SECOND,
  window_priority        IN VARCHAR2              DEFAULT 'LOW',
  comments               IN VARCHAR2              DEFAULT NULL)
```

```
PROCEDURE create_window (
  window_name            IN VARCHAR2,
  resource_plan          IN VARCHAR2,
  start_date             IN TIMESTAMP WITH TIME ZONE DEFAULT NULL,
  repeat_interval        IN VARCHAR2,
  end_date               IN TIMESTAMP WITH TIME ZONE DEFAULT NULL,
  duration               IN INTERVAL DAY TO SECOND,
  window_priority        IN VARCHAR2                 DEFAULT 'LOW',
  comments               IN VARCHAR2                 DEFAULT NULL)
```

The parameters associated with these procedures and their usage are as follows:

- *window_name* - A name that uniquely identifies the window.

- *resource_plan* - The resource plan associated with the window. When the window opens, the system switches to use the associated resource plan. When the window closes, the system switches back to the previous resource plan.

- *schedule_name* - The name of the schedule associated with the window. If this is specified, the *start_date, repeat_interval* and *end_date* must be NULL.

- *start_date* - The date when this window will take effect. This may be in the future if the window is to be setup in advance.

- *repeat_interval* - The definition of how often the window should open. A value of NULL indicates that the window should only open once.

- *end_date* - The date when this window will stop. This combined with the *start_date* parameter enables a window to be scheduled for a finite period of time.

- *duration* - The length of time in minutes the window should remain open.

- *window_priority* - The priority (LOW or HIGH) of the window. In the event of multiple windows opening at the same time, windows with a high priority take precedence over windows with a low priority, which is the default.

- *comments* - Free text allowing the user to record additional information.

The following code shows how the *create_window* procedures can be used:

```
BEGIN
  -- Window with a predefined schedule.
  DBMS_SCHEDULER.create_window (
    window_name      => 'test_window_1',
    resource_plan    => NULL,
    schedule_name    => 'TEST_HOURLY_SCHEDULE',
    duration         => INTERVAL '30' MINUTE,
```

```
      window_priority => 'LOW',
      comments        => 'Window with a predefined schedule.');
END;
/

BEGIN
  -- Window with an inline schedule.
  DBMS_SCHEDULER.create_window (
    window_name     => 'test_window_2',
    resource_plan   => NULL,
    start_date      => SYSTIMESTAMP,
    repeat_interval => 'freq=hourly; byminute=0',
    end_date        => NULL,
    duration        => INTERVAL '30' MINUTE,
    window_priority => 'LOW',
    comments        => 'Window with an inline schedule.');
END;
/
```

The SYS user is the owner of all windows, so any schedules referenced by them must also be owned by SYS.

Figure 2.13 shows the Create Window screen in the OEM 10g DB Control.

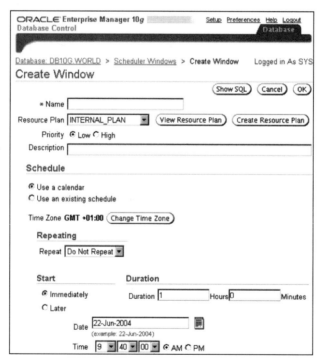

Figure 2.13 – *OEM 10g DB Control: Create Window*

Information about windows can be displayed using the *dba_scheduler_windows* view. The following script uses this view:

💾 **windows.sql**

```
-- ***************************************************
-- Copyright © 2005 by Rampant TechPress
-- This script is free for non-commercial purposes
-- with no warranties.  Use at your own risk.
--
-- To license this script for a commercial purpose,
-- contact info@rampant.cc
-- ***************************************************

select
    window_name,
    resource_plan,
    enabled,
    active
from
    dba_scheduler_windows
;
```

The output from the windows.sql script is displayed below.

```
job_user@db10g> @windows

WINDOW_NAME                      RESOURCE_PLAN            ENABL ACTIV
-------------------------------- ------------------------ ----- -----
TEST_WINDOW_1                                             TRUE  FALSE
TEST_WINDOW_2                                             TRUE  FALSE
WEEKEND_WINDOW                                            TRUE  TRUE
WEEKNIGHT_WINDOW                                          TRUE  FALSE

4 rows selected.
```

Figure 2.14 shows the Scheduler Windows screen in the OEM 10g DB Control.

Overview of dbms_scheduler Functions   **77**

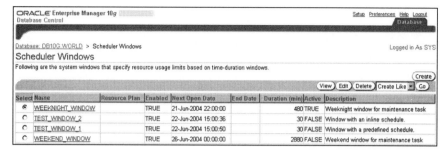

Figure 2.14 – *OEM 10g DB Control: Scheduler Windows*

The server normally controls the opening and closing of windows, but they also can be opened and closed manually using the *open_window* and *close_window* procedures.

```
PROCEDURE open_window (
    window_name            IN VARCHAR2,
    duration               IN INTERVAL DAY TO SECOND,
    force                  IN BOOLEAN DEFAULT FALSE)

PROCEDURE close_window (
    window_name            IN VARCHAR2)
```

The parameters associated with these procedures and their usage are as follows:

- *window_name* - A name that uniquely identifies the window.

- *duration* - The length of time, in minutes, the window should remain open.

- *force* - When set to FALSE, attempting to open a window when one is already open will result in an error unless the currently open window is the one that is attempting to open. In this case, the close time is set to the current system time plus the specified duration.

Closing a window causes all jobs associated with that window to be stopped.

The following example opens then closes *test_window_2*. Notice how the active window switches back to weekend_window when *test_window_2* is closed.

```
BEGIN
    -- Open window.
    DBMS_SCHEDULER.open_window (
        window_name => 'test_window_2',
```

```
     duration      => INTERVAL '1' MINUTE,
     force         => TRUE);
END;
/

SQL> @windows

WINDOW_NAME                          RESOURCE_PLAN          ENABL ACTIV
---------------------------------    --------------------   ----- -----
TEST_WINDOW_1                                               TRUE  FALSE
TEST_WINDOW_2                                               TRUE  TRUE
WEEKEND_WINDOW                                              TRUE  FALSE
WEEKNIGHT_WINDOW                                            TRUE  FALSE

4 rows selected.

BEGIN
  -- Close window.
  DBMS_SCHEDULER.close_window (
    window_name => 'test_window_2');
END;
/

SQL> @windows

WINDOW_NAME                          RESOURCE_PLAN          ENABL ACTIV
---------------------------------    --------------------   ----- -----
TEST_WINDOW_1                                               TRUE  FALSE
TEST_WINDOW_2                                               TRUE  FALSE
WEEKEND_WINDOW                                              TRUE  TRUE
WEEKNIGHT_WINDOW                                            TRUE  FALSE

4 rows selected.
```

Windows can be removed using the drop_window procedure.

```
PROCEDURE drop_window (
   window_name                IN VARCHAR2,
   force                      IN BOOLEAN DEFAULT FALSE)
```

The parameters associated with this procedure and their usage are as follows:

- *window_name* - A single or comma separated list of window names. If a window group name is specified, all windows within that group will be dropped. In addition, all jobs that use the specified window or window group as a schedule will be disabled, although running jobs will complete normally.

- *force* - When set to FALSE, attempting to drop an open window will result in an error. When set to TRUE the open window is closed before it is dropped.

The following example drops the two test windows that were created earlier:

```
BEGIN
  DBMS_SCHEDULER.drop_window (
    window_name => 'test_window_1,test_window_2',
    force       => TRUE);
END;
/
```

The output from the windows.sql script confirms that the windows have been removed successfully.

```
SQL> @windows

WINDOW_NAME              RESOURCE_PLAN      ENABL ACTIV
-----------------------  -----------------  ----- -----
WEEKEND_WINDOW                              TRUE  TRUE
WEEKNIGHT_WINDOW                            TRUE  FALSE

2 rows selected.
```

The following section will show how to group related windows together using window groups.

Window Groups

A window group is a collection of related windows, which can be assigned to the *schedule_name* parameter of a job instead of a schedule object. It can be created with zero, one or many windows as group members using the *create_window_group* procedure.

```
PROCEDURE create_window_group(
  group_name          IN VARCHAR2,
  window_list         IN VARCHAR2 DEFAULT NULL,
  comments            IN VARCHAR2 DEFAULT NULL)
```

The parameters associated with this procedure and their usage are as follows:

- *group_name* - A name that uniquely identifies the window group.

- *window_list* - A comma separated list of windows associated with the window group.

- *comments* - Free text allowing the user to record additional information.

The following code creates a window group and assigns the two test windows defined in the previous section.

```
BEGIN
  DBMS_SCHEDULER.create_window_group (
    group_name  => 'test_window_group',
    window_list => 'test_window_1, test_window_2',
    comments    => 'A test window group');
END;
/
```

Figure 2.15 shows the Create Window Group screen in the OEM 10g DB
Control.

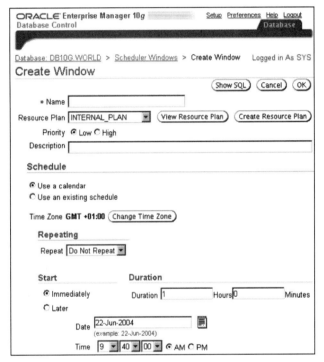

Figure 2.15 – *OEM 10g DB Control: Create Window Group*

Information about window groups can be displayed using the
dba_scheduler_window_groups and *dba_scheduler_wingroup_members* views. The
following script uses both views to display a summary of window group
information.

🖫 window_groups.sql

```
-- ****************************************************
-- Copyright © 2005 by Rampant TechPress
-- This script is free for non-commercial purposes
-- with no warranties.  Use at your own risk.
--
-- To license this script for a commercial purpose,
-- contact info@rampant.cc
-- ****************************************************

prompt
prompt WINDOW GROUPS
prompt --------------

select
   window_group_name,
   enabled,
   number_of_windowS
from
   dba_scheduler_window_groups
;

prompt
prompt WINDOW GROUP MEMBERS
prompt --------------------

select
   window_group_name,
   window_name
from
   dba_scheduler_wingroup_members
;
```

The output from the *window_groups.sql* script shows that the window group was created successfully.

```
SQL> @window_groups

WINDOW GROUPS
------------

WINDOW_GROUP_NAME                 ENABL NUMBER_OF_WINDOWS
------------------------------    ----- -----------------
MAINTENANCE_WINDOW_GROUP          TRUE                  2
TEST_WINDOW_GROUP                 TRUE                  2

2 rows selected.
```

```
WINDOW GROUP MEMBERS
-------------------

WINDOW_GROUP_NAME                WINDOW_NAME
------------------------------   --------------------------------
MAINTENANCE_WINDOW_GROUP         WEEKEND_WINDOW
MAINTENANCE_WINDOW_GROUP         WEEKNIGHT_WINDOW
TEST_WINDOW_GROUP                TEST_WINDOW_1
TEST_WINDOW_GROUP                TEST_WINDOW_2

4 rows selected.
```

Figure 2.16 shows the Scheduler Window Groups screen in the OEM 10g DB Control.

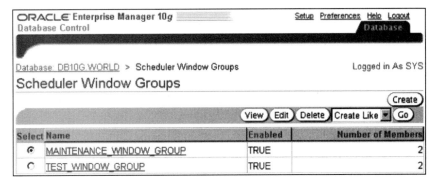

Figure 2.16 – *OEM 10g DB Control: Scheduler Window Groups*

Windows can be added and removed from a group using the *add_window_group_member* and *remove_window_group_member* procedures, respectively.

```
PROCEDURE add_window_group_member (
   group_name            IN VARCHAR2,
   window_list           IN VARCHAR2)

PROCEDURE remove_window_group_member (
   group_name            IN VARCHAR2,
   window_list           IN VARCHAR2)
```

The parameters associated with these procedures and their usage are as follows:

- *group_name* - A name that uniquely identifies the window group.

- *window_list* - A comma separated list of windows to be added or removed from the window group.

The following example creates a new window, adds it to a group and then removes it from the group.

Figure 2.17 shows the Edit Window Group screen in the OEM 10g DB Control. Windows can be added and removed from a window group using this screen.

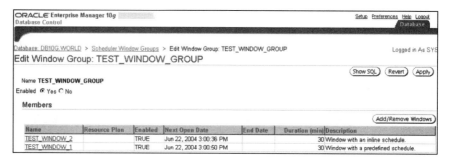

Figure 2.17 – *OEM 10g DB Control: Edit Window Group*

Windows groups are removed using the *drop_window_group* procedure.

```
PROCEDURE drop_window_group (
  group_name            IN VARCHAR2,
  force                 IN BOOLEAN DEFAULT FALSE)
```

The parameters associated with this procedure and their usage are as follows.

- *group_name* - A name that uniquely identifies the window group.

- *force* - When set to FALSE, an error is produced if any jobs reference the specified window group. When set to TRUE, any dependant jobs are disabled.

The following example shows how to drop a window group:

```
BEGIN
  DBMS_SCHEDULER.drop_window_group (
    group_name => 'test_window_group',
    force       => TRUE);
END;
/
```

The output from the *window_groups.sql* script shows that the window group has been removed.

```
SQL> @window_groups

WINDOW GROUPS
-------------

WINDOW_GROUP_NAME               ENABL NUMBER_OF_WINDOWS
------------------------------- ----- -----------------
MAINTENANCE_WINDOW_GROUP        TRUE                  2

1 row selected.


WINDOW GROUP MEMBERS
--------------------

WINDOW_GROUP_NAME               WINDOW_NAME
------------------------------- ---------------------------
MAINTENANCE_WINDOW_GROUP        WEEKEND_WINDOW
MAINTENANCE_WINDOW_GROUP        WEEKNIGHT_WINDOW

2 rows selected.
```

The following section will explain common procedures and functions for managing the scheduler objects that have been created.

Enabling, Disabling and Setting Attributes of Scheduler Objects

All applicable scheduler objects can be enabled and disabled using the enable and disable procedures respectively.

```
PROCEDURE disable(
   name                 IN VARCHAR2,
   force                IN BOOLEAN DEFAULT FALSE)

PROCEDURE enable(
   name                 IN VARCHAR2)
```

The parameters associated with these procedures and their usage are as follows:

- *name* - A name that uniquely identifies the scheduler object: program; job; window; or window group.

- *force* - When set to FALSE, an error is produced if the object has any dependants. When set to TRUE, the object is disabled, but any dependents remain unaltered.

The following example shows their usage:

```
BEGIN
  -- Enable programs and jobs.
  DBMS_SCHEDULER.enable (
    name  => 'test_stored_procedure_prog');

  DBMS_SCHEDULER.enable (
    name  => 'test_full_job_definition');

  -- Disable programs and jobs.
  DBMS_SCHEDULER.disable (
    name  => 'test_stored_procedure_prog',
    force => TRUE);

  DBMS_SCHEDULER.disable (
    name  => 'test_full_job_definition',
    force => TRUE);
END;
/
```

The values for individual attributes of all scheduler objects can be altered using one of the *set_attribute* overloads.

```
BEGIN
  DBMS_SCHEDULER.set_attribute (
    name      => 'test_hourly_schedule',
    attribute => 'repeat_interval',
    value     => 'freq=hourly; byminute=30');
END;
/
```

Attribute values are set to NULL using the *set_attribute_null* procedures.

```
BEGIN
  DBMS_SCHEDULER.set_attribute_null (
    name      => 'test_hourly_schedule',
    attribute => 'repeat_interval');
END;
/
```

Since the creation and maintenance of the scheduler objects has been explained in the previous section, discovering how to identify which dictionary views are available to view information about them will be presented in the following section.

Data Dictionary Views Related to *dbms_scheduler*

The main views relating to the *dbms_scheduler* package and their comments can be displayed using the *table_comments.sql* script as follows:

```
SQL> @table_comments sys dba_scheduler

TABLE NAME                          COMMENTS
--------------------------------    -------------------------------------------
DBA_SCHEDULER_GLOBAL_ATTRIBUTE      All scheduler global attributes
DBA_SCHEDULER_JOBS                  All scheduler jobs in the database
DBA_SCHEDULER_JOB_ARGS              All arguments with set values of all sch
                                    eduler jobs in the database

DBA_SCHEDULER_JOB_CLASSES           All scheduler classes in the database
DBA_SCHEDULER_JOB_LOG               Logged information for all scheduler jobs

DBA_SCHEDULER_JOB_RUN_DETAILS       The details of a job run
DBA_SCHEDULER_PROGRAMS              All scheduler programs in the database
DBA_SCHEDULER_PROGRAM_ARGS          All arguments of all scheduler programs
                                    in the database

DBA_SCHEDULER_RUNNING_JOBS
DBA_SCHEDULER_SCHEDULES             All schedules in the database
DBA_SCHEDULER_WINDOWS               All scheduler windows in the database
DBA_SCHEDULER_WINDOW_DETAILS        The details of a window
DBA_SCHEDULER_WINDOW_GROUPS         All scheduler window groups in the datab
                                    ase

DBA_SCHEDULER_WINDOW_LOG            Logged information for all scheduler win
                                    dows

DBA_SCHEDULER_WINGROUP_MEMBERS      Members of all scheduler window groups i
                                    n the database

15 rows selected.
```

The columns and associated comments for each view can be displayed using the *column_comments.sql* script. Below is an example of how it is used.

```
SQL> @column_comments sys dba_scheduler_window_groups

COLUMN_NAME            COMMENTS
-------------------    --------------------------------------------------
COMMENTS               An optional comment about this window group
ENABLED                Whether the window group is enabled
NUMBER_OF_WINDOWS      Number of members in this window group
WINDOW_GROUP_NAME      Name of the window group

4 rows selected.
```

This script can be used against the other scheduler views to give some indication of their usage.

For further examples of using the scheduler views, refer to Chapter 5.

Conclusion

This chapter presented the following topics:

- How to set the initialization parameters necessary for the scheduler to function properly.

- How to set up a test environment to explore the functionality of the Oracle scheduler.

- How to create and maintain scheduled jobs using both the *dbms_job* package and the *dbms_scheduler* package.

- How to create and maintain scheduled jobs using both Oracle Enterprise Manager (OEM) and OEM 10g Database Control.

- How to identify the data dictionary views that allow information about the scheduled jobs that have been created to be examined.

In addition to basic scheduling of jobs, the links between jobs and the resource manager have been introduced. Additional details will be presented in further detail later in this book.

The next chapter will explore how to define complex job schedules using *dbms_job* and the calendar syntax in *dbms_scheduler*.

Time-Based Job Scheduling

Time to take a closer look at Dates and Times

Introduction

In order to understand how repeat intervals of jobs are specified, a review of how Oracle handles date-time information is warranted. This chapter will present information on how to use dates, timestamps and intervals along with the Oracle10g calendar syntax to define repeat intervals for scheduled jobs.

The use of the DATE datatype used by the *dbms_job* package will be examined in the following section.

Dates

The DATE datatype is used by Oracle to store all datetime information in which a precision greater than one second is not needed. Oracle uses a seven byte binary date format which allows Julian dates to be stored within the range of 01-Jan-4712 BC to 31-Dec-4712 AD. Table 3.1 shows how each of the seven bytes is used to store the date information:

BYTE	MEANING	NOTATION	EXAMPLE (10-JUL-2004 17:21:30)
1	Century	Divided by 100, excess-100	120
2	Year	Modulo 100, excess-100	104
3	Month	0 base	7
4	Day	0 base	10
5	Hour	excess-1	18
6	Minute	excess-1	22
7	Second	excess-1	31

Table 3.1 - *How each of the seven bytes is used to store the date information*

The following example uses the *dump* function to show the contents of a stored date:

```
alter session set nls_date_format = 'DD-MON-YYYY HH24:MI:SS';

drop table date_test;

create table date_test as
select
    sysdate as now
from
    dual
;

select
    now,
    dump (now)
from
    date_test
;

NOW
-------------------
DUMP(NOW)
-----------------------------------------
10-JUL-2004 17:21:30
Typ=12 Len=7: 120,104,7,10,18,22,31

1 row selected.
```

When comparing the *date* and *dump* values, subtracting 100 from the century component, then multiplying the resulting value by 100 gives a value of 2000. Subtracting the 100 from the year component gives a value of 4. The month and day components need no modification, while subtracting one from the hour, minute and second components (18, 22 and 31) give values of 17, 21 and 30.

Jobs scheduled using the *dbms_job* package use dates to define time related information, as seen in the *dbms_job.submit* procedure and the *dba_jobs* view shown below.

```
PROCEDURE submit (
   job        OUT BINARY_INTEGER,
   what       IN  VARCHAR2,
   next_date  IN  DATE DEFAULT sysdate,
   interval   IN  VARCHAR2 DEFAULT 'null',
   no_parse   IN  BOOLEAN DEFAULT FALSE,
   instance   IN  BINARY_INTEGER DEFAULT 0,
   force      IN  BOOLEAN DEFAULT FALSE)

SQL> describe dba_jobs
 Name                            Null?     Type
 ------------------------------- --------  ------------------------
 JOB                             NOT NULL  NUMBER
 LOG_USER                        NOT NULL  VARCHAR2(30)
 PRIV_USER                       NOT NULL  VARCHAR2(30)
 SCHEMA_USER                     NOT NULL  VARCHAR2(30)
 LAST_DATE                                 DATE
 LAST_SEC                                  VARCHAR2(8)
 THIS_DATE                                 DATE
 THIS_SEC                                  VARCHAR2(8)
 NEXT_DATE                       NOT NULL  DATE
 NEXT_SEC                                  VARCHAR2(8)
 TOTAL_TIME                                NUMBER
 BROKEN                                    VARCHAR2(1)
 INTERVAL                        NOT NULL  VARCHAR2(200)
 FAILURES                                  NUMBER
 WHAT                                      VARCHAR2(4000)
 NLS_ENV                                   VARCHAR2(4000)
 MISC_ENV                                  RAW(32)
 INSTANCE                                  NUMBER
```

It is also the datatype that must be returned by the expression defined in the *interval* parameter of jobs scheduled using the *dbms_job* package.

Since dates are actually numbers, certain simple mathematical operations can be performed on them. Adding a whole number to a date is like adding the equivalent number of days, while adding a fraction to a date is like adding that fraction of a day to the date. The same is true in reverse for subtraction. Table 3.2 below shows how each specific time period can be calculated. All three expressions equate to the same value, allowing the DBA to pick a preferred method.

PERIOD	EXPRESSION 1	EXPRESSION 2	EXPRESSION 3	VALUE
1 Day	1	1	1	1
1 Hour	1/24	1/24	1/24	.041666667
1 Minute	1/24/60	1/(24*60)	1/1440	.000694444
1 Second	1/24/60/60	1/(24*60*60)	1/86400	.000011574

Table 3.2 - *How each specific time period can be calculated.*

The following query shows how these expressions might be used to modify the value of the current operating system date:

```
alter session set nls_date_format='DD/MM/YYYY HH24:MI:SS';

select
   sysdate as current_date,
   sysdate + 1 as plus_1_day,
   sysdate + 2/24 as plus_2_hours,
   sysdate + 10/24/60 as plus_10_minutes,
   sysdate + 30/24/60/60 as plus_30_seconds
from
   dual;

alter session set nls_date_format='DD-MON-YYYY HH24:MI:SS';
```

The results of this query are listed below.

```
CURRENT_DATE        PLUS_1_DAY          PLUS_2_HOURS
PLUS_10_MINUTES     PLUS_30_SECONDS
------------------- ------------------- ------------------- --------
10/07/2004 17:57:30 11/07/2004 17:57:30 10/07/2004 19:57:30
10/07/2004 18:07:30 10/07/2004 17:58:00

1 row selected.
```

Oracle provides several date functions to make date manipulation simpler. Table 3.3 below lists a selection of those date functions and the examples of their usage:

DATE FUNCTION	USAGE

sysdate	Returns the current date-time from the operating system of the database server.
	
	``
	select
	   sysdate
	from
	   dual;
	
	SYSDATE
	------------------ 	
	10/07/2004 18:34:12
	
	1 row selected.
	``

current_date	Similar to the *sysdate* function, but returns the current date-time within the session's time zone.
	
	``
	select
	   current_date
	from
	   dual;
	
	CURRENT_DATE
	------------------ 	
	10/07/2004 18:36:24
	
	1 row selected.
	``

add_months(date, months)	Adds or subtracts the specified number of months from the specified date.
	
	``
	select
	   sysdate,
	   add_months(sysdate, 2)
	from
	   dual;
	
	SYSDATE ADD_MONTHS(SYSDATE,
	------------------ ------------------
	10/07/2004 18:40:46 10/09/2004 18:40:46
	
	1 row selected.
	``

DATE FUNCTION	USAGE

last_day(date)	Returns the last day of the month that contains the specified date.
	
	``
	select
	    sysdate,
	    last_day(sysdate)
	from
	    dual;
	
	SYSDATE LAST_DAY(SYSDATE)
	------------------ ------------------
	10/07/2004 18:42:14 31/07/2004 18:42:14
	
	1 row selected.
	``

next_day(date, day)	Returns the date of the first day that matches the specified day that occurs after the specified date.
	
	``
	select
	    sysdate,
	    next_day(sysdate, 'MONDAY')
	from
	    dual;
	
	SYSDATE NEXT_DAY(SYSDATE,'M
	------------------ ------------------
	10/07/2004 18:43:44 12/07/2004 18:43:44
	
	1 row selected.
	``

new_time(date, timezone1, timezone2)	Converts a date from timezone1 into the appropriate date for timezone2.
	
	``
	select
	    sysdate,
	    new_time(sysdate, 'GMT', 'EST')
	from
	    dual;
	
	SYSDATE NEW_TIME(SYSDATE,'G
	------------------ ------------------
	10/07/2004 18:46:12 10/07/2004 13:46:12
	
	1 row selected.
	``

DATE FUNCTION	USAGE

to_char(date, format)	Converts a specified date to a string using the specified format mask. If the format mask is omitted, the *nls_date_format* value is used. There is also an overload of this function to deal with timestamps where the default format mask is taken from the *nls_timestamp_format* or *nls_timestamp_tz_format* value.
	
	``
	select
	    to_char(sysdate, 'DD/MM/YY HH24:MI')
	from
	    dual;
	
	TO_CHAR(SYSDAT
	-------------- 	
	10/07/04 18:48
	
	1 row selected.
	``

to_date(date_string, format)	Converts a specified string to a date using the specified format mask. If the format mask is omitted, the *nls_date_format* value is used.
	
	``
	select
	    to_date('10/07/2004 13:31:45',
	'DD/MM/YYYY HH24:MI:SS')
	from
	    dual;
	
	TO_DATE('10/07/2004
	------------------- 	
	10/07/2004 13:31:45
	
	1 row selected.
	``

round(date, format)	Returns a date rounded to the level specified by the format. The default value for the format is DD, returning the date without the fractional (time) component, making it represent midnight on the specified date or the following date depending on the rounding.
	
	``
	select
	    sysdate,
	    round(sysdate, 'HH24')
	from
	    dual;
	
	SYSDATE ROUND(SYSDATE,'HH24
	------------------- -------------------
	10/07/2004 18:54:24 10/07/2004 19:00:00
	
	1 row selected.
	``

DATE FUNCTION	USAGE
	Returns a date truncated to the level specified by the format. The default value for the format is DD, truncating the fractional (time) component, making it represent midnight on the specified date. Using the *trunc* function allows comparison of dates without the time components distracting from the true meaning of the comparison. It is similar to the round function, except that it always rounds down.
| *trunc(date, format)* | ```
select
    sysdate,
    trunc(sysdate, 'HH24')
from
    dual;

SYSDATE              TRUNC(SYSDATE,'HH24
-------------------- --------------------
10/07/2004 18:55:44 10/07/2004 18:00:00

1 row selected.
``` |

Table 3.3 - *Select date functions and examples of their usage*

The *round* and *trunc* functions can be especially useful; therefore, their format models will be included in more detail. Table 3.4 below lists the format models, their meanings and examples of their usage. The dates have been adjusted, where necessary, to show the difference between the return values of the functions.

FORMAT MODEL	ROUNDING OR TRUNCATING UNIT
	To the first year of the century (1901, 2001, 2101 etc.)
| CC SCC | ```
select
    sysdate,
    trunc(sysdate, 'CC'),
    round(sysdate, 'CC')
from
    dual;

SYSDATE              TRUNC(SYSDATE,'CC')  ROUND(SYSDATE,'CC')
-------------------- -------------------- --------------------
16-JAN-1999 08:48:09 01-JAN-1901 00:00:00 01-JAN-2001 00:00:00

1 row selected.
``` |

FORMAT MODEL	ROUNDING OR TRUNCATING UNIT
	To the year. Rounds up on July 1st.
| SYYYY<br>YYYY<br>YEAR<br>SYEAR<br>YYY<br>YY<br>Y | ```
select
  sysdate,
  trunc(sysdate, 'YY'),
  round(sysdate, 'YY')
from
  dual;

SYSDATE             TRUNC(SYSDATE,'YY') ROUND(SYSDATE,'YY')
------------------- ------------------- -------------------
08-JUL-2004 08:08:49 01-JAN-2004 00:00:00 01-JAN-2005 00:00:00

1 row selected.
``` |
| | **To the ISO Year.** |
| IYYY<br>IY<br>IY<br>I | ```
select
  sysdate,
  trunc(sysdate, 'IY'),
  round(sysdate, 'IY')
from
  dual;

SYSDATE             TRUNC(SYSDATE,'IY') ROUND(SYSDATE,'IY')
------------------- ------------------- -------------------
08-JUL-2004 08:10:39 29-DEC-2003 00:00:00 03-JAN-2005 00:00:00

1 row selected.
``` |
| | **To the quarter, rounding up on the 16th day of the second month.** |
| Q | ```
select
  sysdate,
  trunc(sysdate, 'Q'),
  round(sysdate, 'Q')
from
  dual;

SYSDATE             TRUNC(SYSDATE,'Q')  ROUND(SYSDATE,'Q')
------------------- ------------------- -------------------
22-AUG-2004 08:23:56 01-JUL-2004 00:00:00 01-OCT-2004 00:00:00

1 row selected.
``` |
```

FORMAT MODEL	ROUNDING OR TRUNCATING UNIT
	To the month, rounding up on the 16th day.
| MONTH<br>MON<br>MM<br>RM | ```
select
  sysdate,
  trunc(sysdate, 'MM'),
  round(sysdate, 'MM')
from
  dual;

SYSDATE              TRUNC(SYSDATE,'MM')  ROUND(SYSDATE,'MM')
-------------------  -------------------  -------------------
16-JUL-2004 08:15:31 01-JUL-2004 00:00:00 01-AUG-2004 00:00:00

1 row selected.
``` |
| | **To the same day of the week as the first day of the year.** |
| WW | ```
select
  sysdate,
  trunc(sysdate, 'WW'),
  round(sysdate, 'WW')
from
  dual;

SYSDATE              TRUNC(SYSDATE,'WW')  ROUND(SYSDATE,'WW')
-------------------  -------------------  -------------------
12-JUL-2004 08:20:28 08-JUL-2004 00:00:00 15-JUL-2004 00:00:00

1 row selected.
``` |
| | **To the same day of the week as the first day of the ISO year.** |
| IW | ```
select
  sysdate,
  trunc(sysdate, 'IW'),
  round(sysdate, 'IW')
from
  dual;

SYSDATE              TRUNC(SYSDATE,'IW')  ROUND(SYSDATE,'IW')
-------------------  -------------------  -------------------
16-JUL-2004 08:26:02 12-JUL-2004 00:00:00 19-JUL-2004 00:00:00

1 row selected.
``` |
```

FORMAT MODEL	ROUNDING OR TRUNCATING UNIT

To the same day of the week as the first day of the month.

W

```
select
  sysdate,
  trunc(sysdate, 'W'),
  round(sysdate, 'W')
from
  dual;

SYSDATE              TRUNC(SYSDATE,'W')   ROUND(SYSDATE,'W')
-------------------- -------------------- --------------------
13-JUL-2004 08:28:10 08-JUL-2004 00:00:00 15-JUL-2004 00:00:00

1 row selected.
```

To the day.

DDD
DD
J

```
select
  sysdate,
  trunc(sysdate, 'DD'),
  round(sysdate, 'DD')
from
  dual;

SYSDATE              TRUNC(SYSDATE,'DD')  ROUND(SYSDATE,'DD')
-------------------- -------------------- --------------------
08-JUL-2004 20:34:24 08-JUL-2004 00:00:00 09-JUL-2004 00:00:00

1 row selected.
```

To the starting day of the week.

DAY
DY
D

```
select
  sysdate,
  trunc(sysdate, 'D'),
  round(sysdate, 'D')
from
  dual;

SYSDATE              TRUNC(SYSDATE,'D')   ROUND(SYSDATE,'D')
-------------------- -------------------- --------------------
09-JUL-2004 08:33:01 04-JUL-2004 00:00:00 11-JUL-2004 00:00:00

1 row selected.
```

To the hour.

HH
HH12
HH24

```
select
  sysdate,
  trunc(sysdate, 'HH'),
  round(sysdate, 'HH')
from
  dual;

SYSDATE              TRUNC(SYSDATE,'HH')  ROUND(SYSDATE,'HH')
-------------------- -------------------- --------------------
08-JUL-2004 08:36:22 08-JUL-2004 08:00:00 08-JUL-2004 09:00:00

1 row selected.
```

FORMAT MODEL	ROUNDING OR TRUNCATING UNIT

MI	To the minute.
	
	``
	select
	  sysdate,
	  trunc(sysdate, 'MI'),
	  round(sysdate, 'MI')
	from
	  dual;
	
	SYSDATE TRUNC(SYSDATE,'HH') ROUND(SYSDATE,'HH')
	------------------- -------------------- --------------------
	08-JUL-2004 08:37:32 08-JUL-2004 08:37:00 08-JUL-2004 08:38:00
	
	1 row selected.
	``

Table 3.4 - *Format models, their meanings and examples of usage*

This introduction to the DATE datatype is a good foundation for the information presented on the TIMESTAMP datatype in the following section. The TIMESTAMP datatype is similar to the DATE datatype in many ways.

Timestamps

The TIMESTAMP datatype is an extension on the DATE datatype. In addition to the datetime elements of the DATE datatype, the TIMESTAMP datatype holds fractions of a second to a precision between zero and nine decimal places, the default being six. There are also two variants called TIMESTAMP WITH TIME ZONE and TIMESTAMP WITH LOCAL TIME ZONE. As their names imply, these timestamps also store time zone offset information.

Like dates, timestamps are stored using a binary date format. A TIMESTAMP is 11 bytes long; while those variants with time zone information require 13 bytes. Table 3.5 below shows how each of the 11-13 bytes is used to store the timestamp information:

BYTE	MEANING	NOTATION	EXAMPLE (10-JUL-2004 17:21:30.662509 +01:00)
1	Century	Divided by 100, excess-100	120

BYTE	MEANING	NOTATION	EXAMPLE (10-JUL-2004 17:21:30.662509 +01:00)
2	Year	Modulo 100, excess-100	104
3	Month	0 base	7
4	Day	0 base	10
5	Hour	excess-1 (-offset)	17
6	Minute	excess-1	22
7	Second	excess-1	31
8			
9	Fraction of a second	9 digit integer stored in 4 bytes	39,125,21,200
10			
11			
12	Timezone Hour	excess-20	21
13	Timezone Min	excess-60	60

Table 3.5 - *How the 11-13 bytes are used to store timestamp information*

The following example uses the *dump* function to show the contents of a stored timestamp:

```
alter session set nls_timestamp_tz_format = 'DD-MON-YYYY
HH24:MI:SS.FF TZH:TZM';

drop table timestamp_test;
create table timestamp_test as
select
   systimestamp as now
from
   dual
;
select
   now,
   dump (now)
from
   timestamp_test
;

NOW
-----------------------------------------------------
DUMP(NOW)
-----------------------------------------------------
31-JUL-04 11.15.05.662509 +01:00
Typ=181 Len=13: 120,104,7,31,11,16,6,39,125,21,200,21,60

1 row selected.
```

Although they can look confusing due to the action of the offset, the first seven components match those of the DATE datatype. In this example, the offset of +01:00 makes the hour component appear to be in zero base notation, rather than excess-1; however, when the offset is added, it is clear to see that it is not.. The offset component represents the number of minutes the time is offset due to the time zone.

The 10g scheduler uses timestamps to define time-related information about scheduled jobs, as seen in the *dbms_scheduler.create_schedule* procedure and the *dba_scheduler_schedules* view shown below.

```
PROCEDURE create_schedule (
   schedule_name            IN VARCHAR2,
   start_date               IN TIMESTAMP WITH TIME ZONE   DEFAULT NULL,
   repeat_interval          IN VARCHAR2,
   end_date                 IN TIMESTAMP WITH TIME ZONE   DEFAULT NULL,
   comments                 IN VARCHAR2                   DEFAULT NULL)

SQL> describe dba_scheduler_schedules
 Name                          Null?      Type
 ----------------------------- --------   ------------------------
 OWNER                         NOT NULL   VARCHAR2(30)
 SCHEDULE_NAME                 NOT NULL   VARCHAR2(30)
 START_DATE                               TIMESTAMP(6) WITH TIME ZONE
 REPEAT_INTERVAL                          VARCHAR2(4000)
 END_DATE                                 TIMESTAMP(6) WITH TIME ZONE
 COMMENTS                                 VARCHAR2(240)
```

The mathematical operations and most of the date functions mentioned previously are also valid for timestamps. In addition to the date functions, Oracle provides several timestamp specific functions listed in Table 3.6 below.

TIMESTAMP FUNCTION	USAGE

systimestamp(precision)	Returns the current TIMESTAMP from the operating system of the database server to the specified precision. If no precision is specified, the default is 6.
	
	``
	select
	  systimestamp(3)
	from
	  dual;
	
	SYSTIMESTAMP(3)
	--------------------------- 	
	10-JUL-04 19.09.35.793 +01:00
	
	1 row selected.
	``

current_timestamp(precision)	Similar to the *systimestamp* function, but returns the current TIMSTAMP WITH TIME ZONE within the sessions time zone to the specified precision. If no precision is specified, the default is 6.
	
	``
	select
	  current_timestamp(3)
	from
	  dual;
	
	CURRENT_TIMESTAMP(3)
	--------------------------- 	
	10-JUL-04 19.11.12.686 +01:00
	
	1 row selected.
	``

localtimestamp(precision)	Similar to the *current_timestamp* function, but returns the current TIMESTAMP with time zone within the sessions time zone to the specified precision. If no precision is specified, the default is six.
	
	``
	select
	  localtimestamp(3)
	from
	  dual;
	
	LOCALTIMESTAMP(3)
	--------------------- 	
	10-JUL-04 19.12.21.859
	
	1 row selected.
	``

TIMESTAMP FUNCTION	USAGE

to_timestamp(string, format)	Converts a specified string to a TIMESTAMP using the specified format mask. If the format mask is omitted, the *nls_timestamp_format* or *nls_timestamp_tz_format* value is used depending on the context.
	
	``select
	  to_timestamp('10/07/2004',
	'DD/MM/YYYY')
	from
	  dual;
	
	TO_TIMESTAMP('10/07/2004','DD/MM/
	YYYY')
	--------------------------------- 	
	10-JUL-04 00.00.00.000000000
	
	1 row selected.```

to_timestamp_tz(string, format)	Converts a specified string to a TIMESTAMP WITH TIME ZONE using the specified format mask. If the format mask is omitted, the *nls_timestamp_format* or *nls_timestamp_tz_format* value is used depending on the context.
	
	``select
	  to_timestamp_tz('10/07/2004',
	'DD/MM/YYYY')
	from
	  dual;
	
	TO_TIMESTAMP_TZ('10/07/2004','DD/MM/YYYY')
	-- 	
	10-JUL-04 00.00.00.000000000 +01:00
	
	1 row selected.```

from_tz(timestamp, timezone)	Converts a TIMESTAMP and a string representing the time zone to a TIMESTAMP WITH TIME ZONE.
	
	``select
	  from_tz(localtimestamp, '3:00')
	from
	  dual;
	
	FROM_TZ(LOCALTIMESTAMP,'3:00')
	--------------------------------- 	
	10-JUL-04 19.19.07.385684 +03:00
	
	1 row selected.```

TIMESTAMP FUNCTION	USAGE

dbtimezone	Returns the database time zone.
	
	``
	select
	  dbtimezone
	from
	  dual;
	
	DBTIME
	------ 	
	+00:00
	
	1 row selected.
	``

sessiontimezone	Returns the current session's time zone.
	
	``
	select
	  sessiontimezone
	from
	  dual;
	
	SESSIONTIMEZONE
	--------------- 	
	+01:00
	
	1 row selected.
	``

sys_extract_utc(timestamp)	Returns the UTC, or GMT timestamp from a specified TIMESTAMP WITH TIME ZONE.
	
	``
	select
	  sys_extract_utc(systimestamp)
	from
	  dual;
	
	SYS_EXTRACT_UTC(SYSTIMESTAMP)
	----------------------------- 	
	10-JUL-04 18.23.09.393478
	
	1 row selected.
	``

extract(datepart from date)	Extracts the specified datepart from the specified timestamp.
	
	``
	select
	  extract(hour from
	systimestamp)
	from
	  dual;
	
	EXTRACT(HOURFROMSYSTIMESTAMP)
	----------------------------- 	
	                           18
	
	1 row selected.
	``

Table 3.6 – *Oracle timestamp specific functions*

In the Oracle10g scheduler, the repeat interval of a job can be defined by a PL/SQL expression or by using a new calendar syntax, which will be presented later in this chapter.

Now that the two datetime values of DATE and TIMESTAMP have been introduced, the following section will illustrate how intervals can be stored in the database and defined using the interval literal syntax.

Intervals and Interval Literals

Intervals provide a way of storing a specific period of time that separates two datetime values. There is no need to store any intervals to use the Oracle scheduler, but an explanation of them will help put the information on interval literals into context.

There are currently two supported types of intervals. One specifies intervals in years and months, and the other specifies intervals in days, hours, minutes and seconds. The syntax of these datatypes is shown below.

```
INTERVAL YEAR [(year_precision)] TO MONTH
INTERVAL DAY [(day_precision)] TO SECOND
[(fractional_seconds_precision)]
```

The precision elements are defined as follows:

- *year_precision* - The maximum number of digits in the year component of the interval, such that a precision of three limits the interval to a maximum of 999 years. The default value is two.

- *day_precision* - The maximum number of digits in the day component of the interval, such that a precision of four limits the interval to a maximum of 9999 days. The day precision can accept a value from zero to nine, with the default value being two.

- *fraction_second_precision* - The number of digits in the fractional component of the interval. Values between zero and nine are allowed, with the default value being six.

In the following example, a table is created to show how intervals can be used as column definitions:

```
create table test_interval_table (
  id              number(10),
  time_period_1   interval year to month,
  time_period_2   interval day to second,
  time_period_3   interval year (3) to month,
  time_period_4   interval day (4) to second (9)
);

SQL> describe test_interval_table
 Name                                     Null?    Type
 --------------------------------- -------- -----------------------
 ID                                                 NUMBER(10)
 TIME_PERIOD_1                                      INTERVAL YEAR(2) TO MONTH
 TIME_PERIOD_2                                      INTERVAL DAY(2) TO
SECOND(6)
 TIME_PERIOD_3                                      INTERVAL YEAR(3) TO MONTH
 TIME_PERIOD_4                                      INTERVAL DAY(4) TO
SECOND(9)
```

Interval literals are used to define intervals in an easy to understand manner. There are two separate syntax definitions, one for each type of interval. The full syntax definitions can be a little confusing so they will be skipped in favor of examples that make their usage more clear.

The YEAR TO MONTH interval literal syntax will be presented first. The default precision for the fields is listed below, along with the allowable values if specified as a trailing field.

- YEAR - Number of years with a default precision of two digits.

- MONTH - Number of months with a default precision of four digits. If specified as a trailing field, it has allowable values of zero to 11.

INTERVAL LITERAL	MEANING
INTERVAL '21-2' YEAR TO MONTH	An interval of 21 years and two months.
INTERVAL '100-5' YEAR(3) TO MONTH	An interval of 100 years and five months. The leading precision is specified, as it is greater than the default of two.
INTERVAL '1' YEAR	An interval of one year.
INTERVAL '20' MONTH	An interval of 20 months.
INTERVAL '100' YEAR(3)	An interval of 100 years. The precision must be specified as this value is beyond the default precision.
INTERVAL '10000' MONTH(5)	An interval of 10,000 months. The precision must be specified as this value is beyond the default precision.

INTERVAL LITERAL	MEANING
INTERVAL '1-13' YEAR TO MONTH	Error produced. When the leading field is YEAR the allowable values for MONTH are zero to 11.

Table 3.7 – *YEAR TO MONTH intervals and their meanings*

These intervals from Table 3.7 can be tested by substituting them into the following query. The month syntax is converted into a years and months value.

```
select
    interval '20' month
from
    dual
;

INTERVAL'20'MONTH
----------------------------------------------------------------------
+01-08

1 row selected.
```

A YEAR TO MONTH interval can be added to or subtracted from, with the result being another YEAR TO MONTH interval.

```
select
    interval '1' year - interval '1' month
from
    dual
;

INTERVAL'1'YEAR-INTERVAL'1'MONTH
----------------------------------------------------------------------
+000000000-11

1 row selected.
```

The following examples relate to the DAY TO SECOND interval literal syntax. As with the previous example, if a trailing field is specified, it must be less significant than the previous field.

- DAY - Number of days with a default precision of two digits.

- HOUR - Number of hours with a default precision of three digits. If specified as a trailing field it has allowable values of zero to 23.

- MINUTE - Number of minutes with a default precision of five digits. If specified as a trailing field it has allowable values of zero to 59.

- SECOND - Number of seconds with a default precision of seven digits before the decimal point and six digits after. If specified as a trailing field, it has allowable values of zero to 59.999999999.

INTERVA LITERAL	MEANING
INTERVAL '2 3:04:11.333' DAY TO SECOND(3)	2 days, 3 hours, 4 minutes, 11 seconds and 333 thousandths of a second.
INTERVAL '2 3:04' DAY TO MINUTE	2 days, 3 hours, 4 minutes.
INTERVAL '2 3' DAY TO HOUR	2 days, 3 hours.
INTERVAL '2' DAY	2 days.
INTERVAL '03:04:11.333' HOUR TO SECOND	3 hours, 4 minutes, 11 seconds and 333 thousandths of a second.
INTERVAL '03:04' HOUR TO MINUTE	3 hours, 4 minutes.
INTERVAL '40' HOUR	40 hours.
INTERVAL '04:11.333' MINUTE TO SECOND	4 minutes, 11 seconds and 333 thousandths of a second.
INTERVAL '70' MINUTE	70 minutes.
INTERVAL '70' SECOND	70 seconds.
INTERVAL '03:70' HOUR TO MINUTE	Error produced. When the leading field is specified the allowable values for the trailing field must be within normal range.

Table 3.8 - *DAY TO SECOND intervals and their meanings*

Substituting the intervals from Table 3.8 into the following query will allow those intervals to be tested. The default precision for seconds is used because it has not been to three decimal places.

```
select
    interval '2 3:04:11.333' day to second
from
    dual
;

INTERVAL'23:04:11.333'DAYTOSECOND
-------------------------------------------------------------------
+02 03:04:11.333000

1 row selected.
```

A DAY TO SECOND interval can be added to or subtracted from, with the result being another DAY TO SECOND interval.

```
select
   interval '1' day - interval '1' second
from
   dual
;

INTERVAL'1'DAY-INTERVAL'1'SECOND
--------------------------------------------------------------------
+000000000 23:59:59.000000000

1 row selected.
```

Intervals can also be combined with dates to manipulate date values. The
following query shows how this is done:

```
select
   sysdate,
   sysdate + interval '1' month + interval '1' day - interval '3'
second
from
   dual
;

SYSDATE              SYSDATE+INTERVAL'1'M
-------------------- --------------------
10-JUL-2004 19:55:53 11-AUG-2004 19:55:50

1 row selected.
```

Oracle provides several interval specific functions, which are listed in Table
3.9 below.

INTERVAL FUNCTION	USAGE

numtoyminterval (integer, unit)	Converts the specified integer to a YEAR TO MONTH interval in which the integer represents the number of units.
	
	``
	Select
	   numtoyminterval(2, 'MONTH')
	from
	   dual;
	
	NUMTOYMINTERVAL(2,'MONTH')
	+000000000-02
	
	1 row selected.
	``

INTERVAL FUNCTION	USAGE

numtodsinterval (integer, unit)	Converts the specified integer to DAY TO SECOND interval in which the integer represents the number of units.
	
	``
	Select
	    numtodsinterval(2, 'HOUR')
	from
	    dual;
	``
	
	NUMTODSINTERVAL(2,'HOUR')
	+000000000 02:00:00.000000000
	
	1 row selected.

to_yminterval (interval_string)	Converts a string representing an interval into a YEAR TO MONTH interval.
	
	``
	Select
	    to_yminterval('3-10')
	from
	    dual;
	``
	
	TO_YMINTERVAL('3-10')
	+000000003-10
	
	1 row selected.

to_dsinterval (interval_string)	Converts a string representing an interval into a DAY TO SECOND interval.
	
	``
	Select
	    to_dsinterval('2 10:3:45.123')
	from
	    dual;
	``
	
	TO_DSINTERVAL('210:3:45.123')
	+000000002 10:03:45.123000000
	
	1 row selected.

extract(datepart from interval)	Extracts the specified datepart from the specified interval.
	
	``
	Select
	    extract(hour from
	                numtodsinterval(2,
	'HOUR'))
	from
	    dual;
	``
	
	EXTRACT(HOURFROMNUMTODSINTERVAL(2,'HOUR'))
	2
	
	1 row selected.

Table 3.9 – *Interval Specific Functions provided by Oracle*

Now that the groundwork for using PL/SQL expressions has been covered, the calendaring syntax available in Oracle10g will be presented in the following section.

Calendar Syntax in Oracle10g

Oracle10g introduced a calendar syntax allowing complex job execution cycles to be defined in a simple and clear manner. The calendar syntax is listed below:

```
repeat_interval = freq=?
  [; interval=?] [; bymonth=?] [; byweekno=?]
  [; byyearday=?] [; bymonthday=?] [; byday=?]
  [; byhour=?] [; byminute=?] [; bysecond=?]
```

Before investigating what the individual clauses of this syntax mean, how the calendar strings can be tested should be explained. The *evaluate_calendar_string* procedure from the *dbms_scheduler* package returns run timestamps by evaluating a specified calendar string.

```
PROCEDURE evaluate_calendar_string (
   calendar_string    IN  VACRHAR2,
   start_date         IN  TIMESTAMP WITH TIME ZONE,
   return_date_after  IN  TIMESTAMP WITH TIME ZONE,
   next_run_date      OUT TIMESTAMP WITH TIME ZONE);
```

The parameters associated with this procedure and their usage are as follows:

- *calendar_string* - The calendar string to be evaluated.

- *start_date* - The date the calendar string becomes valid. If elements of the calendar string are missing, they may be derived from elements of this date.

- *return_after_date* - Only dates after this date will be returned by the procedure. If no date is specified, the current systimestamp is used.

- *next_run_date* - The first date that matches the *calendar_string* and *start_date* and is greater than the *run_after_date*.

The *test_calendar_string.sql* procedure, listed below, uses the *evaluate_calendar_string* procedure to display a list of run dates. For convenience, the *start_date* and *run_after_date* parameters are defaulted.

```
-- **************************************************
-- Copyright © 2005 by Rampant TechPress
-- This script is free for non-commercial purposes
-- with no warranties.  Use at your own risk.
--
-- To license this script for a commercial purpose,
-- contact info@rampant.cc
-- **************************************************

set serveroutput on;
alter session set nls_timestamp_format = 'DD-MON-YYYY HH24:MI:SS';

CREATE OR REPLACE PROCEDURE test_calendar_string(
  p_calendar_string  IN  VARCHAR2,
  p_iterations       IN  NUMBER DEFAULT 5)
AS
  l_start_date            TIMESTAMP := TO_TIMESTAMP('01-JAN-2004
03:04:32',
                                      'DD-MON-YYYY
HH24:MI:SS');
  l_return_date_after  TIMESTAMP := l_start_date;
  l_next_run_date      TIMESTAMP;
BEGIN
  FOR i IN 1 .. p_iterations LOOP
    DBMS_SCHEDULER.evaluate_calendar_string (
      calendar_string   => p_calendar_string,
      start_date        => l_start_date,
      return_date_after => l_return_date_after,
      next_run_date     => l_next_run_date);

    DBMS_OUTPUT.put_line('Next Run Date: ' || l_next_run_date);
    l_return_date_after := l_next_run_date;
  END LOOP;
END;
/
```

The individual clauses that make up a calendar string are explained in Table 3.10 below. The *test_calendar_string* procedure is used to display sample run timestamps to make the element usage clear.

PARAMETER	MEANING
Freq	Specifies the frequency, or type of recurrence, and is the only mandatory clause. Its allowable values are: yearly, monthly, weekly, daily, hourly, minutely and secondly. ``` SQL> -- Run every second. SQL> exec test_calendar_string('freq=secondly'); Next Run Date: 01-JAN-2004 03:04:33 Next Run Date: 01-JAN-2004 03:04:34 Next Run Date: 01-JAN-2004 03:04:35 Next Run Date: 01-JAN-2004 03:04:36 Next Run Date: 01-JAN-2004 03:04:37 PL/SQL procedure successfully completed. ```

interval	Specifies the interval associated with the specified frequency, such that an interval of 2 on a minutely frequency would cause the job to execute every other minute, while an interval of 10 would cause it to execute every 10 minutes. The allowable values are 1 to 999, with a default value of 1.
	
	``
	SQL> -- Run every 30 minutes
	SQL> exec test_calendar_string('freq=minutely;
	interval=30');
	Next Run Date: 01-JAN-2004 03:34:32
	Next Run Date: 01-JAN-2004 04:04:32
	Next Run Date: 01-JAN-2004 04:34:32
	Next Run Date: 01-JAN-2004 05:04:32
	Next Run Date: 01-JAN-2004 05:34:32
	PL/SQL procedure successfully completed.
	``

bymonth	Specifies the month or months on which the job should execute. The month can be specified using the month number (1-12) or using the three letter abbreviation (jan-dec).
	
	``
	SQL> -- Run on months 1, 2, 11 and 12.
	SQL> exec test_calendar_string('freq=monthly;
	bymonth=1,2,11,12');
	Next Run Date: 01-FEB-2004 03:04:32
	Next Run Date: 01-NOV-2004 03:04:32
	Next Run Date: 01-DEC-2004 03:04:32
	Next Run Date: 01-JAN-2005 03:04:32
	Next Run Date: 01-FEB-2005 03:04:32
	PL/SQL procedure successfully completed.
	
	SQL> -- Run on months JAN, FEB, NOV and DEC.
	SQL> exec test_calendar_string('freq=monthly;
	bymonth=jan,feb,nov,dec');
	Next Run Date: 01-FEB-2004 03:04:32
	Next Run Date: 01-NOV-2004 03:04:32
	Next Run Date: 01-DEC-2004 03:04:32
	Next Run Date: 01-JAN-2005 03:04:32
	Next Run Date: 01-FEB-2005 03:04:32
	PL/SQL procedure successfully completed.
	``

PARAMETER	MEANING
byweekno	Specifies the week or weeks of the year to include for strings with a yearly frequency. Allowable values are one to 52 (or 53), with the week starting on a Monday and finishing on a Sunday.

```
SQL> -- Run on the first Monday of weeks
10,20,30,40,50.
SQL> exec test_calendar_string('freq=yearly;
byweekno=10,20,30,40,50; byday=mon');
Next Run Date: 01-MAR-2004 03:04:32
Next Run Date: 10-MAY-2004 03:04:32
Next Run Date: 19-JUL-2004 03:04:32
Next Run Date: 27-SEP-2004 03:04:32
Next Run Date: 06-DEC-2004 03:04:32

PL/SQL procedure successfully completed.
```

PARAMETER	MEANING
byyearday	Specifies the day or days of the year with valid values from one to 366.

```
SQL> -- Run on the 100th, 200th and 300th days of the
year.
SQL> exec test_calendar_string('freq=yearly;
byyearday=100,200,300');
Next Run Date: 09-APR-2004 03:04:32
Next Run Date: 18-JUL-2004 03:04:32
Next Run Date: 26-OCT-2004 03:04:32
Next Run Date: 10-APR-2005 03:04:32
Next Run Date: 19-JUL-2005 03:04:32

PL/SQL procedure successfully completed.
```

PARAMETER	MEANING
bymonthday	Specifies the day or days of the month with valid values from one to 31. Using a negative number results in a count backwards from the end of the month such that -1 means the last day of the month.

```
SQL> -- Run on the first two days of the month.
SQL> exec test_calendar_string('freq=monthly;
bymonthday=1,2');
Next Run Date: 02-JAN-2004 03:04:32
Next Run Date: 01-FEB-2004 03:04:32
Next Run Date: 02-FEB-2004 03:04:32
Next Run Date: 01-MAR-2004 03:04:32
Next Run Date: 02-MAR-2004 03:04:32

PL/SQL procedure successfully completed.

SQL> -- Run on the last two days of the month.
SQL> exec test_calendar_string('freq=monthly;
bymonthday=-1,-2');
Next Run Date: 30-JAN-2004 03:04:32
Next Run Date: 31-JAN-2004 03:04:32
Next Run Date: 28-FEB-2004 03:04:32
Next Run Date: 29-FEB-2004 03:04:32
Next Run Date: 30-MAR-2004 03:04:32

PL/SQL procedure successfully completed.
```

PARAMETER	MEANING
byday	Specifies the day or days of the week with reference to the frequency using the three letter abbreviation. When used with a yearly or monthly frequency, the day can be prefixed with a number. Prefixing the day with a number indicates the occurrence of that number within the frequency, with negative numbers providing a backwards count.

```
SQL> -- Run on the thirty fifth Monday of the year.
SQL> exec test_calendar_string('freq=yearly;
byday=35MON');
Next Run Date: 30-AUG-2004 03:04:32
Next Run Date: 29-AUG-2005 03:04:32
Next Run Date: 28-AUG-2006 03:04:32
Next Run Date: 27-AUG-2007 03:04:32
Next Run Date: 01-SEP-2008 03:04:32

PL/SQL procedure successfully completed.

SQL> -- Run on the second Monday of the month.
SQL> exec test_calendar_string('freq=monthly;
byday=2MON');
Next Run Date: 12-JAN-2004 03:04:32
Next Run Date: 09-FEB-2004 03:04:32
Next Run Date: 08-MAR-2004 03:04:32
Next Run Date: 12-APR-2004 03:04:32
Next Run Date: 10-MAY-2004 03:04:32

PL/SQL procedure successfully completed.

SQL> -- Run on the last Wednesday of the month.
SQL> exec test_calendar_string('freq=monthly; byday=-
1WED');
Next Run Date: 28-JAN-2004 03:04:32
Next Run Date: 25-FEB-2004 03:04:32
Next Run Date: 31-MAR-2004 03:04:32
Next Run Date: 28-APR-2004 03:04:32
Next Run Date: 26-MAY-2004 03:04:32

PL/SQL procedure successfully completed.
```

byhour	Specifies the hour or hours of the day with valid values from zero to 23. Negative numbers result in a backwards count.

```
-- Run on the first hour of every day.
SQL> exec test_calendar_string('freq=daily;
byhour=1');
Next Run Date: 02-JAN-2004 01:04:32
Next Run Date: 03-JAN-2004 01:04:32
Next Run Date: 04-JAN-2004 01:04:32
Next Run Date: 05-JAN-2004 01:04:32
Next Run Date: 06-JAN-2004 01:04:32

PL/SQL procedure successfully completed.
```

PARAMETER	MEANING
byminute	Specifies the minute or minutes of the hour with valid values from zero to 59.

```
-- Run on the first minute of every hour.
SQL> exec test_calendar_string('freq=hourly;
byminute=1');
Next Run Date: 01-JAN-2004 04:01:32
Next Run Date: 01-JAN-2004 05:01:32
Next Run Date: 01-JAN-2004 06:01:32
Next Run Date: 01-JAN-2004 07:01:32
Next Run Date: 01-JAN-2004 08:01:32

PL/SQL procedure successfully completed.
```

PARAMETER	MEANING
bysecond	Specifies the second or seconds of the minute with valid values from zero to 59. Negative numbers result in a backwards count.

```
-- Run on the first second of every minute.
SQL> exec test_calendar_string('freq=minutely;
bysecond=1');
Next Run Date: 01-JAN-2004 03:05:01
Next Run Date: 01-JAN-2004 03:06:01
Next Run Date: 01-JAN-2004 03:07:01
Next Run Date: 01-JAN-2004 03:08:01
Next Run Date: 01-JAN-2004 03:09:01

PL/SQL procedure successfully completed.
```

Table 3.10 – *Calendar parameters and their meanings*

The following points contain general guidance information for the use of calendar syntax during scheduling:

- The calendar string must contain a frequency as the first clause. All other clauses are optional and can be placed in any order.

- Each clause can only be present once and must be separated by a semi-colon.

- The calendar strings are not case sensitive and white spaces between clauses are allowed.

- Where a BY clause contains a list of values, the order of the list is not important.

- When there are not enough clauses to determine the precise run date, the missing clauses are derived from the *start_date*. For example, if there is no *bysecond* clause in the calendar string, the value of seconds from the *start_date* is used to create one.

- When a number range is not fixed, the last value of the range can be determined using a negative integer as a count-back. As such *bymonthday=-1* equates to the last day of the month. The documentation states that count-backs are not supported for fixed number ranges such as those used by the bymonth, byhour, byminute and bysecond clauses, but they do appear to work consistently.

- The first day of the week is Monday.

- A calendar string cannot specify time zones. Instead the time zone is derived from one of the following places in this order: the *start_date*, the current session's time zone, the DEFAULT_TIMEZONE scheduler attribute, or time zone returned by the *systimestamp* function.

Now that calendar syntax has been introduced in detail, the following section will compare the use of PL/SQL expressions and the use of calendar syntax for scheduling jobs.

Complex Date Rules for Job Execution

Prior to Oracle10g, the only way to define a jobs repeat interval was to use a PL/SQL expression that evaluated to a date. In Oracle10g, the calendar syntax is the preferred way to define a jobs repeat interval, although PL/SQL expression can still be used if they evaluate to a timestamp. In this section we will compare how each method works.

The previous section used the *test_calendar_string.sql* procedure to display the run schedule expected for a specific calendar string. Before any comparisons between the possible scheduling methods can be done, a way to test the PL/QSL expressions that are used to schedule jobs using dates and timestamps is needed. The *test_date_string* procedure listed below is similar to the *test_calendar_string* procedure, but it displays run dates defined by interval strings that might be used when scheduling jobs via the *dbms_job* package.

🖫 **test_date_string.sql**

```
-- ************************************************
-- Copyright © 2005 by Rampant TechPress
-- This script is free for non-commercial purposes
-- with no warranties.  Use at your own risk.
--
-- To license this script for a commercial purpose,
-- contact info@rampant.cc
-- ************************************************
```

```
set serveroutput on;
alter session set nls_date_format = 'DD-MON-YYYY HH24:MI:SS';

CREATE OR REPLACE PROCEDURE test_date_string(
  p_interval    IN  VARCHAR2,
  p_iterations  IN  NUMBER DEFAULT 5)
AS
  l_interval            VARCHAR2(1000) := p_interval;
  l_start_date          DATE := TO_DATE('01-JAN-2004 03:04:32',
                                         'DD-MON-YYYY HH24:MI:SS');

  l_next_run_date       DATE;
  l_start_date_str      VARCHAR2(100);
BEGIN
  FOR i IN 1 .. p_iterations LOOP
    l_start_date_str := 'TO_DATE(''' ||
                         TO_CHAR(l_start_date, 'DD-MON-YYYY
HH24:MI:SS') ||
                           ''',''DD-MON-YYYY HH24:MI:SS'')';
    l_interval := REPLACE(LOWER(p_interval), 'sysdate',
l_start_date_str);
    EXECUTE IMMEDIATE 'SELECT ' || l_interval || ' INTO :return FROM
dual'
      INTO l_next_run_date;

    DBMS_OUTPUT.put_line('Next Run Date: ' || l_next_run_date);
    l_start_date := l_next_run_date;
  END LOOP;
END;
/
```

The *test_timestamp_string* procedure listed below is a copy of the *test_date_string* procedure that has been adjusted to work with timestamps.

🖫 test_timestamp_string.sql

```
-- *************************************************
-- Copyright © 2005 by Rampant TechPress
-- This script is free for non-commercial purposes
-- with no warranties.  Use at your own risk.
--
-- To license this script for a commercial purpose,
-- contact info@rampant.cc
-- *************************************************

set serveroutput on;
alter session set nls_timestamp_format = 'DD-MON-YYYY HH24:MI:SS';

CREATE OR REPLACE PROCEDURE test_timestamp_string(
  p_interval    IN  VARCHAR2,
  p_iterations  IN  NUMBER DEFAULT 5)
AS
  l_interval            VARCHAR2(1000) := p_interval;
```

```
    l_start_ts          TIMESTAMP := TO_TIMESTAMP('01-JAN-2004
03:04:32',
                                        'DD-MON-YYYY
HH24:MI:SS');

    l_next_run_ts       TIMESTAMP;
    l_start_ts_str      VARCHAR2(100);
BEGIN
  FOR i IN 1 .. p_iterations LOOP
    l_start_ts_str := 'TO_TIMESTAMP('' ||
                      TO_CHAR(l_start_ts, 'DD-MON-YYYY HH24:MI:SS')
||
                      '','''DD-MON-YYYY HH24:MI:SS'')';
    l_interval := REPLACE(LOWER(p_interval), 'systimestamp',
l_start_ts_str);
    EXECUTE IMMEDIATE 'SELECT ' || l_interval || ' INTO :return FROM
dual'
      INTO l_next_run_ts;

    DBMS_OUTPUT.put_line('Next Run Date: ' || l_next_run_ts);
    l_start_ts := l_next_run_ts;
  END LOOP;
END;
/
```

The best way to come to grips with defining repeat intervals and comparing the different methods available is looking at some examples. Table 3.11 below lists a range of repeat intervals along with expressions than can be used to achieve them. The date expressions can be used to schedule jobs using the *dbms_job* package, while the timestamp and calendar syntax expressions can be used for jobs scheduled using the *dbms_scheduler* package in Oracle10g. Where possible, a literal and interval literal example is given along with an example of the output generated by the test procedures.

INTERVAL	EXPRESSION
Every day.	'sysdate + 1'
	'systimestamp + 1'
	'sysdate + interval "1" day'
	'systimestamp + interval "1" day'
	'freq=daily;'

```
            Next Run Date: 02-JAN-2004 03:04:32
            Next Run Date: 03-JAN-2004 03:04:32
            Next Run Date: 04-JAN-2004 03:04:32
            Next Run Date: 05-JAN-2004 03:04:32
            Next Run Date: 06-JAN-2004 03:04:32
```

INTERVAL	EXPRESSION

Midnight every night.	'trunc(sysdate) + 1'
	'trunc(systimestamp) + 1'
	
	'trunc(sysdate) + interval "1" day'
	'trunc(systimestamp) + interval "1" day'
	
	'freq=daily; byhour=0; byminute=0; bysecond=0;'
	
	`Next Run Date: 02-JAN-2004 00:00:00`
	`Next Run Date: 03-JAN-2004 00:00:00`
	`Next Run Date: 04-JAN-2004 00:00:00`
	`Next Run Date: 05-JAN-2004 00:00:00`
	`Next Run Date: 06-JAN-2004 00:00:00`

6:00 AM every day.	'trunc(sysdate) + 1 + 6/24'
	'trunc(systimestamp) + 1 + 6/24'
	
	'trunc(sysdate) + interval "1 6" day to hour '
	'trunc(systimestamp) + interval "1 6" day to hour'
	
	'freq=daily; byhour=6; byminute=0; bysecond=0;'
	
	`Next Run Date: 01-JAN-2004 06:00:00`
	`Next Run Date: 02-JAN-2004 06:00:00`
	`Next Run Date: 03-JAN-2004 06:00:00`
	`Next Run Date: 04-JAN-2004 06:00:00`
	`Next Run Date: 05-JAN-2004 06:00:00`

Every hour.	'sysdate + 1/24'
	'systimestamp + 1/24'
	
	'sysdate + interval "1" hour'
	'systimestamp + interval "1" hour'
	
	'freq=hourly;'
	
	`Next Run Date: 01-JAN-2004 04:04:32`
	`Next Run Date: 01-JAN-2004 05:04:32`
	`Next Run Date: 01-JAN-2004 06:04:32`
	`Next Run Date: 01-JAN-2004 07:04:32`
	`Next Run Date: 01-JAN-2004 08:04:32`

INTERVAL	EXPRESSION
Every hour, on the hour.	'trunc(sysdate, ''HH24'') + 1/24' 'trunc(systimestamp, ''HH24'') + 1/24' 'trunc(sysdate, ''HH24'') + interval ''1'' hour' 'trunc(systimestamp, ''HH24'') + interval ''1'' hour' 'freq=hourly; byminute=0; bysecond=0;' ``` Next Run Date: 01-JAN-2004 04:00:00 Next Run Date: 01-JAN-2004 05:00:00 Next Run Date: 01-JAN-2004 06:00:00 Next Run Date: 01-JAN-2004 07:00:00 Next Run Date: 01-JAN-2004 08:00:00 ```
Every minute.	'sysdate + 1/24/60' 'systimestamp + 1/24/60' 'sysdate + interval ''1'' minute' 'systimestamp + interval ''1'' minute' 'freq=minutely;' ``` Next Run Date: 01-JAN-2004 03:05:32 Next Run Date: 01-JAN-2004 03:06:32 Next Run Date: 01-JAN-2004 03:07:32 Next Run Date: 01-JAN-2004 03:08:32 Next Run Date: 01-JAN-2004 03:09:32 ```
Every minute, on the minute.	'trunc(sysdate, ''MI'') + 1/24/60' 'trunc(systimestamp, ''MI'') + 1/24/60' 'trunc(sysdate, ''MI'') + interval ''1'' minute' 'trunc(systimestamp, ''MI'') + interval ''1'' minute' 'freq=minutely; bysecond=0;' ``` Next Run Date: 01-JAN-2004 03:05:00 Next Run Date: 01-JAN-2004 03:06:00 Next Run Date: 01-JAN-2004 03:07:00 Next Run Date: 01-JAN-2004 03:08:00 Next Run Date: 01-JAN-2004 03:09:00 ```

INTERVAL	EXPRESSION
Every hour.	'sysdate + 1/24' 'systimestamp + 1/24' 'sysdate + interval ''1'' hour' 'systimestamp + interval ''1'' hour' 'freq=hourly;' ``` Next Run Date: 01-JAN-2004 04:04:32 Next Run Date: 01-JAN-2004 05:04:32 Next Run Date: 01-JAN-2004 06:04:32 Next Run Date: 01-JAN-2004 07:04:32 Next Run Date: 01-JAN-2004 08:04:32 ```
Every hour, on the hour.	'trunc(sysdate, ''HH24'') + 1/24' 'trunc(systimestamp, ''HH24'') + 1/24' 'trunc(sysdate, ''HH24'') + interval ''1'' hour' 'trunc(systimestamp, ''HH24'') + interval ''1'' hour' 'freq=hourly; byminute=0; bysecond=0;' ``` Next Run Date: 01-JAN-2004 04:00:00 Next Run Date: 01-JAN-2004 05:00:00 Next Run Date: 01-JAN-2004 06:00:00 Next Run Date: 01-JAN-2004 07:00:00 Next Run Date: 01-JAN-2004 08:00:00 ```
Every Monday at 9:00 AM	'trunc(next_day(sysdate, ''MONDAY'')) + 9/24' 'trunc(next_day(systimestamp, ''MONDAY'')) + 9/24' 'trunc(next_day(sysdate, ''MONDAY'')) + interval ''9'' hour' 'trunc(next_day(systimestamp, ''MONDAY'')) + interval ''9''hour' 'freq=weekly; byday=mon; byhour=9; byminute=0; bysecond=0;' ``` Next Run Date: 05-JAN-2004 09:00:00 Next Run Date: 12-JAN-2004 09:00:00 Next Run Date: 19-JAN-2004 09:00:00 Next Run Date: 26-JAN-2004 09:00:00 Next Run Date: 02-FEB-2004 09:00:00 ```

Complex Date Rules for Job Execution   **123**

INTERVAL	EXPRESSION
Every Monday, Wednesday and Friday at 6:00 AM	'trunc(least(next_day(sysdate, "monday"), next_day(sysdate, "wednesday"), next_day(sysdate, "friday"))) + (6/24)'
	'trunc(least(next_day(systimestamp, "monday"), next_day(systimestamp, "wednesday"), next_day(systimestamp, "friday"))) + (6/24)'
	'trunc(least(next_day(sysdate,"monday"), next_day(sysdate, "wednesday"), next_day(sysdate, "friday"))) + interval "6" hour'
	'trunc(least(next_day(systimestamp, "monday"), next_day(systimestamp, "wednesday"), next_day(systimestamp, "friday"))) + interval "6" hour'
	'freq=weekly; byday=mon,wed,fri; byhour=6; byminute=0; bysecond=0;'
	``` Next Run Date: 02-JAN-2004 06:00:00 Next Run Date: 05-JAN-2004 06:00:00 Next Run Date: 07-JAN-2004 06:00:00 Next Run Date: 09-JAN-2004 06:00:00 Next Run Date: 12-JAN-2004 06:00:00 ```
First Monday of each quarter	'next_day(add_months(trunc(sysdate, "q"), 3), "monday")' 'next_day(add_months(trunc(systimestamp, "q"), 3), "monday")'
	'freq=monthly; bymonth=1,4,7,10; byday=1mon'
	``` Next Run Date: 05-APR-2004 00:00:00 Next Run Date: 05-JUL-2004 00:00:00 Next Run Date: 04-OCT-2004 00:00:00 Next Run Date: 03-JAN-2005 00:00:00 Next Run Date: 04-APR-2005 00:00:00 ```

Table 3.11 - *Repeat intervals and the expressions than can be used to achieve them.*

It would appear that all of the above expressions give exactly the same run schedule regardless of which syntax is used. In practice this not true because PL/SQL expressions can allow the run schedules of jobs to slide.

The scheduler attempts to execute all jobs on time, but in practice there is often a small delay. When a job is executed, the first thing that happens is the next run date is calculated using the specified repeat interval. Since most PL/SQL expressions use either the *sysdate* or *systimestamp* functions, the actual start date may be slightly later than the jobs original next run date. Over several iterations of the job, this could add up to a noticeable difference between the times the job is expected to run and when it actually does run. Table 3.12 gives an example of the sort of slide that might be seen if the scheduler is consistently 10 seconds late in executing a job that was originally intended to run a 09:00:00 each day.

RUN	ACTUAL START DATE	NEXT RUN DATE
1	01-JAN-2004 09:00:10	02-JAN-2004 09:00:10
2	02-JAN-2004 09:00:20	03-JAN-2004 09:00:20
3	03-JAN-2004 09:00:30	04-JAN-2004 09:00:30
4	04-JAN-2004 09:00:40	05-JAN-2004 09:00:40
5	05-JAN-2004 09:00:50	06-JAN-2004 09:00:50
6	06-JAN-2004 09:01:00	07-JAN-2004 09:01:00

Table 3.12 – *The time slide phenomenon*

This issue becomes even more noticeable on shorter repeat intervals such as hourly runs. This behavior can be prevented by always defining PL/SQL expressions that result in a specific time, rather than one relative to the current time. This is typically done using the *trunc* and *round* functions to remove the variable components. For example, 'trunc(sysdate) + 1 + 6/24' is always 06:00 tomorrow morning no matter what time it is evaluated because the time component has been truncated. The earlier examples regularly make use of the *trunc* function for the same reason.

The calendar syntax does not suffer from the problem of sliding schedules as the repeat intervals it defines are always time specific. If a component of the calendar string is not defined explicitly, it is defaulted using values from the start date specified when the job or schedule was defined. For example, a schedule with a start date of 01-JAN-2004 09:45:31 and a calendar string with no *byminute* clause would actually be assigned *byminute=45*. As a result, every *next_run_date* evaluated using this schedule would have a value of 45 minutes past the hour.

Sometimes it is either not possible or very difficult to define a repeat interval using the calendar syntax or a PL/SQL expression. In these situations, it might be easier to use a database function which returns a date or timestamp as required. The *my_schedule_function.sql* script creates a function which returns a different time interval depending on the contents of the database.

```
-- ***************************************************
-- Copyright © 2005 by Rampant TechPress
-- This script is free for non-commercial purposes
-- with no warranties.  Use at your own risk.
--
-- To license this script for a commercial purpose,
-- contact info@rampant.cc
-- ***************************************************

-- Requires the following grant:
--    grant select on v_$database to job_user;
-- ********************************************************
CREATE OR REPLACE FUNCTION my_schedule_function (
  p_timestamp  IN   TIMESTAMP)
  RETURN TIMESTAMP
AS
  l_db_name      v$database.name%TYPE;
  l_timestamp  TIMESTAMP;
BEGIN
  SELECT name
  INTO   l_db_name
  FROM   v$database;

  CASE l_db_name
    WHEN 'PROD' THEN l_timestamp := p_timestamp + INTERVAL '10'
MINUTE;
    WHEN 'TEST' THEN l_timestamp := p_timestamp + INTERVAL '1' HOUR;
    ELSE l_timestamp := p_timestamp + INTERVAL '1' DAY;
  END CASE;

  RETURN l_timestamp;
END;
/
```

When this script is run against the development environment with a database name of DB10G, the following run schedule is produced:

```
SQL1> exec
test_timestamp_string('my_schedule_function(systimestamp)');
Next Run Date: 02-JAN-2004 03:04:32
Next Run Date: 03-JAN-2004 03:04:32
Next Run Date: 04-JAN-2004 03:04:32
Next Run Date: 05-JAN-2004 03:04:32
Next Run Date: 06-JAN-2004 03:04:32

PL/SQL procedure successfully completed.
```

The same result could be achieved by running a different schedule in each environment, but it serves to illustrate the point.

It should now be obvious that there is an almost limitless combination of possible calendar string and PL/SQL expression variations. The only way to become really confident with repeat intervals is to try as many variations as possible. The test procedures presented in this chapter will allow this to be done without having to actually schedule jobs, which in turn will save lots of time.

Conclusion

In this chapter, a number of areas both directly and indirectly related to repeat intervals of scheduled jobs have been covered. The topics include:

- The use of the DATE datatype, including modification of dates using literals and date functions.

- The use of the TIMESTAMP datatype, including the use of timestamp functions.

- The use of the INTERVAL datatype, the interval literal syntax and interval functions.

- The calendar syntax in Oracle10g.

- Complex date rules for job execution in jobs scheduled using the *dbms_job* and *dbms_scheduler* packages.

The next chapter will investigate a number of techniques that can be implemented to make job scheduling more robust.

Chaining Oracle Jobs Together

You can chain Oracle Jobs?

This chapter will introduce a number of techniques that can be used to create dependencies between jobs and make job executions more robust. An explanation of how a job chain is created is a good place to start.

Creating a Job Chain

Jobs are often defined as individual tasks that are performed in isolation; however, in some circumstances, a job consists of several tasks that must be performed as a whole in a specific sequence. Typically, this would be accomplished by combining the tasks into a single job like the one defined below.

```
DBMS_SCHEDULER.create_job (
    job_name       => 'single_job',
    job_type       => 'PLSQL_BLOCK',
    job_action     => 'BEGIN
                        task1;
                        task2;
```

```
                        task3;
                      END;',
  start_date        => SYSTIMESTAMP,
  repeat_interval   => 'freq=daily; byhour=9; byminute=0;
bysecond=0;',
  end_date          => NULL,
  enabled           => TRUE,
  comments          => 'Single job.');
```

The problem arises when not all tasks can be performed at the same time. For example, a batch of orders might process at midnight and produce the necessary billing paperwork at 9:00 a.m. If no dependencies are defined between these tasks, any delays in the order processing may result in the generation of the billing paperwork before the orders are complete.

In these circumstances, a job chain needs to be created such that each task in the chain is performed in sequence and the failure of a single task breaks the chain. This can be achieved in many ways, but the following methods are preferred:

- Conditional job creation.

- Conditional job enabling.

- Conditional job runs using Oracle Advanced Queuing.

- Conditional job runs using a custom table solution.

Most of the examples in this chapter will use the Oracle10g *dbms_scheduler* package, but there are earlier versions of Oracle in which the *dbms_job* package can be used effectively in its place.

Conditional Job Creation

In this method, the first task in the chain is scheduled as a regular repeating job, but all subsequent tasks are not scheduled. Instead, as each task in the chain completes successfully, it schedules the next task as a one-off job.

In the order and billing example, the time between tasks was long and the run times were fixed, excluding delays. An example like this would not be very useful here since it would require a significant amount of time for the chain to complete successfully. Instead, assume that a process made up of three tasks must run in sequence. For the purposes of testing, the times between tasks should be relatively short and instead of fixed times, rolling times should be used.

In this example, each task will simply insert a record into a table, which can be created using the following script:

🖫 job_chain_table.sql

```
-- ***************************************************
-- Copyright © 2005 by Rampant TechPress
-- This script is free for non-commercial purposes
-- with no warranties.  Use at your own risk.
--
-- To license this script for a commercial purpose,
-- contact info@rampant.cc
-- ***************************************************

CREATE TABLE job_chain (
  created_timestamp  TIMESTAMP,
  task_name          VARCHAR2(20)
);
```

The *job_chain_create.sql* script creates a package specification and body that will do all the work for the example job chain.

🖫 job_chain_create.sql

```
-- ***************************************************
-- Copyright © 2005 by Rampant TechPress
-- This script is free for non-commercial purposes
-- with no warranties.  Use at your own risk.
--
-- To license this script for a commercial purpose,
-- contact info@rampant.cc
-- ***************************************************

CREATE OR REPLACE PACKAGE job_chain_create AS

PROCEDURE task_1;
PROCEDURE task_2;
PROCEDURE task_3;

END job_chain_create;
/
SHOW ERRORS

CREATE OR REPLACE PACKAGE BODY job_chain_create AS

-- --------------------------------------------------------------------
PROCEDURE task_1 AS
-- --------------------------------------------------------------------
BEGIN
  DELETE FROM job_chain;
  INSERT INTO job_chain (created_timestamp, task_name)
```

```
      VALUES (systimestamp, 'TASK_1');
      COMMIT;

      -- Uncomment the following line to force a failure.
      --RAISE_APPLICATION_ERROR(-20000,
      --   'This is a fake error to prevent task_2 being executed');

      -- The work has comleted successfully so create task_2
      -- Oracle10g
      DBMS_SCHEDULER.create_job (
         job_name        => 'job_chain_create_task_2',
         job_type        => 'STORED_PROCEDURE',
         job_action      => 'job_chain_create.task_2',
         start_date      => SYSTIMESTAMP + INTERVAL '2' MINUTE,
         repeat_interval => NULL,
         end_date        => NULL,
         enabled         => TRUE,
         comments        => 'Second task in the create chain.');

      -- Pre Oracle10g
      /*
      DBMS_JOB.isubmit (
         job       => 1001,
         what      => 'BEGIN job_chain_create.task_2; END;' ,
         next_date => SYSDATE + INTERVAL '2' MINUTE);

      COMMIT;
      */

EXCEPTION
   WHEN OTHERS THEN
      -- Don't create task_2.
      NULL;
END task_1;
-- ---------------------------------------------------------------------
PROCEDURE task_2 AS
-- ---------------------------------------------------------------------
BEGIN

   INSERT INTO job_chain (created_timestamp, task_name)
   VALUES (systimestamp, 'TASK_2');
   COMMIT;

   -- Uncomment the following line to force a failure.
   --RAISE_APPLICATION_ERROR(-20000,
   --   'This is a fake error to prevent task_3 being executed');

   -- The work has comleted successfully so create task_3
   -- Oracle10g
   DBMS_SCHEDULER.create_job (
      job_name        => 'job_chain_create_task_3',
      job_type        => 'STORED_PROCEDURE',
      job_action      => 'job_chain_create.task_3',
      start_date      => SYSTIMESTAMP + INTERVAL '2' MINUTE,
      repeat_interval => NULL,
      end_date        => NULL,
```

```
      enabled          => TRUE,
      comments         / => 'Third task in the create chain.');

   -- Pre Oracle10g
   /*
   DBMS_JOB.isubmit (
      job        => 1002,
      what       => 'BEGIN job_chain_create.task_3; END;' ,
      next_date => SYSDATE + INTERVAL '2' MINUTE);

   COMMIT;
   */

EXCEPTION
   WHEN OTHERS THEN
      -- Don't create task_3.
      NULL;
END task_2;
-- ----------------------------------------------------------------
PROCEDURE task_3 AS
-- ----------------------------------------------------------------
BEGIN

   INSERT INTO job_chain (created_timestamp, task_name)
   VALUES (systimestamp, 'TASK_3');
   COMMIT;

END task_3;
-- ----------------------------------------------------------------

END job_chain_create;
/
SHOW ERRORS
```

Both task_1 and task_2 schedule a one-off job on successful completion. Any exceptions are caught by the exception handler, which does not schedule the next job in the chain.

With the table and code in place, a job to call the first task using the *job_chain_create_job.sql* script can be scheduled.

🖫 job_chain_create_job.sql

```
-- ****************************************************
-- Copyright © 2005 by Rampant TechPress
-- This script is free for non-commercial purposes
-- with no warranties.  Use at your own risk.
--
-- To license this script for a commercial purpose,
-- contact info@rampant.cc
-- ****************************************************
```

```
-- Oracle10g
BEGIN
  DBMS_SCHEDULER.create_job (
    job_name        => 'job_chain_create_task_1',
    job_type        => 'STORED_PROCEDURE',
    job_action      => 'job_chain_create.task_1',
    start_date      => SYSTIMESTAMP,
    repeat_interval => NULL,
    end_date        => NULL,
    enabled         => TRUE,
    comments        => 'First task in the create chain.');
END;
/

-- Pre Oracle10g
/*
BEGIN
  DBMS_JOB.isubmit (
    job       => 1000,
    what      => 'BEGIN job_chain_create.task_1; END;',
    next_date => SYSDATE);
  COMMIT;
END;
/
*/
```

The *repeat_interval* (or *interval*) parameter of this job definition is set to NULL making it a one-off job. Under normal circumstances, this job is expected to be scheduled with a repeat interval since it is the first task in the chain. However, for the purposes of this example, the less clutter on the system the better, so no unnecessary repeating jobs are scheduled.

The progress of the job can be monitored using the following query:

💾 job_chain_query.sql

```
-- ************************************************
-- Copyright © 2005 by Rampant TechPress
-- This script is free for non-commercial purposes
-- with no warranties.  Use at your own risk.
--
-- To license this script for a commercial purpose,
-- contact info@rampant.cc
-- ************************************************

alter session set nls_timestamp_format = 'DD-MON-YYYY
HH24:MI:SS.FF';

set linesize 100
column created_timestamp format a27
column task_name format a20
```

```
select
    *
from
    job_chain
order by
    created_timestamp
;
```

On completion of the chain, the following output from the query is expected:

```
SQL> @job_chain_query.sql

CREATED_TIMESTAMP              TASK_NAME
--------------------------     --------------------
07-AUG-2004 10:49:42.701000    TASK_1
07-AUG-2004 10:51:42.858000    TASK_2
07-AUG-2004 10:53:43.093000    TASK_3

3 rows selected.
```

The result of breaks in the chain can be tested by uncommenting the lines in the code containing the *raise_application_error* procedure calls. Uncommenting this line in task_1 would cause the chain to break during task_1 resulting in the following query output:

```
SQL> @job_chain_query.sql

CREATED_TIMESTAMP              TASK_NAME
--------------------------     --------------------
07-AUG-2004 11:03:11.827000    TASK_1

1 row selected.
```

Commenting out the statement in task_1 and uncommenting it in task_2 would cause the chain to break in task_2 resulting in the following query output:

```
SQL> job_chain_query.sql

CREATED_TIMESTAMP              TASK_NAME
--------------------------     --------------------
07-AUG-2004 11:10:42.746000    TASK_1
07-AUG-2004 11:12:42.956000    TASK_2

2 rows selected.
```

Conditional Job Enabling

In this method, all tasks in the chain are scheduled as regular repeating jobs, but only the first job in the chain is enabled. All subsequent jobs in the chain are disabled or marked as broken prior to Oracle10g. As each task in the chain completes successfully, it enables the next task in the chain by enabling its associated job. Every time the first task runs, it disables the chain before starting again.

The *job_chain_enable.sql* script creates a package specification and body that will do all the work for the example job chain.

🖫 job_chain_enable.sql

```
-- ************************************************
-- Copyright © 2005 by Rampant TechPress
-- This script is free for non-commercial purposes
-- with no warranties.  Use at your own risk.
--
-- To license this script for a commercial purpose,
-- contact info@rampant.cc
-- ************************************************

CREATE OR REPLACE PACKAGE job_chain_enable AS

PROCEDURE task_1;
PROCEDURE task_2;
PROCEDURE task_3;

END job_chain_enable;
/
SHOW ERRORS


CREATE OR REPLACE PACKAGE BODY job_chain_enable AS

-- ------------------------------------------------------------
PROCEDURE task_1 AS
-- ------------------------------------------------------------
BEGIN

  -- Disable dependant jobs
  -- Oracle10g
  DBMS_SCHEDULER.disable ('job_chain_enable_task_2');
  DBMS_SCHEDULER.disable ('job_chain_enable_task_3');

  -- Pre Oracle10g
  /*
  DBMS_JOB.broken (1001, TRUE);
  DBMS_JOB.broken (1002, TRUE);
```

```
  COMMIT;
  */

  DELETE FROM job_chain;

  INSERT INTO job_chain (created_timestamp, task_name)
  VALUES (systimestamp, 'TASK_1');
  COMMIT;

  -- Uncomment the following line to force a failure.
  --RAISE_APPLICATION_ERROR(-20000,
  --   'This is a fake error to prevent task_2 being executed');

  -- The work has comleted successfully so enable task_2
  -- Oracle10g
  DBMS_SCHEDULER.enable ('job_chain_enable_task_2');

  -- Pre Oracle10g
  /*
  DBMS_JOB.broken (1001, FALSE, SYSDATE + INTERVAL '2' MINUTE);
  COMMIT;
  */

EXCEPTION
  WHEN OTHERS THEN
    -- Don't enable task_2.
    NULL;
END task_1;
-- ---------------------------------------------------------------------

-- ---------------------------------------------------------------------
PROCEDURE task_2 AS
-- ---------------------------------------------------------------------
BEGIN

  INSERT INTO job_chain (created_timestamp, task_name)
  VALUES (systimestamp, 'TASK_2');
  COMMIT;

  -- Uncomment the following line to force a failure.
  --RAISE_APPLICATION_ERROR(-20000,
  --   'This is a fake error to prevent task_3 being executed');

  -- The work has comleted successfully so enable task_3
  -- Oracle10g
  DBMS_SCHEDULER.enable ('job_chain_enable_task_3');

  -- Pre Oracle10g
  /*
  DBMS_JOB.broken (1002, FALSE, SYSDATE + INTERVAL '2' MINUTE);
  COMMIT;
  */

EXCEPTION
  WHEN OTHERS THEN
    -- Don't enable task_3.
```

```
     NULL;
END task_2;
-- -----------------------------------------------------------------


-- -----------------------------------------------------------------
PROCEDURE task_3 AS
-- -----------------------------------------------------------------
BEGIN

   INSERT INTO job_chain (created_timestamp, task_name)
   VALUES (systimestamp, 'TASK_3');
   COMMIT;

END task_3;
-- -----------------------------------------------------------------

END job_chain_enable;
/
SHOW ERRORS
```

Since no jobs are created by the code, they must all be created in advance using the *job_chain_enable_jobs.sql* script. The jobs must persist, so they are generated with repeat intervals. These repeat intervals schedule them to run at 06:00, 12:00 and 18:00 respectively. Commands to remove the jobs are included and should be run once the example is completed.

💾 job_chain_enable_jobs.sql

```
-- ***************************************************
-- Copyright © 2005 by Rampant TechPress
-- This script is free for non-commercial purposes
-- with no warranties.  Use at your own risk.
--
-- To license this script for a commercial purpose,
-- contact info@rampant.cc
-- ***************************************************

-- Oracle10g
BEGIN
   DBMS_SCHEDULER.create_job (
     job_name        => 'job_chain_enable_task_1',
     job_type        => 'STORED_PROCEDURE',
     job_action      => 'job_chain_enable.task_1',
     start_date      => SYSTIMESTAMP,
     repeat_interval => 'freq=daily; byhour=6; byminute=0;
bysecond=0;',
     end_date        => NULL,
     enabled         => TRUE,
     comments        => 'First task in the enable chain.');
END;
/
```

```
BEGIN
  DBMS_SCHEDULER.create_job (
    job_name        => 'job_chain_enable_task_2',
    job_type        => 'STORED_PROCEDURE',
    job_action      => 'job_chain_enable.task_2',
    start_date      => SYSTIMESTAMP,
    repeat_interval => 'freq=daily; byhour=12; byminute=0;
bysecond=0;',
    end_date        => NULL,
    enabled         => FALSE,
    comments        => 'Second task in the enable chain.');
END;
/

BEGIN
  DBMS_SCHEDULER.create_job (
    job_name        => 'job_chain_enable_task_3',
    job_type        => 'STORED_PROCEDURE',
    job_action      => 'job_chain_enable.task_3',
    start_date      => SYSTIMESTAMP,
    repeat_interval => 'freq=daily; byhour=18; byminute=0;
bysecond=0;',
    end_date        => NULL,
    enabled         => FALSE,
    comments        => 'Third task in the enable chain.');
END;
/

-- Pre Oracle10g
/*
BEGIN
  DBMS_JOB.isubmit (
    job       => 1000,
    what      => 'BEGIN job_chain_create.task_1; END;',
    next_date => SYSDATE,
    interval  => 'TRUNC(SYSDATE) + INTERVAL ''1 6'' DAY TO HOUR');

  DBMS_JOB.isubmit (
    job       => 1001,
    what      => 'BEGIN job_chain_create.task_2; END;',
    next_date => SYSDATE,
    interval  => 'TRUNC(SYSDATE) + INTERVAL ''1 12'' DAY TO HOUR');

  DBMS_JOB.broken(1001, TRUE);

  DBMS_JOB.isubmit (
    job       => 1002,
    what      => 'BEGIN job_chain_create.task_3; END;',
    next_date => SYSDATE,
    interval  => 'TRUNC(SYSDATE) + INTERVAL ''1 18'' DAY TO HOUR');

  DBMS_JOB.broken(1002, TRUE);

  COMMIT;
END;
/
```

```
*/
-- Cleanup
/*
-- Oracle10g
BEGIN
  DBMS_SCHEDULER.drop_job ('job_chain_enable_task_3');
  DBMS_SCHEDULER.drop_job ('job_chain_enable_task_2');
  DBMS_SCHEDULER.drop_job ('job_chain_enable_task_1');
END;
/

-- Pre Oracle10g
BEGIN
  DBMS_JOB.remove(1002);
  DBMS_JOB.remove(1001);
  DBMS_JOB.remove(1000);
  COMMIT;
END;
/
*/
```

The current job schedules for this example can be queried using the *job_queue_query.sql* script listed below.

💾 job_queue_query.sql

```
--     **************************************************
-- Copyright © 2005 by Rampant TechPress
-- This script is free for non-commercial purposes
-- with no warranties.  Use at your own risk.
--
-- To license this script for a commercial purpose,
-- contact info@rampant.cc
--     **************************************************

set feedback off
alter session set nls_date_format = 'DD-MON-YYYY HH24:MI:SS';
alter session set nls_timestamp_format = 'DD-MON-YYYY
HH24:MI:SS.FF';
alter session set nls_timestamp_tz_format = 'DD-MON-YYYY
HH24:MI:SS.FF TZH:TZM';
set feedback on

set linesize 100
column created_timestamp format a27
column next_run_date format a34
column next_date format a20

prompt
prompt USER_SCHEDULER_JOBS
select
   job_name,
```

```
      enabled,
      next_run_date
from
      user_scheduler_jobs
order by
      job_name
;

prompt USER_JOBS
select
      job,
      broken,
      next_date
from
      user_jobs
order by
      job
;
```

The output of this script along with the output of the *job_chain_query.sql* script is listed below.

```
SQL> @job_chain_query.sql

no rows selected

SQL> @job_queue_query.sql

USER_SCHEDULER_JOBS

JOB_NAME                        ENABL NEXT_RUN_DATE
------------------------------- ----- -----------------------------------
JOB_CHAIN_ENABLE_TASK_1         TRUE  08-AUG-2004 06:00:00.800000 +01:00
JOB_CHAIN_ENABLE_TASK_2         FALSE
JOB_CHAIN_ENABLE_TASK_3         FALSE

3 rows selected.
```

At this point, the first task is scheduled but has not been executed, hence no results in the *job_chain* table. Rather than waiting until 6:00, it can be forced to run immediately. The results below show that the first task has run, and the second job has been enabled.

```
SQL> exec dbms_scheduler.run_job ('job_chain_enable_task_1');

PL/SQL procedure successfully completed.

SQL> @job_queue_query.sql

USER_SCHEDULER_JOBS
```

```
JOB_NAME                    ENABL NEXT_RUN_DATE
-------------------------   ----- ------------------------------------
JOB_CHAIN_ENABLE_TASK_1     TRUE  08-AUG-2004 06:00:00.800000 +01:00
JOB_CHAIN_ENABLE_TASK_2     TRUE  08-AUG-2004 12:00:00.200000 +01:00
JOB_CHAIN_ENABLE_TASK_3     FALSE

3 rows selected.

USER_JOBS

no rows selected

SQL> @job_chain_query.sql

CREATED_TIMESTAMP          TASK_NAME
-------------------------  --------------------
07-AUG-2004 13:52:28.227000 TASK_1

1 row selected.
```

Next, run the second job manually. The results below show that the second task has run and the third job has been enabled.

```
SQL> exec dbms_scheduler.run_job ('job_chain_enable_task_2');

PL/SQL procedure successfully completed.

SQL> @job_chain_query.sql

CREATED_TIMESTAMP          TASK_NAME
-------------------------  --------------------
07-AUG-2004 13:52:28.227000 TASK_1
07-AUG-2004 13:59:16.666000 TASK_2

2 rows selected.

SQL> @job_queue_query.sql

USER_SCHEDULER_JOBS

JOB_NAME                    ENABL NEXT_RUN_DATE
-------------------------   ----- ------------------------------------
JOB_CHAIN_ENABLE_TASK_1     TRUE  08-AUG-2004 06:00:00.800000 +01:00
JOB_CHAIN_ENABLE_TASK_2     TRUE  08-AUG-2004 12:00:00.200000 +01:00
JOB_CHAIN_ENABLE_TASK_3     TRUE  07-AUG-2004 18:00:00.700000 +01:00

3 rows selected.

USER_JOBS

no rows selected
```

Next, run the third job manually. The results below show that the third task has run successfully.

```
SQL> exec dbms_scheduler.run_job ('job_chain_enable_task_3');

PL/SQL procedure successfully completed.

SQL> @job_chain_query.sql

CREATED_TIMESTAMP           TASK_NAME
-------------------------   --------------------
07-AUG-2004 13:52:28.227000 TASK_1
07-AUG-2004 13:59:16.666000 TASK_2
07-AUG-2004 14:02:10.948000 TASK_3

3 rows selected.

SQL> @job_queue_query.sql

USER_SCHEDULER_JOBS

JOB_NAME                    ENABL NEXT_RUN_DATE
-------------------------   ----- ----------------------------------
JOB_CHAIN_ENABLE_TASK_1     TRUE  08-AUG-2004 06:00:00.800000 +01:00
JOB_CHAIN_ENABLE_TASK_2     TRUE  08-AUG-2004 12:00:00.200000 +01:00
JOB_CHAIN_ENABLE_TASK_3     TRUE  07-AUG-2004 18:00:00.700000 +01:00

3 rows selected.

USER_JOBS

no rows selected
```

Finally, run the first job again to see that the subsequent jobs have been enabled or disabled appropriately.

```
SQL> exec dbms_scheduler.run_job ('job_chain_enable_task_1');

PL/SQL procedure successfully completed.

SQL> @job_chain_query.sql

CREATED_TIMESTAMP           TASK_NAME
-------------------------   --------------------
07-AUG-2004 14:03:55.683000 TASK_1

1 row selected.

SQL> @job_queue_query.sql

USER_SCHEDULER_JOBS

JOB_NAME                    ENABL NEXT_RUN_DATE
-------------------------   ----- ----------------------------------
JOB_CHAIN_ENABLE_TASK_1     TRUE  08-AUG-2004 06:00:00.800000 +01:00
JOB_CHAIN_ENABLE_TASK_2     TRUE  08-AUG-2004 12:00:00.700000 +01:00
JOB_CHAIN_ENABLE_TASK_3     FALSE 07-AUG-2004 18:00:00.700000 +01:00
```

```
3 rows selected.

USER_JOBS

no rows selected
```

Care must be taken when running the pre-10g version of this code due to the way the broken procedure works. When a job has its broken flag set to FALSE, its next run date is set to the value specified by the *next_date* parameter. If this is not specified, it defaults to the current datetime. As a result, the enabled job will not run at the expected time. In this example, the *next_date* parameter has been specified as a two minute interval for the convenience of testing, but in a real example, it must be set to an appropriate datetime value.

Conditional Job Runs Using Oracle Advanced Queuing

In this method, all tasks in the chain are scheduled as regular repeating jobs. When a task completes successfully, it places a message on a queue for the next task to read. With the exception of the first task, the first operation a task performs is read from its queue. If there is a message on the queue, the task can proceed; otherwise, it waits indefinitely for the message to arrive.

Before any code can be written, a queuing infrastructure needs to be set up using the *job_chain_aq_setup.sql* script and background information must be introduced. A full introduction to Oracle Advanced Queuing is beyond the scope of this book, so explanations will be limited to just those elements necessary to build a simple working system.

🖫 job_chain_aq_setup.sql

```
-- *************************************************
-- Copyright © 2005 by Rampant TechPress
-- This script is free for non-commercial purposes
-- with no warranties.  Use at your own risk.
--
-- To license this script for a commercial purpose,
-- contact info@rampant.cc
-- *************************************************
-- Grant necessary permissions
conn sys/password as sysdba

-- Create the queue payload
CREATE OR REPLACE TYPE job_user.job_chain_msg_type AS OBJECT (
```

```
  message    VARCHAR2(10)
)
/
-- Create the queue table and queues
BEGIN
  DBMS_AQADM.create_queue_table (
     queue_table          => 'job_user.job_chain_queue_tab',
     queue_payload_type   => 'job_user.job_chain_msg_type');

  DBMS_AQADM.create_queue (
     queue_name           => 'job_user.task_2_queue',
     queue_table          => 'job_user.job_chain_queue_tab');

  DBMS_AQADM.create_queue (
     queue_name           => 'job_user.task_3_queue',
     queue_table          => 'job_user.job_chain_queue_tab');

  DBMS_AQADM.start_queue (
     queue_name           => 'job_user.task_2_queue',
     enqueue              => TRUE);

  DBMS_AQADM.start_queue (
     queue_name           => 'job_user.task_3_queue',
     enqueue              => TRUE);
END;
/
grant execute on dbms_aq to job_user;

conn job_user/job_user
```

Advanced Queuing (AQ) is Oracle's implementation of a messaging system which can be used as a replacement for the *dbms_pipe* package and other bespoke solutions. The basic unit of any messaging system is a message with the most important element of the message being its contents, or payload. In order to define a queue table, the payload of the messages that will be stored within it must first be defined. The *job_chain_aq_setup.sql* script contains a definition of an object type called *job_chain_msg_type* that will act as the payload. The creation of object types requires the CREATE TYPE privilege.

The payload of the message can be as simple or complicated as desired. In this case, the only concern is that the message has been sent. The particular contents are not important at this time, so the message is extremely simple.

Administration of queues is done using the *dbms_aqadm* package and requires the *aq_administrator_role* to be granted to the administrator. Alternatively, all administration can be performed by a privileged user such as SYS or SYSTEM. With the payload object defined, the queue table is created using the *create_queue_table* procedure.

Once the queue table has been created, the individual queues are created and started using the *create_queue* and *start_queue* procedures respectively. A single queue table can hold many queues as long as each queue uses the same type for its payload.

Messages are queued and de-queued using the *dbms_aq* package. Access to this package can be granted using the *aq_user_role* role. However, access to it from a stored procedure is achieved by using the *job_chain_aq_setup.sql* script, which grants the privilege on this object directly to the test user.

The contents of the queue table can be monitored using the *job_chain_aq_query.sql* script.

🖫 job_chain_aq_query.sql

```
-- ****************************************************
-- Copyright © 2005 by Rampant TechPress
-- This script is free for non-commercial purposes
-- with no warranties.  Use at your own risk.
--
-- To license this script for a commercial purpose,
-- contact info@rampant.cc
-- ****************************************************

select
    queue,
    count(*) as messages
from
    aq$job_chain_queue_taB
group by
    queue
order by
    queue
;
```

The point has been reach at which coding the specific example is desired. The *job_chain_aq.sql* script creates a package specification and body that will do all the work for the example job chain.

🖫 job_chain_aq.sql

```
-- ****************************************************
-- Copyright © 2005 by Rampant TechPress
-- This script is free for non-commercial purposes
-- with no warranties.  Use at your own risk.
--
-- To license this script for a commercial purpose,
```

```
-- contact info@rampant.cc
-- **************************************************

CREATE OR REPLACE PACKAGE job_chain_aq AS

PROCEDURE task_1;
PROCEDURE task_2;
PROCEDURE task_3;
PROCEDURE enqueue_message (p_queue_name  IN  VARCHAR2);
PROCEDURE dequeue_message (p_queue_name  IN  VARCHAR2);

END job_chain_aq;
/
SHOW ERRORS

CREATE OR REPLACE PACKAGE BODY job_chain_aq AS

-- -------------------------------------------------------------------
PROCEDURE task_1 AS
-- -------------------------------------------------------------------
BEGIN

  DELETE FROM job_chain;

  INSERT INTO job_chain (created_timestamp, task_name)
  VALUES (systimestamp, 'TASK_1');
  COMMIT;

  -- Uncomment the following line to force a failure.
  --RAISE_APPLICATION_ERROR(-20000,
  --   'This is a fake error to prevent task_2 being executed');

  -- The work has comleted successfully so signal task_2
  enqueue_message (p_queue_name => 'task_2_queue');

EXCEPTION
  WHEN OTHERS THEN
    -- Don't signal task_2.
    NULL;
END task_1;
-- -------------------------------------------------------------------


-- -------------------------------------------------------------------
PROCEDURE task_2 AS
-- -------------------------------------------------------------------
BEGIN

  dequeue_message (p_queue_name => 'task_2_queue');

  INSERT INTO job_chain (created_timestamp, task_name)
  VALUES (systimestamp, 'TASK_2');
  COMMIT;

  -- Uncomment the following line to force a failure.
  --RAISE_APPLICATION_ERROR(-20000,
  --   'This is a fake error to prevent task_3 being executed');
```

```
      -- The work has comleted successfully so signal task_3
      enqueue_message (p_queue_name => 'task_3_queue');

EXCEPTION
   WHEN OTHERS THEN
      -- Don't signal task_3.
      NULL;
END task_2;
-- -----------------------------------------------------------------


-- -----------------------------------------------------------------
PROCEDURE task_3 AS
-- -----------------------------------------------------------------
BEGIN

   dequeue_message (p_queue_name => 'task_3_queue');

   INSERT INTO job_chain (created_timestamp, task_name)
   VALUES (systimestamp, 'TASK_3');
   COMMIT;

END task_3;
-- -----------------------------------------------------------------


-- -----------------------------------------------------------------
PROCEDURE enqueue_message (p_queue_name  IN  VARCHAR2) AS
-- -----------------------------------------------------------------
   l_enqueue_options      DBMS_AQ.enqueue_options_t;
   l_message_properties   DBMS_AQ.message_properties_t;
   l_message_handle       RAW(16);
   l_job_chain_msg        job_chain_msg_type;
BEGIN
   l_job_chain_msg := job_chain_msg_type('GO');

   DBMS_AQ.enqueue(queue_name             => 'job_user.' ||
p_queue_name,
                   enqueue_options        => l_enqueue_options,
                   message_properties     => l_message_properties,
                   payload                => l_job_chain_msg,
                   msgid                  => l_message_handle);
END enqueue_message;
-- -----------------------------------------------------------------


-- -----------------------------------------------------------------
PROCEDURE dequeue_message (p_queue_name  IN  VARCHAR2) AS
-- -----------------------------------------------------------------
   l_dequeue_options      DBMS_AQ.dequeue_options_t;
   l_message_properties   DBMS_AQ.message_properties_t;
   l_message_handle       RAW(16);
   l_job_chain_msg        job_chain_msg_type;
BEGIN
   DBMS_AQ.dequeue(queue_name             => 'job_user.' ||
p_queue_name,
                   dequeue_options        => l_dequeue_options,
                   message_properties     => l_message_properties,
```

```
                    payload              => l_job_chain_msg,
                    msgid                => l_message_handle);
   END dequeue_message;
-- ------------------------------------------------------------

END job_chain_aq;
/
SHOW ERRORS
```

Next, the jobs associated with each task are scheduled. Unlike the previous example, the job sequence is protected by the queue, so all the jobs can be enabled.

🖫 job_chain_aq_jobs.sql

```
-- ***************************************************
-- Copyright © 2005 by Rampant TechPress
-- This script is free for non-commercial purposes
-- with no warranties.  Use at your own risk.
--
-- To license this script for a commercial purpose,
-- contact info@rampant.cc
-- ***************************************************

-- Oracle10g
BEGIN
  DBMS_SCHEDULER.create_job (
    job_name        => 'job_chain_aq_task_1',
    job_type        => 'STORED_PROCEDURE',
    job_action      => 'job_chain_aq.task_1',
    start_date      => SYSTIMESTAMP,
    repeat_interval => 'freq=daily; byhour=6; byminute=0;
bysecond=0;',
    end_date        => NULL,
    enabled         => TRUE,
    comments        => 'First task in the AQ chain.');
END;
/
BEGIN
  DBMS_SCHEDULER.create_job (
    job_name        => 'job_chain_aq_task_2',
    job_type        => 'STORED_PROCEDURE',
    job_action      => 'job_chain_aq.task_2',
    start_date      => SYSTIMESTAMP,
    repeat_interval => 'freq=daily; byhour=12; byminute=0;
bysecond=0;',
    end_date        => NULL,
    enabled         => TRUE,
    comments        => 'Second task in the AQ chain.');
END;
/
BEGIN
  DBMS_SCHEDULER.create_job (
```

```
    job_name        => 'job_chain_aq_task_3',
    job_type        => 'STORED_PROCEDURE',
    job_action      => 'job_chain_aq.task_3',
    start_date      => SYSTIMESTAMP,
    repeat_interval => 'freq=daily; byhour=18; byminute=0;
bysecond=0;',
    end_date        => NULL,
    enabled         => TRUE,
    comments        => 'Third task in the AQ chain.');
END;
/

EXEC DBMS_SCHEDULER.run_job ('job_chain_aq_task_1');
-- Pre Oracle10g
/*
BEGIN
  DBMS_JOB.isubmit (
    job      => 1000,
    what     => 'BEGIN job_chain_aq.task_1; END;',
    next_date => SYSDATE,
    interval => 'TRUNC(SYSDATE) + INTERVAL ''1 6'' DAY TO HOUR');

  DBMS_JOB.isubmit (
    job      => 1001,
    what     => 'BEGIN job_chain_aq.task_2; END;',
    next_date => SYSDATE,
    interval => 'TRUNC(SYSDATE) + INTERVAL ''1 12'' DAY TO HOUR');

  DBMS_JOB.isubmit (
    job      => 1002,
    what     => 'BEGIN job_chain_aq.task_3; END;',
    next_date => SYSDATE,
    interval => 'TRUNC(SYSDATE) + INTERVAL ''1 18'' DAY TO HOUR');
  COMMIT;
END;
/
*/
-- Cleanup
/*
-- Oracle10g
BEGIN
  DBMS_SCHEDULER.drop_job ('job_chain_aq_task_3');
  DBMS_SCHEDULER.drop_job ('job_chain_aq_task_2');
  DBMS_SCHEDULER.drop_job ('job_chain_aq_task_1');
END;
/
-- Pre Oracle10g
BEGIN
  DBMS_JOB.remove(1002);
  DBMS_JOB.remove(1001);
  DBMS_JOB.remove(1000);
  COMMIT;
END;
/
*/
```

At this point, the tasks are scheduled but have not been executed; therefore, there are no results in the *job_chain* table or the *job_chain_queue_tab* table. Rather than waiting until 6:00, the first job is forced to run immediately. The results below show that the first task has run and there is a message waiting in the queue table on the *task_2_queue*.

```
SQL> exec dbms_scheduler.run_job ('job_chain_aq_task_1');

PL/SQL procedure successfully completed.

job_user@db10g> @job_chain_query.sql

CREATED_TIMESTAMP              TASK_NAME
----------------------------   --------------------
07-AUG-2004 18:18:36.136000    TASK_1

1 row selected.

SQL> @job_chain_aq_query.sql

QUEUE                                MESSAGES
-----------------------------        ----------
TASK_2_QUEUE                                1

1 row selected.
```

If the run of the second job is forced; the second task has read a message from its queue, completed its processing and placed a message on the queue for the third task.

```
SQL> exec dbms_scheduler.run_job ('job_chain_aq_task_2');

PL/SQL procedure successfully completed.

SQL> @job_chain_query.sql

CREATED_TIMESTAMP              TASK_NAME
----------------------------   --------------------
07-AUG-2004 18:18:36.136000    TASK_1
07-AUG-2004 18:23:08.771000    TASK_2

2 rows selected.

SQL> @job_chain_aq_query.sql

QUEUE                                MESSAGES
-----------------------------        ----------
TASK_3_QUEUE                                1

1 row selected.
```

If the run of the third job is forced; the third task has read a message from its queue and completed its processing.

```
SQL> exec dbms_scheduler.run_job ('job_chain_aq_task_3');

PL/SQL procedure successfully completed.

SQL> @job_chain_query.sql

CREATED_TIMESTAMP              TASK_NAME
-------------------------      --------------------
07-AUG-2004 18:18:36.136000    TASK_1
07-AUG-2004 18:23:08.771000    TASK_2
07-AUG-2004 18:26:04.972000    TASK_3

3 rows selected.

SQL> @job_chain_aq_query.sql

no rows selected
```

If manually attempting to start jobs out of sequence; the sessions hang until the appropriate message is sent.

Conditional Job Runs using a Custom Table Solution

If none of the previous methods seem suitable, a specific solution to meet specific needs can always be built.. The following example could be used as a starting point for such a solution.

The sequence of jobs is protected using the *job_chain_locks* table. The RETRIES column specifies the number of times a task should check the locks before it gives up and re-schedules itself. The RETRY_DELAY column specifies the number of minutes between retries. The TASK_NAME and LOCKED columns are self-explanatory.

🖫 job_chain_locks.sql

```
-- ****************************************************
-- Copyright © 2005 by Rampant TechPress
-- This script is free for non-commercial purposes
-- with no warranties.  Use at your own risk.
--
-- To license this script for a commercial purpose,
-- contact info@rampant.cc
-- ****************************************************
```

```
CREATE TABLE job_chain_locks (
  task_name    VARCHAR2(20)                 NOT NULL,
  locked       VARCHAR2(1)   DEFAULT 'Y'    NOT NULL,
  retries      NUMBER(3)     DEFAULT 0      NOT NULL,
  retry_delay  NUMBER(3)     DEFAULT 1      NOT NULL,
  CONSTRAINT job_chain_locks_pk PRIMARY KEY (task_name)
);

INSERT INTO job_chain_locks (task_name, locked, retries,
retry_delay)
VALUES ('task_2', 'Y', 5, 1);

INSERT INTO job_chain_locks (task_name, locked, retries,
retry_delay)
VALUES ('task_3', 'Y', 3, 1);

COMMIT;
```

The contents of the *job_chain_locks* table can be monitored using the *job_chain_locks_query.sql* script.

🖫 job_chain_locks_query.sql

```
-- ****************************************************
-- Copyright © 2005 by Rampant TechPress
-- This script is free for non-commercial purposes
-- with no warranties.  Use at your own risk.
--
-- To license this script for a commercial purpose,
-- contact info@rampant.cc
-- ****************************************************

select
   *
from
   job_chain_locks
order by
   task_name
;
```

The *job_chain_custom.sql* script creates a package specification and body which will do all the work for the example job chain.

🖫 job_chain_custom_sql

```
-- ****************************************************
-- Copyright © 2005 by Rampant TechPress
-- This script is free for non-commercial purposes
-- with no warranties.  Use at your own risk.
--
```

```
-- To license this script for a commercial purpose,
-- contact info@rampant.cc
-- ************************************************

CREATE OR REPLACE PACKAGE job_chain_custom AS

PROCEDURE task_1;
PROCEDURE task_2;
PROCEDURE task_3;
PROCEDURE lock_task (p_task_name   IN
job_chain_locks.task_name%TYPE,
                     p_lock        IN  BOOLEAN DEFAULT TRUE);
FUNCTION unlocked (p_task_name  IN  job_chain_locks.task_name%TYPE)
  RETURN BOOLEAN;

END job_chain_custom;
/
SHOW ERRORS


CREATE OR REPLACE PACKAGE BODY job_chain_custom AS

-- ------------------------------------------------------------------
PROCEDURE task_1 AS
-- ------------------------------------------------------------------
BEGIN

  DELETE FROM job_chain;

  INSERT INTO job_chain (created_timestamp, task_name)
  VALUES (systimestamp, 'TASK_1');
  COMMIT;

  -- Uncomment the following line to force a failure.
  --RAISE_APPLICATION_ERROR(-20000,
  --  'This is a fake error to prevent task_2 being executed');

  -- The work has comleted successfully so unlock task_2
  lock_task ('task_2', FALSE);

EXCEPTION
  WHEN OTHERS THEN
    -- Don't unlock task_2.
    NULL;
END task_1;
-- ------------------------------------------------------------------

-- ------------------------------------------------------------------
PROCEDURE task_2 AS
-- ------------------------------------------------------------------
BEGIN

  IF unlocked('task_2') THEN
    lock_task ('task_2');

    INSERT INTO job_chain (created_timestamp, task_name)
```

```
        VALUES (systimestamp, 'TASK_2');
        COMMIT;

        -- Uncomment the following line to force a failure.
        --RAISE_APPLICATION_ERROR(-20000,
        --  'This is a fake error to prevent task_3 being executed');

        -- The work has comleted successfully so unlock task_3
        lock_task ('task_3', FALSE);
      END IF;

EXCEPTION
  WHEN OTHERS THEN
    -- Don't unlock task_3.
    NULL;
END task_2;
-- -------------------------------------------------------------------

-- -------------------------------------------------------------------
PROCEDURE task_3 AS
-- -------------------------------------------------------------------
BEGIN

  IF unlocked('task_3') THEN
    lock_task ('task_3');

    INSERT INTO job_chain (created_timestamp, task_name)
    VALUES (systimestamp, 'TASK_3');
    COMMIT;
  END IF;

END task_3;
-- -------------------------------------------------------------------

-- -------------------------------------------------------------------
PROCEDURE lock_task (p_task_name   IN
job_chain_locks.task_name%TYPE,
                     p_lock        IN  BOOLEAN DEFAULT TRUE) AS
-- -------------------------------------------------------------------
  PRAGMA AUTONOMOUS_TRANSACTION;
BEGIN
  UPDATE job_chain_locks
  SET    locked = 'Y'
  WHERE  task_name = p_task_name;
  COMMIT;
END lock_task;
-- -------------------------------------------------------------------

-- -------------------------------------------------------------------
FUNCTION unlocked (p_task_name   IN   job_chain_locks.task_name%TYPE)
  RETURN BOOLEAN AS
-- -------------------------------------------------------------------
  l_jcl_row   job_chain_locks%ROWTYPE;
BEGIN
  SELECT *
  INTO   l_jcl_row
```

```
FROM    job_chain_locks
WHERE   task_name = p_task_name;

IF l_jcl_row.locked != 'Y' THEN
  RETURN TRUE;
END IF;

FOR i IN 1 .. l_jcl_row.retries LOOP
  DBMS_LOCK.sleep(60 * l_jcl_row.retry_delay);

  SELECT locked
  INTO   l_jcl_row.locked
  FROM   job_chain_locks
  WHERE  task_name = p_task_name;

  IF l_jcl_row.locked != 'Y' THEN
    RETURN TRUE;
  END IF;
END LOOP;

RETURN FALSE;
EXCEPTION
  WHEN NO_DATA_FOUND THEN
    RETURN FALSE;
END unlocked;
-- ------------------------------------------------------------------

END job_chain_custom;
/
SHOW ERRORS
```

Next, the jobs associated with each task are scheduled.

🖫 job_chain_custom_jobs.sql

```
-- *****************************************************
-- Copyright © 2005 by Rampant TechPress
-- This script is free for non-commercial purposes
-- with no warranties.  Use at your own risk.
--
-- To license this script for a commercial purpose,
-- contact info@rampant.cc
-- *****************************************************

-- Oracle10g
BEGIN
  DBMS_SCHEDULER.create_job (
    job_name        => 'job_chain_custom_task_1',
    job_type        => 'STORED_PROCEDURE',
    job_action      => 'job_chain_custom.task_1',
    start_date      => SYSTIMESTAMP,
    repeat_interval => 'freq=daily; byhour=6; byminute=0;
bysecond=0;',
    end_date        => NULL,
```

```
      enabled         => TRUE,
      comments        => 'First task in the AQ chain.');
END;
/

BEGIN
  DBMS_SCHEDULER.create_job (
    job_name        => 'job_chain_custom_task_2',
    job_type        => 'STORED_PROCEDURE',
    job_action      => 'job_chain_custom.task_2',
    start_date      => SYSTIMESTAMP,
    repeat_interval => 'freq=daily; byhour=12; byminute=0;
bysecond=0;',
    end_date        => NULL,
    enabled         => TRUE,
    comments        => 'Second task in the AQ chain.');
END;
/

BEGIN
  DBMS_SCHEDULER.create_job (
    job_name        => 'job_chain_custom_task_3',
    job_type        => 'STORED_PROCEDURE',
    job_action      => 'job_chain_custom.task_3',
    start_date      => SYSTIMESTAMP,
    repeat_interval => 'freq=daily; byhour=18; byminute=0;
bysecond=0;',
    end_date        => NULL,
    enabled         => TRUE,
    comments        => 'Third task in the AQ chain.');
END;
/

-- Pre Oracle10g
/*
BEGIN
  DBMS_JOB.isubmit (
    job       => 1000,
    what      => 'BEGIN job_chain_custom.task_1; END;',
    next_date => SYSDATE,
    interval  => 'TRUNC(SYSDATE) + INTERVAL ''1 6'' DAY TO HOUR');

  DBMS_JOB.isubmit (
    job       => 1001,
    what      => 'BEGIN job_chain_custom.task_2; END;',
    next_date => SYSDATE,
    interval  => 'TRUNC(SYSDATE) + INTERVAL ''1 12'' DAY TO HOUR');

  DBMS_JOB.isubmit (
    job       => 1002,
    what      => 'BEGIN job_chain_custom.task_3; END;',
    next_date => SYSDATE,
    interval  => 'TRUNC(SYSDATE) + INTERVAL ''1 18'' DAY TO HOUR');

  COMMIT;
END;
```

```
/
*/

-- Cleanup
/*
-- Oracle10g
BEGIN
  DBMS_SCHEDULER.drop_job ('job_chain_custom_task_3');
  DBMS_SCHEDULER.drop_job ('job_chain_custom_task_2');
  DBMS_SCHEDULER.drop_job ('job_chain_custom_task_1');
END;
/

-- Pre Oracle10g
BEGIN
  DBMS_JOB.remove(1002);
  DBMS_JOB.remove(1001);
  DBMS_JOB.remove(1000);
  COMMIT;
END;
/
*/
```

At this point, the tasks are scheduled but have not been executed; hence, no results in the *job_chain* table. Rather than waiting until 6:00, the first job can be forced to run immediately. The results below show that the first task has run and second task has been unlocked.

```
SQL> exec dbms_scheduler.run_job ('job_chain_custom_task_1');

PL/SQL procedure successfully completed.

SQL> @job_chain_query.sql

CREATED_TIMESTAMP              TASK_NAME
--------------------------     --------------------
07-AUG-2004 19:54:51.010000    TASK_1

1 row selected.

SQL> @job_chain_locks_query.sql

TASK_NAME             L    RETRIES  RETRY_DELAY
--------------------  -    -------- -----------
task_2                N          5            1
task_3                Y          3            1

2 rows selected.
```

Running the second job manually results in the second task being relocked and the third task being unlocked.

```
SQL> exec dbms_scheduler.run_job ('job_chain_custom_task_2');

PL/SQL procedure successfully completed.

SQL> @job_chain_query.sql

CREATED_TIMESTAMP               TASK_NAME
--------------------------      --------------------
07-AUG-2004 19:54:51.010000     TASK_1
07-AUG-2004 19:57:29.636000     TASK_2

2 rows selected.

SQL> @job_chain_locks_query.sql

TASK_NAME           L    RETRIES RETRY_DELAY
------------------  -    ------- -----------
task_2              Y          5           1
task_3              N          3           1

2 rows selected.
```

Running the third job manually results in the second task being relocked.

```
SQL> exec dbms_scheduler.run_job ('job_chain_custom_task_3');

PL/SQL procedure successfully completed.

SQL> @job_chain_query.sql

CREATED_TIMESTAMP               TASK_NAME
--------------------------      ---------------------
07-AUG-2004 19:54:51.010000     TASK_1
07-AUG-2004 19:57:29.636000     TASK_2
07-AUG-2004 19:59:11.184000     TASK_3

3 rows selected.

SQL> @job_chain_locks_query.sql

TASK_NAME           L    RETRIES RETRY_DELAY
------------------  -    ------- -----------
task_2              Y          5           1
task_3              Y          3           1

2 rows selected.
```

Attempting to run a job out of order will result in the session hanging until
the task is unlocked or the appropriate number of retries has been attempted;
at which point the job is rescheduled.

```
SQL> set timing on
SQL> exec dbms_scheduler.run_job ('job_chain_custom_task_3');
```

```
PL/SQL procedure successfully completed.

Elapsed: 00:03:04.50
```

The DBA now has a variety of tools available with which to build job chains. The next section will introduce the error handling requirements associated with job scheduling.

Implementing Error Checking Routines

Proper error handling is an import part of implementing robust job scheduling. Depending on the scheduling mechanism job failures can have differing effects.

For jobs scheduled using the *dbms_job* package, 16 consecutive failures will result in the job being marked as broken. The following definition creates a job that will fail on every run.

create_job_failure.sql

```
-- *************************************************
-- Copyright © 2005 by Rampant TechPress
-- This script is free for non-commercial purposes
-- with no warranties. Use at your own risk.
--
-- To license this script for a commercial purpose,
-- contact info@rampant.cc
-- *************************************************

BEGIN
  DBMS_JOB.isubmit (1000,
                'BEGIN RAISE_APPLICATION_ERROR(-20000, ''Error'');
END;' ,
                SYSDATE,
                'SYSDATE + INTERVAL ''1'' SECOND');
  COMMIT;
END;
/
```

The *job_failures.sql* script queries the *dba_jobs* view allowing the progress of the job to be monitored.

🖫 job_failures.sql

```
-- **************************************************
-- Copyright © 2005 by Rampant TechPress
-- This script is free for non-commercial purposes
-- with no warranties.  Use at your own risk.
--
-- To license this script for a commercial purpose,
-- contact info@rampant.cc
-- **************************************************
select
   job,
   broken,
   failures
from
   dba_jobs
where
   job = DECODE(UPPER('&1'), 'ALL', job, &1)
;
```

The output of this query is displayed below.

```
SQL> @job_failures.sql 1000

      JOB B    FAILURES
---------- - ----------
      1000 N          14

1 row selected.
```

After 16 failures, the *broken* flag has been set.

```
SQL> @job_failures.sql 1000

      JOB B    FAILURES
---------- - ----------
      1000 Y          16

1 row selected.
```

Once the problem with the job is rectified, it could be restarted using the *broken* procedure.

```
SQL> exec dbms_job.broken(1000, false);

PL/SQL procedure successfully completed.

SQL> @job_failures.sql 1000
```

```
     JOB B   FAILURES
---------- - ----------
     1000 N         16
```

1 row selected.

Alternatively, the job could be dropped using the *remove* procedure.

```
SQL> exec dbms_job.remove(1000);

PL/SQL procedure successfully completed.

SQL> commit;

Commit complete.
```

By default, a job scheduled using the *dbms_scheduler* package does not have a limit on the maximum number of failures. If this functionality is required, it can be enforced by setting the *max_failures* attribute of the job. The *create_10g_job_failure.sql* script is the 10g equivalent of the *create_job_failure.sql* script. Notice that the *auto_drop* parameter has been set to FALSE to prevent the job from being dropped once it is disabled.

🖫 create_10g_job_failure.sql

```
-- *************************************************
-- Copyright © 2005 by Rampant TechPress
-- This script is free for non-commercial purposes
-- with no warranties.  Use at your own risk.
--
-- To license this script for a commercial purpose,
-- contact info@rampant.cc
-- *************************************************
BEGIN
  DBMS_SCHEDULER.create_job (
    job_name        => 'force_error_job',
    job_type        => 'PLSQL_BLOCK',
    job_action      => 'BEGIN RAISE_APPLICATION_ERROR(-20000,
''Error''); END;',
    start_date      => SYSTIMESTAMP,
    repeat_interval => 'freq=secondly;',
    end_date        => NULL,
    enabled         => TRUE,
    auto_drop       => FALSE,
    comments        => 'Job containing a forced error.');
  DBMS_SCHEDULER.set_attribute (
    name      => 'force_error_job',
    attribute => 'max_failures',
    value     => 16);
END;
/
```

The *job_run_failures_10g.sql* script queries the *dba_scheduler_jobs* view and can be used to monitor the progress of the 10g job.

💾 job_run_failures_10g.sql

```
-- *************************************************
-- Copyright © 2005 by Rampant TechPress
-- This script is free for non-commercial purposes
-- with no warranties.  Use at your own risk.
--
-- To license this script for a commercial purpose,
-- contact info@rampant.cc
-- *************************************************
select
   job_name,
   enabled,
   run_count,
   max_runs,
   failure_count,
   max_failures
from
   dba_scheduler_jobs
where
   job_name = DECODE(UPPER('&1'), 'ALL', job_name, UPPER('&1'))
;
```

The output from this script is listed below.

```
SQL> @job_run_failures_10g.sql force_error_job

JOB_NAME        ENABL RUN_COUNT  MAX_RUNS FAILURE_COUNT MAX_FAILURES
--------------- ----- ---------- --------- ------------- ------------
FORCE_ERROR_JOB TRUE         14                    14           16

1 row selected.
```

Once the maximum number of failures has been reached, the job is disabled. If the *auto_drop* parameter had not been set, the following query would return no rows, as the job would have been dropped.

```
SQL> @job_run_failures_10g.sql force_error_job

JOB_NAME        ENABL RUN_COUNT  MAX_RUNS FAILURE_COUNT MAX_FAILURES
--------------- ----- ---------- --------- ------------- ------------
FORCE_ERROR_JOB FALSE        16                    16           16

1 row selected.
```

Once the problem with the job is rectified, it could be restarted using the *enable* procedure.

```
SQL> exec dbms_scheduler.enable('force_error_job');

PL/SQL procedure successfully completed.
```

Alternatively, the job could be dropped using the *drop_job* procedure.

```
SQL> exec dbms_scheduler.drop_job ('force_error_job');

PL/SQL procedure successfully completed.
```

Although not directly related to errors, the maximum number of runs for a job can be limited by setting the *max_runs* parameter for a job.

🖫 create_10g_job_max_runs.sql

```
-- ***************************************************
-- Copyright © 2005 by Rampant TechPress
-- This script is free for non-commercial purposes
-- with no warranties.  Use at your own risk.
--
-- To license this script for a commercial purpose,
-- contact info@rampant.cc
-- ***************************************************

BEGIN
  DBMS_SCHEDULER.create_job (
    job_name        => 'max_runs_job',
    job_type        => 'PLSQL_BLOCK',
    job_action      => 'BEGIN NULL; END;',
    start_date      => SYSTIMESTAMP,
    repeat_interval => 'freq=secondly;',
    end_date        => NULL,
    enabled         => TRUE,
    auto_drop       => FALSE,
    comments        => 'Job limiting maximum runs.');

  DBMS_SCHEDULER.set_attribute (
    name      => 'max_runs_job',
    attribute => 'max_runs',
    value     => 16);
END;
/
```

By monitoring the job, it can be seen that the job is disabled once it reaches its maximum number of runs.

```
SQL> @job_run_failures_10g.sql max_runs_job

JOB_NAME          ENABL RUN_COUNT MAX_RUNS FAILURE_COUNT MAX_FAILURES
----------------- ----- --------- -------- ------------- ------------
FORCE_ERROR_JOB   FALSE        16       16            16

1 row selected.
```

The examples above show that having a job fail to complete may introduce two possible problems. The first and most obvious is that the work the job is expected to do will not complete successfully. The second, and possibly most problematic, is that the job may cease to run in future. The simplest way to solve this problem is to trap and handle all errors. In its simplest form, this could be done using an exception handler like the one shown in the *exception_job_proc_1.sql* procedure below.

🖫 exception_job_proc_1.sql

```
-- ***************************************************
-- Copyright © 2005 by Rampant TechPress
-- This script is free for non-commercial purposes
-- with no warranties.  Use at your own risk.
--
-- To license this script for a commercial purpose,
-- contact info@rampant.cc
-- ***************************************************

CREATE OR REPLACE PROCEDURE exception_job_proc_1 AS
BEGIN
  -- Force an error.
  RAISE_APPLICATION_ERROR(-20000, 'Forced error in
exception_job_proc_1');
EXCEPTION
  WHEN OTHERS THEN
    NULL;
END exception_job_proc_1;
/
```

This exception handler will stop the job from failing if a PL/SQL exception is raised, but it will give no indication what caused the job to fail.

```
SQL> EXEC exception_job_proc_1;

PL/SQL procedure successfully completed.
```

Another alternative is to log an error message in the exception handler. First, the *error_logs* table to hold the error messages needs to be created.

```
CREATE TABLE error_logs (
  id                  NUMBER(10)      NOT NULL,
  prefix              VARCHAR2(100),
  data                VARCHAR2(4000)  NOT NULL,
  error_level         NUMBER(2)       NOT NULL,
  created_timestamp   TIMESTAMP       NOT NULL,
  created_by          VARCHAR2(50)    NOT NULL);

ALTER TABLE error_logs ADD (CONSTRAINT error_logs_pk PRIMARY KEY
(id));

CREATE SEQUENCE error_logs_seq;
```

The usages of the table columns are listed below:

- ID - A system generated sequence number used as the primary key.

- PREFIX - An optional string to identify the source of the error. This may be used to identify the job or procedure that the job is running.

- DATA - A string containing information about the error. This could be just the error text or some additional information like the position in the process where the error occurred and any relevant parameters.

- ERROR_LEVEL - A number that can be used as an indicator of the severity of the error. For example, normal errors may be level five, major errors may be level one and minor warnings may be level 10. This has a default value of five.

- CREATED_TIMESTAMP - A timestamp indicating the time the error was logged. This defaults to the current system time.

- CREATED_BY - A reference to the user who created the error. This defaults to the database user.

With the table in place, the logging code starting with the package specification in the *err.pks* script can be created; then the package body in the *err.pkb* script can also be created.

err.pks

```
-- Requirements :
/*
CREATE TABLE error_logs (
  id                NUMBER(10)      NOT NULL,
  prefix            VARCHAR2(100),
  data              VARCHAR2(4000)  NOT NULL,
  error_level       NUMBER(2)       NOT NULL,
  created_timestamp TIMESTAMP       NOT NULL,
  created_by        VARCHAR2(50)    NOT NULL);

ALTER TABLE error_logs ADD (CONSTRAINT error_logs_pk PRIMARY KEY
(id));

CREATE SEQUENCE error_logs_seq;
*/
-- ***********************************************************************

CREATE OR REPLACE PACKAGE err AS

PROCEDURE reset_defaults;

PROCEDURE logs_on;
PROCEDURE logs_off;

PROCEDURE line (p_prefix       IN  error_logs.prefix%TYPE,
                p_data         IN  error_logs.data%TYPE,
                p_error_level  IN  error_logs.error_level%TYPE
DEFAULT 5,
                p_error_user   IN  error_logs.created_by%TYPE
DEFAULT USER);

PROCEDURE line (p_data         IN  error_logs.data%TYPE,
                p_error_level  IN  error_logs.error_level%TYPE
DEFAULT 5,
                p_error_user   IN  error_logs.created_by%TYPE
DEFAULT USER);

END err;
/
SHOW ERRORS
```

🖫 **err.pkb**

```
CREATE OR REPLACE PACKAGE BODY err AS
```

```
-- Package Variables
g_logs_on  BOOLEAN := TRUE;

-- Exposed Methods

-- ---------------------------------------------------------------------
PROCEDURE reset_defaults IS
-- ---------------------------------------------------------------------
BEGIN
  g_logs_on := TRUE;
END;
-- ---------------------------------------------------------------------


-- ---------------------------------------------------------------------
PROCEDURE logs_on IS
-- ---------------------------------------------------------------------
BEGIN
  g_logs_on := TRUE;
END;
-- ---------------------------------------------------------------------


-- ---------------------------------------------------------------------
PROCEDURE logs_off IS
-- ---------------------------------------------------------------------
BEGIN
  g_logs_on := FALSE;
END;
-- ---------------------------------------------------------------------


-- ---------------------------------------------------------------------
PROCEDURE line (p_prefix       IN  error_logs.prefix%TYPE,
                p_data         IN  error_logs.data%TYPE,
                p_error_level  IN  error_logs.error_level%TYPE
DEFAULT 5,
                p_error_user   IN  error_logs.created_by%TYPE
DEFAULT USER) IS
-- ---------------------------------------------------------------------
  PRAGMA AUTONOMOUS_TRANSACTION;
BEGIN
  IF g_logs_on THEN
    INSERT INTO error_logs
    (id,
     prefix,
     data,
     error_level,
     created_timestamp,
     created_by)
    VALUES
    (error_logs_seq.NEXTVAL,
     p_prefix,
     p_data,
     p_error_level,
     SYSTIMESTAMP,
     p_error_user);

    COMMIT;
```

```
   END IF;
END;
-- ----------------------------------------------------------------


-- ----------------------------------------------------------------
PROCEDURE line (p_data         IN  error_logs.data%TYPE,
                p_error_level  IN  error_logs.error_level%TYPE
DEFAULT 5,
                p_error_user   IN  error_logs.created_by%TYPE
DEFAULT USER) IS
-- ----------------------------------------------------------------
BEGIN
  line (p_prefix      => NULL,
        p_data        => p_data,
        p_error_level => p_error_level,
        p_error_user  => p_error_user);
END;
-- ----------------------------------------------------------------


END err;
/
SHOW ERRORS
```

The *line* procedure is overloaded allowing it to be used with or without a prefix. The main procedure is defined as an autonomous transaction, allowing it to commit the logging data without affecting the transactions within the job. In its simplest form, error logging can be achieved by issuing the following command:

```
SQL> execute err.line('This is an error');

PL/SQL procedure successfully completed.
```

The contents of the *error_logs* table can be queried using the *list_error_logs.sql* script listed below.

🖫 list_error_logs.sql

```
-- ****************************************************
-- Copyright © 2005 by Rampant TechPress
-- This script is free for non-commercial purposes
-- with no warranties.  Use at your own risk.
--
-- To license this script for a commercial purpose,
-- contact info@rampant.cc
-- ****************************************************
-- Parameters:
--    1) Specific prefix or "all".
-- **********************************************************************

set feedback off
alter session set nls_timestamp_format='DD-MON-YYYY HH24:MI:SS';
```

```
set feedback on

set linesize 150
set verify off

column id format 99999
column prefix format a20
column data format a30
column created_timestamp format a20
column created_by format a10

select
   id,
   prefix,
   data,
   error_level,
   created_timestamp,
   created_by
from
   error_logs
where
   nvl(prefix, '~') = decode(upper('&1'), 'ALL', nvl(prefix, '~'),
'&1')
order by
   id
;
```

The output from this query is displayed below.

```
SQL> @list_error_logs.sql all

    ID PREFIX  DATA              ERROR_LEVEL CREATED_TIMESTAMP     CREATED_BY
------ ------- ----------------- ----------- --------------------- ----------
     1         This is an error            5 14-AUG-2004 12:58:08  JOB_USER

1 row selected.
```

Armed with this error logging procedure, the *exception_job_proc_1* procedure can be amended to create the *exception_job_proc_2* procedure.

💾 exception_job_proc_2.sql

```
-- *****************************************************
-- Copyright © 2005 by Rampant TechPress
-- This script is free for non-commercial purposes
-- with no warranties.  Use at your own risk.
--
-- To license this script for a commercial purpose,
-- contact info@rampant.cc
-- *****************************************************

CREATE OR REPLACE PROCEDURE exception_job_proc_2 AS
BEGIN
```

```
-- Force an error.
RAISE_APPLICATION_ERROR(-20000, 'Forced error in
exception_job_proc_2');
EXCEPTION
  WHEN OTHERS THEN
    ERR.line(p_prefix => 'exception_job_proc_2',
             P_data   => SQLERRM);
END exception_job_proc_2;
/
```

Running the following procedure results in the generation of the appropriate error log:

```
SQL> exec exception_job_proc_2;

PL/SQL procedure successfully completed.

SQL> @list_error_logs.sql exception_job_proc_2

ID PREFIX       DATA                    ERROR_LEVEL CREATED_TIMESTAMP   CREATED_BY
------ ------------------- --------------------------- ----------- --------------------
  2 exception_job_proc_2 ORA-20000: Forced error in exc   5 14-AUG-2004 13:35:02 JOB_USER
                         eption_job_proc_2

1 row selected.
```

With this mechanism in place, PL/SQL exceptions can be monitored, and their presence will not cause the jobs to fail.

This section has introduced several methods by which error checking can be implemented. Chapter 6 contains additional information on the job run history available in Oracle10g, which has some relevance to monitoring job failures. Next, the following section will focus on mechanisms for sending email notifications of job failures.

Sending Email Notifications of Job Errors

The mechanism for sending email notifications can vary depending on the version of Oracle being used. Oracle10g allows the use of the simpler *utl_mail* package rather than the *utl_smtp* package available in previous versions.

Using UTL_SMTP

The *utl_smtp* package was introduced in Oracle8i to give access to the SMTP protocol from PL/SQL. The package is dependant on the JServer option, which can be loaded using the Database Configuration Assistant (DBCA) or by running the following scripts as the SYS user if it is not already present.

```
CONN sys/password AS SYSDBA
@$ORACLE_HOME/javavm/install/initjvm.sql
@$ORACLE_HOME/rdbms/admin/initplsj.sql
```

Using the package to send an email requires some knowledge of the SMTP protocol, but for the purpose of this text, a simple *send_mail* procedure has been written that should be suitable for most error reporting.

🖫 send_mail.sql

```
--   ****************************************************
-- Copyright © 2005 by Rampant TechPress
-- This script is free for non-commercial purposes
-- with no warranties.  Use at your own risk.
--
-- To license this script for a commercial purpose,
-- contact info@rampant.cc
--   ****************************************************
-- Parameters:
--     1) SMTP mail gateway.
--     2) From email address.
--     3) To email address.
--     4) Subject of email.
--     5) Text body of email.
--   **********************************************************************
CREATE OR REPLACE PROCEDURE send_mail (
  p_mail_host  IN  VARCHAR2,
  p_from       IN  VARCHAR2,
  p_to         IN  VARCHAR2,
  p_subject    IN  VARCHAR2,
  p_message    IN  VARCHAR2)
AS
  l_mail_conn   UTL_SMTP.connection;
BEGIN
  l_mail_conn := UTL_SMTP.open_connection(p_mail_host, 25);
  UTL_SMTP.helo(l_mail_conn, p_mail_host);
  UTL_SMTP.mail(l_mail_conn, p_from);
  UTL_SMTP.rcpt(l_mail_conn, p_to);

  UTL_SMTP.open_data(l_mail_conn);

  UTL_SMTP.write_data(l_mail_conn, 'Date: ' || TO_CHAR(SYSDATE, 'DD-
MON-YYYY HH24:MI:SS') || Chr(13));
  UTL_SMTP.write_data(l_mail_conn, 'From: ' || p_from || Chr(13));
  UTL_SMTP.write_data(l_mail_conn, 'Subject: ' || p_subject ||
Chr(13));
  UTL_SMTP.write_data(l_mail_conn, 'To: ' || p_to || Chr(13));
  UTL_SMTP.write_data(l_mail_conn, '' || Chr(13));
  UTL_SMTP.write_data(l_mail_conn, p_message || Chr(13));

  UTL_SMTP.close_data(l_mail_conn);
```

```
    UTL_SMTP.quit(l_mail_conn);
END send_mail;
/
SHOW ERRORS
```

The following code shows how the *send_mail* procedure can be used to send an email. Obviously, one will need to substitute the appropriate parameter values.

```
BEGIN
  send_mail(p_mail_host => 'smtp.mycompany.com',
            p_from      => 'me@mycompany.com',
            p_to        => 'you@mycompany.com',
            p_subject   => 'Test SEND_MAIL Procedure',
            p_message   => 'If you are reading this it worked!');
END;
/
```

The *p_mail_host* parameter specifies the SMTP gateway that actually sends the message.

Now that the email mechanism has been presented, how to capture errors and produce email notifications will be explained.

The simplest way to achieve this is to place all the code related to the job into a database procedure or preferably, a packaged procedure. This allows the capture of errors using an exception handler and the generation of an appropriate email. As an example, assume there is a need for a procedure to gather database statistics for an Oracle 8i or 9i instance. A procedure like the one below might be defined.

🖫 automated_email_alert.sql

```
-- ***************************************************
-- Copyright © 2005 by Rampant TechPress
-- This script is free for non-commercial purposes
-- with no warranties.  Use at your own risk.
--
-- To license this script for a commercial purpose,
-- contact info@rampant.cc
-- ***************************************************

CREATE OR REPLACE PROCEDURE automated_email_alert AS
  l_mail_host  VARCHAR2(50) := 'smtp.mycompany.com';
  l_from       VARCHAR2(50) := 'jobs@mycompany.com';
  l_to         VARCHAR2(50) := 'tim@mycompany.com';
BEGIN
```

```
      DBMS_STATS.gather_database_stats(cascade => TRUE,
                                       options => 'GATHER AUTO');
    send_mail(p_mail_host => l_mail_host,
              p_from      => l_from,
              p_to        => l_to,
              p_subject   => 'AUTOMATED_EMAIL_ALERT (MYSID): Success',
              p_message   => 'AUTOMATED_EMAIL_ALERT (MYSID) completed
successfully!');

EXCEPTION
  WHEN OTHERS THEN
    send_mail(p_mail_host => l_mail_host,
              p_from      => l_from,
              p_to        => l_to,
              p_subject   => 'AUTOMATED_EMAIL_ALERT (MYSID): Error',
              p_message   => 'AUTOMATED_EMAIL_ALERT (MYSID) failed
with the following error:' || SQLERRM);
END automated_email_alert;
/
SHOW ERRORS
```

If this procedure were run as part of a scheduled job, an email notification would be generated whether the job completed successfully or not. In the event of an error, the associated Oracle error would be reported.

Using UTL_MAIL in Oracle10g

Oracle10g introduced the *utl_mail* package, which provides a simpler and more intuitive email API. The package is loaded by running the following scripts as the SYS user.

```
CONN sys/password AS SYSDBA
@$ORACLE_HOME/rdbms/admin/utlmail.sql
@$ORACLE_HOME/rdbms/admin/prvtmail.plb
GRANT EXECUTE ON UTL_MAIL TO test_user;
```

Before the package can be used, the SMTP gateway must be specified by setting the *smtp_out_server* parameter. The parameter is dynamic, but the instance must be restarted before an email can be sent.

```
CONN sys/password AS SYSDBA
ALTER SYSTEM SET smtp_out_server='smtp.mycompany.com';
SHUTDOWN IMMEDIATE
STARTUP
```

With the configuration complete, it is now possible to send an email using the *send* procedure.

```
BEGIN
  UTL_MAIL.send(sender     => 'me@mycompany.com',
                recipients => 'you@mycompany.com',
                subject     => 'Test UTL_MAIL.SEND Procedure',
                message     => 'If you are reading this it worked!');
END;
/
```

As with the *utl_smtp* example, the code related to the job needs to be placed into a database procedure which captures errors using an exception handler and sends the appropriate email. The following procedure is the Oracle10g equivalent of the one used in the *utl_smtp* example.

💾 automated_email_alert_10g.sql

```
-- *****************************************************
-- Copyright © 2005 by Rampant TechPress
-- This script is free for non-commercial purposes
-- with no warranties.  Use at your own risk.
--
-- To license this script for a commercial purpose,
-- contact info@rampant.cc
-- *****************************************************

CREATE OR REPLACE PROCEDURE automated_email_alert_10g AS
  l_mail_host  VARCHAR2(50) := 'smtp.mycompany.com';
  l_from       VARCHAR2(50) := 'jobs@mycompany.com';
  l_to         VARCHAR2(50) := 'tim@mycompany.com';
BEGIN
  DBMS_STATS.gather_database_stats(cascade => TRUE,
                                   options => 'GATHER AUTO');

  UTL_MAIL.send(sender     => l_from,
                recipients => l_to,
                subject     => 'AUTOMATED_EMAIL_ALERT_10G (MYSID):
Success',
                message     => 'AUTOMATED_EMAIL_ALERT_10G (MYSID)
completed successfully!');
EXCEPTION
  WHEN OTHERS THEN
    UTL_MAIL.send(sender     => l_from,
                  recipients => l_to,
                  subject     => 'AUTOMATED_EMAIL_ALERT_10G (MYSID):
Error',
                  message     => 'AUTOMATED_EMAIL_ALERT_10G (MYSID)
failed with the following error:' || SQLERRM);
END automated_email_alert_10g;
/
SHOW ERRORS
```

Next, a mechanism for running operating system commands and scripts from within PL/SQL will be introduced.

If combining these techniques with the error logging method described previously, one may wish to send additional information in the email (prefix, start and end timestamps) to help pinpoint the errors in the *error_logs* table.

Running OS Commands and Scripts from PL/SQL

Not all jobs that can be scheduled are written as stored procedures. Sometimes it is necessary to schedule jobs to run operating system commands or batch scripts. Typically, these types of jobs have been scheduled using an operating system scheduler, such as CRON, since it is not possible to call operating system command or executable scripts natively from PL/SQL. Splitting job scheduling between two schedulers can get confusing, so many database administrators resign themselves to only using the operating system scheduler.

The scheduler in Oracle10g can be used to schedule operating system commands and scripts natively, giving the option of avoiding the operating system scheduler. This is great if using Oracle10g, but what can be done if using Oracle 8i and 9i? One method is to use Java stored procedures to do the work.

First, the Java stored procedure that will actually do the work needs to be created.

🖫 Host.java

```
-- **************************************************
-- Copyright © 2005 by Rampant TechPress
-- This script is free for non-commercial purposes
-- with no warranties.  Use at your own risk.
--
-- To license this script for a commercial purpose,
-- contact info@rampant.cc
-- **************************************************
-- Parameters:
--    1) Host command or executable file to execute.
-- *********************************************************************

CREATE OR REPLACE AND COMPILE JAVA SOURCE NAMED "Host" AS
import java.io.*;
public class Host {
  public static void void executeCommand(String command) {
```

```
    try {
      String[] finalCommand;
      if (isWindows()) {
        finalCommand = new String[4];
        finalCommand[0] = "C:\\winnt\\system32\\cmd.exe";
        finalCommand[1] = "/y";
        finalCommand[2] = "/c";
        finalCommand[3] = command;
      }
      else {
        finalCommand = new String[3];
        finalCommand[0] = "/bin/sh";
        finalCommand[1] = "-c";
        finalCommand[2] = command;
      }

      final Process pr = Runtime.getRuntime().exec(finalCommand);
      new Thread(new Runnable() {
        public void run() {
          try {
            BufferedReader br_in = new BufferedReader(new
InputStreamReader(pr.getInputStream()));
            String buff = null;
            while ((buff = br_in.readLine()) != null) {
              System.out.println(buff);
              try {Thread.sleep(100); } catch(Exception e) {}
            }
            br_in.close();
          }
          catch (IOException ioe) {
            System.out.println("Exception caught printing process
output.");
            ioe.printStackTrace();
          }
        }
      }).start();

      new Thread(new Runnable() {
        public void run() {
          try {
            BufferedReader br_err = new BufferedReader(new
InputStreamReader(pr.getErrorStream()));
            String buff = null;
            while ((buff = br_err.readLine()) != null) {
              System.out.println(buff);
              try {Thread.sleep(100); } catch(Exception e) {}
            }
            br_err.close();
          }
          catch (IOException ioe) {
            System.out.println("Exception caught printing process
error.");
            ioe.printStackTrace();
          }
        }
      }).start();
```

```
      }
    catch (Exception ex) {
      System.out.println(ex.getLocalizedMessage());
    }
  }

  public static boolean isWindows() {
    if
(System.getProperty("os.name").toLowerCase().indexOf("windows") != -
1)
      return true;
    else
      return false;
  }

};
/

show errors java source "Host"
```

The *Host.java* procedure is loaded in the same way as a PL/SQL stored procedure.

```
SQL> @Host.java
```

In order to call the Java stored procedure, a PL/SQL call specification must be published. This is essentially a PL/SQL wrapper with the correct parameter list which allows the Java code to be called as if it were a PL/SQL procedure or function.

💾 host_command.sql

```
-- *************************************************
-- Copyright © 2005 by Rampant TechPress
-- This script is free for non-commercial purposes
-- with no warranties.  Use at your own risk.
--
-- To license this script for a commercial purpose,
-- contact info@rampant.cc
-- *************************************************
-- Parameters:
--    1) Host command or executable file to execute.
-- *****************************************************************

CREATE OR REPLACE PROCEDURE host_command (p_command   IN   VARCHAR2)
AS LANGUAGE JAVA
NAME 'Host.executeCommand (java.lang.String)';
/
```

By default, the JServer has very little access to the operating system of the database server. To make sure there are no problems accessing the file system and operating system commands, the appropriate permissions using the *grant_permission* procedure of the *dbms_java* package must be given to the user.

```
PROCEDURE grant_permission (
  grantee           IN  VARCHAR2,
  permission_type   IN  VARCHAR2,
  permission_name   IN  VARCHAR2,
  permission_action IN  VARCHAR2)
```

Assuming that *job_user* is the schema that owns the *Host* Java stored procedure, the following permissions need to be granted:

```
BEGIN
  DBMS_JAVA.grant_permission ('JOB_USER', 'java.io.FilePermission',
                              '<>', 'read ,write, execute, delete');

  DBMS_JAVA.grant_permission ('JOB_USER',
'SYS:java.lang.RuntimePermission',
                              'writeFileDescriptor', '');

  DBMS_JAVA.grant_permission ('JOB_USER',
'SYS:java.lang.RuntimePermission',
                              'readFileDescriptor', '');
END;
/
```

The effects of these permissions are only seen when the grantee reconnects.

The *host_command* procedure can be tested as follows:

```
SET SERVEROUTPUT ON SIZE 1000000
CALL DBMS_JAVA.SET_OUTPUT(1000000);
BEGIN
  host_command (p_command => 'touch /u01/app/oracle/test_file');
END;
/
```

With the *host_command* procedure in place, the OS commands can now be scheduled using the *dbms_job* package the same way any normal PL/SQL procedure is used.

 Care should be taken over who gets access to the *host_command* procedure as it runs OS commands and executable scripts as the operating system user that owns the Oracle software. As such, it can be the cause of security vulnerabilities if used incorrectly.

Conclusion

This chapter presented several topics related to managing job dependencies and making job schedules more robust including the following:

- Creating a job chain using several methods.

- Implementing error checking routines.

- Sending email notifications of error messages.

- Running OS commands and scripts from PL/SQL.

The next chapter will describe how the execution of job schedules can be monitored.

Monitoring Oracle Job Execution

Monitoring Jobs in Oracle 10g is much easier

Introduction

This chapter will introduce how Oracle jobs can be monitored using both database views and Oracle Enterprise Manager (OEM). The scheduler available in Oracle10g is radically different from the one available in previous versions of Oracle. For this reason, it will be dealt with separately.

Explanations of the *dbms_application_info* and *dbms_system* packages are included as they can simplify the identification and monitoring of sessions related to scheduled jobs.

The monitoring of jobs scheduled using the *dbms_job* package will be presented first.

Monitoring Jobs Prior to 10g

The OEM GUI provided with Oracle9i includes very little support for jobs and scheduling. Chapter 2 of this text explained that jobs can be created and edited via OEM, but there is no support for monitoring running jobs directly.

This leaves only the *dba_jobs_running* view to identify running jobs. The following *jobs_running.sql* script lists the currently running jobs:

🖫 **jobs_running.sql**

```
-- *************************************************
-- Copyright © 2005 by Rampant TechPress
-- This script is free for non-commercial purposes
-- with no warranties.  Use at your own risk.
--
-- To license this script for a commercial purpose,
-- contact info@rampant.cc
-- *************************************************

set feedback off
alter session set nls_date_format='DD-MON-YYYY HH24:MI:SS';
set feedback on

select
   jr.job,
   s.username,
   s.sid,
   s.lockwait,
   s.logon_time
from
   dba_jobs_running jr,
   v$session s
where
   jr.sid = s.sid
order by
   jr.job
;
```

The type of output that might be expected from this script is listed below.

```
SQL> @jobs_running

       JOB USERNAME        SID LOCKWAIT   LOGON_TIME
---------- --------- ---------- ---------- --------------------
        42 JOB_USER         265            23-JUN-2004 08:21:25
        99 JOB_USER         272            23-JUN-2004 08:55:35

2 rows selected.
```

Identifying the sessions that are executing jobs will allow closer monitoring of what the jobs are actually doing.

There is no job history associated with jobs scheduled using the *dbms_job* package, unlike those scheduled using the *dbms_sheduler* package in Oracle10g. It is possible to create a job history by mimicking the Oracle10g job history.

To do this, schema objects must be created to hold the history records. This achieved by using the *job_run_details_schema.sql* script as shown below.

💾 job_run_details_schema.sql

```
-- ***************************************************
-- Copyright © 2005 by Rampant TechPress
-- This script is free for non-commercial purposes
-- with no warranties.  Use at your own risk.
--
-- To license this script for a commercial purpose,
-- contact info@rampant.cc
-- ***************************************************
conn sys/password as sysdba

grant select on v_$session to job_user;
grant select on dba_jobs_running to job_user;
grant select on v_$sesstat to job_user;
grant select on v_$statname to job_user;

conn job_user/job_user

create table job_run_details (
  log_id               NUMBER,
  log_date             DATE,
  owner                VARCHAR2(30),
  job                  NUMBER,
  status               VARCHAR2(30),
  error#               NUMBER,
  actual_start_date    DATE,
  actual_end_date      DATE,
  run_duration         INTERVAL DAY(3) TO SECOND(0),
  instance_id          NUMBER,
  session_id           VARCHAR2(30),
  cpu_used             NUMBER,
  additional_info      VARCHAR2(4000)
);

alter table job_run_details add (
  constraint job_run_details_pk primary key (log_id)
);

create sequence job_run_details_seq;
```

With the schema objects in place, the supporting packaged procedures available in the *job_run_details_api.sql* script can be compiled as listed below.

🖫 job_run_details_api.sql

```
-- *************************************************
-- Copyright © 2005 by Rampant TechPress
-- This script is free for non-commercial purposes
-- with no warranties.  Use at your own risk.
--
-- To license this script for a commercial purpose,
-- contact info@rampant.cc
-- *************************************************

CREATE OR REPLACE PACKAGE job_run_details_api AS

PROCEDURE start_log;

PROCEDURE end_log;

PROCEDURE error_log;

FUNCTION get_job
  RETURN job_run_details.job%TYPE;

FUNCTION get_cpu_used
  RETURN job_run_details.cpu_used%TYPE;

END job_run_details_api;
/
SHOW ERRORS


CREATE OR REPLACE PACKAGE BODY job_run_details_api AS

g_log_id   job_run_details.log_id%TYPE;

-- ----------------------------------------------------------------
PROCEDURE start_log AS
-- ----------------------------------------------------------------
  PRAGMA AUTONOMOUS_TRANSACTION;
  l_owner         job_run_details.owner%TYPE;
  l_instance_id   job_run_details.instance_id%TYPE;
  l_session_id    job_run_details.session_id%TYPE;
BEGIN
  SELECT job_run_details_seq.NEXTVAL,
         SYS_CONTEXT('USERENV','SESSION_USER'),
         SYS_CONTEXT('USERENV','INSTANCE'),
         SYS_CONTEXT('USERENV','SESSIONID')
  INTO   g_log_id,
         l_owner,
         l_instance_id,
         l_session_id
  FROM   dual;
```

```
    INSERT INTO job_run_details (
      log_id ,
      log_date,
      owner,
      job,
      status,
      actual_start_date,
      instance_id,
      session_id
    )
    VALUES (
      g_log_id,
      SYSDATE,
      l_owner,
      get_job,
      'IN PROGRESS',
      SYSDATE,
      l_instance_id,
      l_session_id
    );

    COMMIT;
END start_log;
-- ------------------------------------------------------------------

-- ------------------------------------------------------------------
PROCEDURE end_log AS
-- ------------------------------------------------------------------
  PRAGMA AUTONOMOUS_TRANSACTION;
BEGIN
  UPDATE job_run_details
  SET    status          = 'COMPLETE',
         actual_end_date = SYSDATE,
         run_duration    = NUMTODSINTERVAL(SYSDATE -
actual_start_date, 'DAY'),
         cpu_used        = get_cpu_used
  WHERE  log_id          = g_log_id;

    COMMIT;
END end_log;
-- ------------------------------------------------------------------

-- ------------------------------------------------------------------
PROCEDURE error_log AS
-- ------------------------------------------------------------------
  PRAGMA AUTONOMOUS_TRANSACTION;
  l_error#           job_run_details.error#%TYPE;
  l_additional_info  job_run_details.additional_info%TYPE;
BEGIN
  l_error#         := SQLCODE;
  l_additional_info := SQLERRM;

  UPDATE job_run_details
  SET    status          = 'ERROR',
         actual_end_date = SYSDATE,
```

```
             run_duration      = NUMTODSINTERVAL(SYSDATE -
actual_start_date, 'DAY'),
             cpu_used          = get_cpu_used,
             error#            = l_error#,
             additional_info   = l_additional_info
   WHERE   log_id              = g_log_id;

   COMMIT;
END error_log;
-- ----------------------------------------------------------------


-- ----------------------------------------------------------------
FUNCTION get_job
   RETURN job_run_details.job%TYPE AS
-- ----------------------------------------------------------------
   l_job      job_run_details.job%TYPE;
BEGIN
   SELECT jr.job
   INTO   l_job
   FROM   dba_jobs_running jr,
          v$session s
   WHERE  jr.sid    = s.sid
   AND    s.audsid = SYS_CONTEXT('USERENV','SESSIONID');
   RETURN l_job;
EXCEPTION
   WHEN OTHERS THEN
      RETURN 0;
END get_job;
-- ----------------------------------------------------------------


-- ----------------------------------------------------------------
FUNCTION get_cpu_used
   RETURN job_run_details.cpu_used%TYPE AS
-- ----------------------------------------------------------------
   l_cpu_used      job_run_details.cpu_used%TYPE;
BEGIN
   SELECT ss.value
   INTO   l_cpu_used
   FROM   v$sesstat ss,
          v$statname sn,
          v$session s
   WHERE  ss.statistic# = sn.statistic#
   and    ss.sid        = s.sid
   AND    sn.name       = 'CPU used by this session'
   AND    s.audsid      = SYS_CONTEXT('USERENV','SESSIONID');
   RETURN l_cpu_used;
EXCEPTION
   WHEN OTHERS THEN
      RETURN 0;
END get_cpu_used;
-- ----------------------------------------------------------------


END job_run_details_api;
/
SHOW ERRORS
```

With the package in place, it is necessary to make some adjustments to the existing job code to make sure the history is gathered correctly. The *job_run_details_template_proc.sql* script provides a template that shows how the *job_run_details_api* package should be used. At the start of the job, the *start_log* procedure is called, which creates the appropriate run entry in the *job_run_details* table. On successful completion of the job, the *end_log* procedure is called to close the run entry. In the event of a problem, the *error_log* procedure is called, which records the error code and the error message.

🖫 job_run_details_template_proc.sql

```
-- ************************************************
-- Copyright © 2005 by Rampant TechPress
-- This script is free for non-commercial purposes
-- with no warranties.  Use at your own risk.
--
-- To license this script for a commercial purpose,
-- contact info@rampant.cc
-- ************************************************

CREATE OR REPLACE PROCEDURE job_run_details_template_proc AS
BEGIN
  job_run_details_api.start_log;

  -- Do something.
  DBMS_LOCK.sleep(30);

  -- Test error (uncomment to test).
  -- RAISE_APPLICATION_ERROR(-20000, 'For a test error!');

  job_run_details_api.end_log;
EXCEPTION
  WHEN OTHERS THEN
    job_run_details_api.error_log;
END job_run_details_template_proc;
/
SHOW ERRORS
```

The *job_run_details_template_job.sql* script creates a test job that calls the template procedure to test the action of the *job_run_details_api* package.

🖫 job_run_details_template_job.sql

```
-- ************************************************
-- Copyright © 2005 by Rampant TechPress
-- This script is free for non-commercial purposes
-- with no warranties.  Use at your own risk.
--
```

```
-- To license this script for a commercial purpose,
-- contact info@rampant.cc
-- ************************************************

VARIABLE l_job NUMBER;

BEGIN
  DBMS_JOB.submit (
    job       => :l_job,
    what      => 'job_run_details_template_proc;',
    next_date => SYSDATE,
    interval  => 'SYSDATE + INTERVAL ''1'' MINUTE');

  COMMIT;
END;
/

PRINT l_job
```

With the job created, the contents of the *job_run_details* table can be queried using the *job_run_details.sql* script as listed below.

💾 job_run_details.sql

```
-- ************************************************
-- Copyright © 2005 by Rampant TechPress
-- This script is free for non-commercial purposes
-- with no warranties.  Use at your own risk.
--
-- To license this script for a commercial purpose,
-- contact info@rampant.cc
-- ************************************************
-- Parameters:
--    1) Specific job or ALL which doesn't limit output.
--    2) Number of records to be displayed.
-- ********************************************************************

set linesize 200
set verify off

column owner format a15
column status format a12
column completion_date format a20
column run_duration format a20

select
   *
from
   (select
       job,
       owner,
       status,
```

```
        TO_CHAR(actual_end_date, 'DD-MON-YYYY HH24:MI:SS') as
completion_date,
        run_duration
    from
        job_run_details
    where
        job = decode(upper('&1'), 'ALL', job, upper('&1'))
    order by
        (actual_end_date) DESC) a
where
  rownum <= &2
;
```

The type of output expected from the script is listed below.

```
SQL> @ job_run_details.sql all 10

JOB OWNER          STATUS        COMPLETION_DATE        RUN_DURATION
--- ------------   -----------   --------------------   ------------------
 30 JOB_USER       IN PROGRESS
 30 JOB_USER       COMPLETE      23-JUN-2004 19:02:26   +000 00:00:34
 30 JOB_USER       COMPLETE      23-JUN-2004 19:01:24   +000 00:00:34
 30 JOB_USER       COMPLETE      23-JUN-2004 19:00:22   +000 00:00:33
 30 JOB_USER       COMPLETE      23-JUN-2004 18:59:21   +000 00:00:34
 30 JOB_USER       COMPLETE      23-JUN-2004 18:58:19   +000 00:00:34
 30 JOB_USER       COMPLETE      23-JUN-2004 18:57:17   +000 00:00:33
 30 JOB_USER       COMPLETE      23-JUN-2004 18:56:16   +000 00:00:34
 30 JOB_USER       COMPLETE      23-JUN-2004 18:55:14   +000 00:00:34
 30 JOB_USER       COMPLETE      23-JUN-2004 18:54:12   +000 00:00:33
```

If the user uncomments the test error in the *job_run_details_template_proc.sql*
script, the resulting error is trapped and recorded. After two runs of the job,
the user would expect to see something like the results listed below.

```
column ADDITIONAL_INFO format a50

select
   error#,
   additional_info,
   status
from
   job_run_details
where
   error# is not null
;
    ERROR# ADDITIONAL_INFO                                      STATUS
---------- -------------------------------------------------- ------
    -20000 ORA-20000: For a test error!                        ERROR
    -20000 ORA-20000: For a test error!                        ERROR

2 rows selected.
```

The *job_run_details* table and supporting code can be extended to include additional system statistics as required.

Now that a way to monitor jobs prior to Oracle10g has been presented, it is time to introduce the new and improved scheduler available in Oracle10g.

Monitoring Jobs in 10g

Chapter 2 noted that Oracle10g includes a new set of *dba_scheduler_%* views to display scheduler information. This section will examine the information that can be gathered regarding scheduled jobs using these views and the OEM 10g DB Control.

The list of currently scheduled jobs is displayed using the *dba_scheduler_jobs* view, which provides list of job names and the basic schedule information. The *scheduled_jobs.sql* script shows how this view is used.

🖫   **scheduled_jobs.sql**

```
-- **************************************************
-- Copyright © 2005 by Rampant TechPress
-- This script is free for non-commercial purposes
-- with no warranties.  Use at your own risk.
--
-- To license this script for a commercial purpose,
-- contact info@rampant.cc
-- **************************************************

set linesize 200

column owner format a15
column next_run_date format a25

select
   job_name,
   owner,
   nvl(to_char(next_run_date, 'DD-MON-YYYY HH24:MI:SS'),
schedule_name) as next_run_date,
   to_char(last_start_date, 'DD-MON-YYYY HH24:MI:SS') as
last_run_date,
   job_class,
   run_count
from
   dba_scheduler_jobs
;
```

The output generated from the *scheduled_jobs.sql* script is shown below.

```
SQL> @scheduled_jobs

JOB_NAME                                  OWNER         NEXT_RUN_DATE             LAST_RUN_DATE
JOB_CLASS                                 RUN_COUNT
-----------------------------         ---------------   -------------------------   -----------------
-- ----------------------------       ----------
GATHER_STATS_JOB                          SYS           MAINTENANCE_WINDOW_GROUP   24-JUN-2004
08:09:39 AUTO_TASKS_JOB_CLASS                               4
PURGE_LOG                                 SYS           24-JUN-2004 03:00:00       23-JUN-2004
03:00:01 DEFAULT_JOB_CLASS                                 19
TEST_FULL_JOB_DEFINITION                  JOB_USER      24-JUN-2004 08:52:00       24-JUN-2004
08:52:00 DEFAULT_JOB_CLASS                                 281
TEST_PROG_SCHED_CLASS_JOB_DEF             JOB_USER      24-JUN-2004 09:00:16       24-JUN-2004
08:09:39 TEST_JOB_CLASS                                    16
ARGUMENT_JOB_DEFINITION                   JOB_USER      24-JUN-2004 09:00:16       24-JUN-2004
08:09:39 DEFAULT_JOB_CLASS                                 16
TEST_SCHED_JOB_DEFINITION                 JOB_USER      24-JUN-2004 09:00:16       24-JUN-2004
08:09:37 DEFAULT_JOB_CLASS                                 16
TEST_PROG_JOB_DEFINITION                  JOB_USER      24-JUN-2004 09:00:09       24-JUN-2004
08:09:38 DEFAULT_JOB_CLASS                                 16
TEST_PROG_SCHED_JOB_DEFINITION JOB_USER                 24-JUN-2004 09:00:16       24-JUN-2004
08:09:39 TEST_JOB_CLASS                                    16

8 rows selected.
```

This information is also available from OEM on the Scheduler Jobs
(Scheduled) page (Administration > Jobs) shown in Figure 5.1.

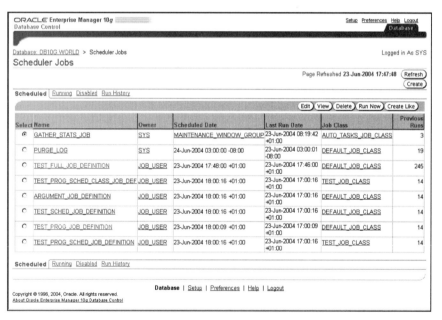

Figure 5.1 – *OEM 10g DB Control: Scheduler Jobs (Scheduled)*

The *dba_scheduler_running_jobs* view is the real starting point for job
monitoring as it displays a list of the currently running jobs. Using this view,

the user is able to identify the session that is actually executing the job, giving the ability to monitor session level information. The *scheduled_jobs_running.sql* script uses this view to identify the currently running jobs. The *extract* function is used to retrieve the elapsed time in seconds from the interval returned by the view.

💾 scheduled_jobs_running.sql

```
--  ****************************************************
-- Copyright © 2005 by Rampant TechPress
-- This script is free for non-commercial purposes
-- with no warranties.  Use at your own risk.
--
-- To license this script for a commercial purpose,
-- contact info@rampant.cc
--  ****************************************************
set linesize 200
column owner format a15
column next_run_date format a20

select
   rj.job_name,
   rj.owner,
   to_char(j.next_run_date, 'DD-MON-YYYY HH24:MI:SS') as
next_run_date,
   extract(second from rj.elapsed_time) as elapsed_time,
   rj.cpu_used,
   rj.session_id,
   rj.resource_consumer_group,
   j.run_count
from
   dba_scheduler_running_jobs rj,
   dba_scheduler_jobs j
where
   rj.job_name = j.job_name
order by
   rj.job_name
;
```

The output generated from the *scheduled_jobs_running.sql* script is shown below.

```
SQL> @scheduled_jobs_running

JOB_NAME                        OWNER           NEXT_RUN_DATE          ELAPSED_TIME  CPU_USED
SESSION_ID RESOURCE_CONSUMER_GROUP          RUN_COUNT
------------------------------- --------------- ---------------------- ------------ ----------
TEST_FULL_JOB_DEFINITION        JOB_USER        24-JUN-2004 09:22:00          20.69          0
272                             296

1 row selected.
```

This information is also available from OEM on the Scheduler Jobs (Running) page (Administration > Jobs) shown in Figure 5.2.

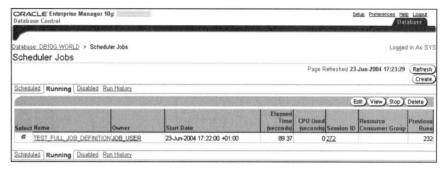

Figure 5.2 – *OEM 10g DB Control: Scheduler Jobs (Running)*

The Scheduler Jobs (Disabled) page of OEM, shown in Figure 5.3, lists all currently disabled jobs. This screen is essentially the same as the Scheduler Jobs (Scheduled) screen except the output from the *dba_scheduler_jobs* view is restricted using the ENABLED column. The *disabled_jobs.sql* script shows how the disabled jobs can be displayed.

💾 **disabled_jobs.sql**

```
-- ***************************************************
-- Copyright © 2005 by Rampant TechPress
-- This script is free for non-commercial purposes
-- with no warranties.  Use at your own risk.
--
-- To license this script for a commercial purpose,
-- contact info@rampant.cc
-- ***************************************************

set linesize 200

column owner format a15
column next_run_date format a25

select
   job_name,
   owner,
   nvl(to_char(next_run_date, 'DD-MON-YYYY HH24:MI:SS'),
schedule_name) as next_run_date,
   to_char(last_start_date, 'DD-MON-YYYY HH24:MI:SS') as
last_run_date,
   job_class,
   run_count
from
```

```
   dba_scheduler_jobs
where
   enabled = 'FALSE'
;
```

If a job is disabled, it will be listed in the output from the *disabled_jobs.sql* script.

```
SQL> exec dbms_scheduler.disable ('test_full_job_definition', true);

PL/SQL procedure successfully completed.

SQL> @disabled_jobs

JOB_NAME                      OWNER           NEXT_RUN_DATE             LAST_RUN_DATE
JOB_CLASS                     RUN_COUNT
----------------------------- --------------- ------------------------- -------------------
-- ---------------------------  ----------
TEST_FULL_JOB_DEFINITION      JOB_USER        26-JUN-2004 13:42:00      26-JUN-2004
13:36:00 DEFAULT_JOB_CLASS               733

1 row selected.
```

The same information is displayed in the Scheduler Jobs (Disabled) page of OEM shown in Figure 5.3.

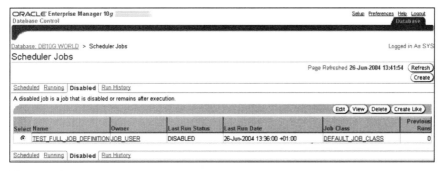

Figure 5.3 – *OEM 10g DB Control: Scheduler Jobs (Disabled)*

The *dba_scheduler_job_run_details* view provides a history of previous job runs. The *job_run_history.sql* script uses a top-n query to return a specified number of records from the history for a specified job, or all jobs.

🖫 job_run_history.sql

```
-- ****************************************************
-- Copyright © 2005 by Rampant TechPress
-- This script is free for non-commercial purposes
-- with no warranties.  Use at your own risk.
--
```

```
-- To license this script for a commercial purpose,
-- contact info@rampant.cc
-- *************************************************

-- **********************************************************************
-- Parameters:
--    1) Specific job name or ALL which doesn't limit output.
--    2) Number of records to be displayed.
-- **********************************************************************

set linesize 200
set verify off

column owner format a15
column status format a10
column completion_date format a20
column run_duration format a20

select
   *
from
   (select
       job_name,
       owner,
       status,
       to_char(actual_start_date + run_duration, 'DD-MON-YYYY
HH24:MI:SS') as completion_date,
       run_duration
    from
       dba_scheduler_job_run_details
    where
       job_name = decode(upper('&1'), 'ALL', job_name, upper('&1'))
    and
       actual_start_date is not null
    order by
       (actual_start_date + run_duration) DESC) a
where
  rownum <= &2
;
```

The following output lists history information from a specific job and all jobs. The output is restricted to five rows by the second parameter.

```
SQL> @job_run_history test_sched_job_definition 5

JOB_NAME                      OWNER           STATUS     COMPLETION_DATE       RUN_DURATION
----------------------------- --------------- ---------- --------------------  ------------
TEST_SCHED_JOB_DEFINITION     JOB_USER        SUCCEEDED  24-JUN-2004 10:01:59             1
TEST_SCHED_JOB_DEFINITION     JOB_USER        SUCCEEDED  24-JUN-2004 09:01:59             1
TEST_SCHED_JOB_DEFINITION     JOB_USER        SUCCEEDED  24-JUN-2004 08:11:21             1
TEST_SCHED_JOB_DEFINITION     JOB_USER        SUCCEEDED  23-JUN-2004 18:01:59             1
TEST_SCHED_JOB_DEFINITION     JOB_USER        SUCCEEDED  23-JUN-2004 17:01:59             1

5 rows selected.
```

```
SQL> @job_run_history all 5

JOB_NAME                       OWNER           STATUS      COMPLETION_DATE       RUN_DURATION
------------------------------ --------------- ----------- --------------------- ------------
TEST_FULL_JOB_DEFINITION       JOB_USER        SUCCEEDED   24-JUN-2004 10:31:43             1
TEST_FULL_JOB_DEFINITION       JOB_USER        SUCCEEDED   24-JUN-2004 10:29:43             1
TEST_FULL_JOB_DEFINITION       JOB_USER        SUCCEEDED   24-JUN-2004 10:27:43             1
TEST_FULL_JOB_DEFINITION       JOB_USER        SUCCEEDED   24-JUN-2004 10:25:43             1
TEST_FULL_JOB_DEFINITION       JOB_USER        SUCCEEDED   24-JUN-2004 10:23:43             1

5 rows selected.
```

The Scheduler Jobs (Run History) page of OEM, shown in Figure 5.4, lists the full job run history.

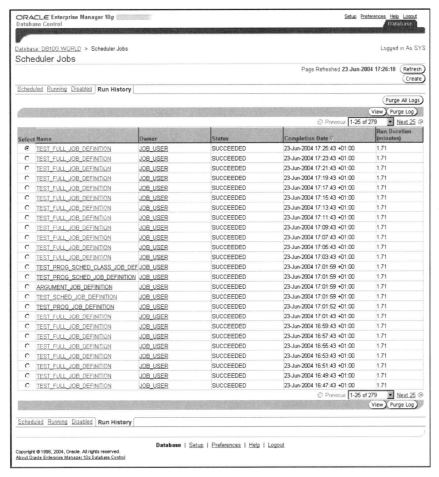

Figure 5.4 – *OEM 10g DB Control: Scheduler Jobs (Run History)*

The *scheduled_job_details.sql* script displays a summary of the information available for a specific job, including a limited job history.

💾 scheduled_job_details.sql

```
-- ************************************************
-- Copyright © 2005 by Rampant TechPress
-- This script is free for non-commercial purposes
-- with no warranties.  Use at your own risk.
--
-- To license this script for a commercial purpose,
-- contact info@rampant.cc
-- ************************************************
-- Parameters:
--    1) Specific job name.
--    2) Number of history records to be displayed.
-- ********************************************************************

set verify off
set feedback off
set linesize 200

column owner format a15
column comments format a50

prompt
prompt GENERAL
prompt --------

select
  job_name,
  owner,
  enabled,
  logging_level,
  job_class,
  comments
from
  dba_scheduler_jobs
where
  job_name = upper('&1');

column repeat_interval format a40
column start_date format a20
column end_date format a20
column next_run_date format a20

prompt
prompt
prompt SCHEDULE
prompt ---------

select
  repeat_interval,
  to_char(start_date, 'DD-MON-YYYY HH24:MI:SS') as start_date,
```

```
  to_char(end_date, 'DD-MON-YYYY HH24:MI:SS') as end_date,
  to_char(next_run_date, 'DD-MON-YYYY HH24:MI:SS') as next_run_date
from
  dba_scheduler_jobs
where
  job_name = upper('&1');

column job_action format a100

prompt
prompt
prompt COMMAND
prompt ---------

select
  job_action
from
  dba_scheduler_jobs
where
  job_name = upper('&1');


column status format a10
column completion_date format a20
column run_duration format a20

prompt
prompt
prompt RUN HISTORY
prompt ------------

select
  *
from
  (select
      job_name,
      owner,
      status,
      to_char(actual_start_date + run_duration, 'DD-MON-YYYY
HH24:MI:SS') as completion_date,
      run_duration
  from
      dba_scheduler_job_run_details
  where
      job_name = decode(upper('&1'), 'ALL', job_name, upper('&1'))
  and
      actual_start_date is not null
  order by
      (actual_start_date + run_duration) DESC) a
where
  rownum <= &2
;
set feedback on
```

An example of the output generated by the script is listed below.

```
SQL> @scheduled_job_details test_full_job_definition 5

GENERAL
-------

JOB_NAME                        OWNER            ENABL LOGG JOB_CLASS
COMMENTS
------------------------------- ---------------- ----- ---- ------------------------------ --
TEST_FULL_JOB_DEFINITION        JOB_USER          TRUE RUNS DEFAULT_JOB_CLASS
Job defined entirely by the CREATE JOB procedure.


SCHEDULE
--------

REPEAT_INTERVAL                             START_DATE           END_DATE
NEXT_RUN_DATE
------------------------------------------- -------------------- -------------------- --------
FREQ=MINUTELY;INTERVAL=2                     23-JUN-2004 09:22:00                       24-JUN-
2004 10:42:00


COMMAND
--------

JOB_ACTION
--------------------------------------------------------------------------------
BEGIN my_job_proc('CREATE_PROGRAM (BLOCK)'); END;


RUN HISTORY
-----------

JOB_NAME                        OWNER            STATUS      COMPLETION_DATE      RUN_DURATION
------------------------------- ---------------- ----------- -------------------- ------------
TEST_FULL_JOB_DEFINITION        JOB_USER         SUCCEEDED   24-JUN-2004 10:41:43            1
TEST_FULL_JOB_DEFINITION        JOB_USER         SUCCEEDED   24-JUN-2004 10:39:43            1
TEST_FULL_JOB_DEFINITION        JOB_USER         SUCCEEDED   24-JUN-2004 10:37:43            1
TEST_FULL_JOB_DEFINITION        JOB_USER         SUCCEEDED   24-JUN-2004 10:35:43            1
TEST_FULL_JOB_DEFINITION        JOB_USER         SUCCEEDED   24-JUN-2004 10:33:43            1
```

Clicking on a job run in the Scheduler Jobs (Run History) page produces the View Job page, shown in Figure 5.5, which contains similar information to the *scheduled_job_details.sql* script.

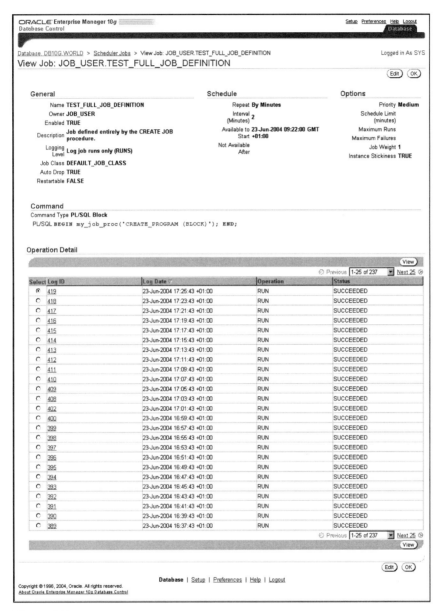

Figure 5.5 – *OEM 10g DB Control: View Job*

Clicking on one of the individual operations in this screen produces the Operation Detail screen, shown in Figure 5.6.

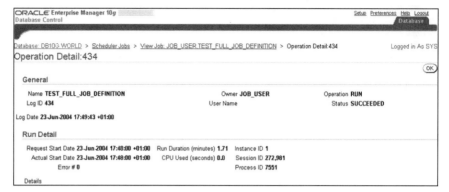

Figure 5.6 – *OEM 10g DB Control: Operation Detail*

The previous two sections showed how running jobs along with their associated sessions can be identified. The next section will focus on monitoring the individual sessions.

Monitoring Sessions

The previous sections explained how to identify the sessions that are executing jobs. This section will discuss the information that can be gathered regarding a specific session. For the most part, session management is the same between Oracle10g and previous versions, so this subject will be dealt with in one block.

The main location for all session information is the *v$session* view. The *sessions.sql* script displays session information using this view along with the *v$process*, *v$sesstat,* and *v$statname* views. The *v$process* view provides information about the background processes that service the sessions, while the *v$sesstat* and *v$statname* provide statistical information about the session.

🖫 **sessions.sql**

```
-- **************************************************
-- Copyright © 2005 by Rampant TechPress
-- This script is free for non-commercial purposes
-- with no warranties.  Use at your own risk.
--
-- To license this script for a commercial purpose,
-- contact info@rampant.cc
-- **************************************************
```

```
set feedback off
alter session set nls_date_format='DD-MON-YYYY HH24:MI:SS';
set feedback on

column username format a15
column osuser format a15
column module format a25
column machine format a25
column program format a25

set linesize 500
set pagesize 1000

select
   a.username,
   a.osuser,
   a.sid,
   a.serial#,
   d.spid,
   a.lockwait,
   a.status,
   trunc(b.value/1024) as pga_kb,
   trunc(e.value/1024) as uga_kb,
   a.module,
   a.machine,
   a.program,
   a.logon_Time
from
   v$session a,
   v$sesstat b,
   v$statname c,
   v$process d,
   v$sesstat e,
   v$statname f
where
   a.paddr      = d.addr
and
   a.sid        = b.sid
and
   b.statistic# = c.statistic#
and
   c.name       = 'session pga memory'
and
   a.sid        = e.sid
and
   e.statistic# = f.statistic#
and
   f.name       = 'session uga memory'
order by
   1,2
;

set pagesize 14
```

A cut-down version of the output expected from this script, is displayed below.

```
SQL> @sessions

USERNAME        OSUSER                    SID   SERIAL# SPID         LOCKWAIT STATUS        PGA_KB    UGA_KB
MODULE                          MACHINE                 PROGRAM                      LOGON_TIME
--------------- ----------------- --------- --------- ------------- -------- -------- ---------- ---------- ---
----------------------- ------------------------        -------------------- --------------------
DBSNMP          oracle                    255    14 4070                      INACTIVE        614       276
emagent@marge (TNS V1-V3) marge                      emagent@marge (TNS V1-V3) 26-JUN-2004 11:53:46
DBSNMP          oracle                    261    28 4105                      ACTIVE         1062       660
emagent@marge (TNS V1-V3) marge                      emagent@marge (TNS V1-V3) 26-JUN-2004 11:53:48
JOB_USER        Administrator             249   287 7340                      ACTIVE         1638       851
SQL*Plus                        WORKGROUP\BART           sqlplusw.exe               26-JUN-2004 13:33:11
SYS                                       272   395 3118                      ACTIVE         1126       148
my_job_proc                                                                         26-JUN-2004 16:49:43
SYSMAN                                    251    13 4052                      INACTIVE        422        84
marge                           oracle@marge (MMAN)      26-JUN-2004 11:51:28
                oracle                    278     1 2903                      ACTIVE         2167        84
marge                           oracle@marge (DBW0)      26-JUN-2004 11:51:28
                oracle                    277     1 2905                      ACTIVE        11430        84
marge                           oracle@marge (LGWR)      26-JUN-2004 11:51:29
                oracle                    276     1 2907                      ACTIVE          877        84
marge                           oracle@marge (CKPT)      26-JUN-2004 11:51:29
                oracle                    270     9 2932                      ACTIVE         1254
  .
  .
  .

32 rows selected.
```

A list of the current sessions can be displayed in the Enterprise Manager by clicking on the 'Sessions' node of the navigator tree (Network > Databases > Database > Instance > Sessions) shown in Figure 5.7.

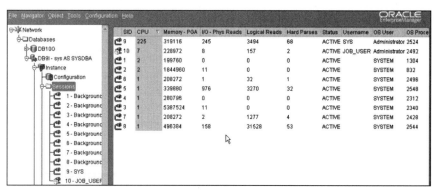

Figure 5.7 – *OEM: Sessions*

In the OEM 10g DB Control, similar information is available on the Top Consumers (Top Sessions) page (Performance > Top Sessions) shown in Figure 5.8.

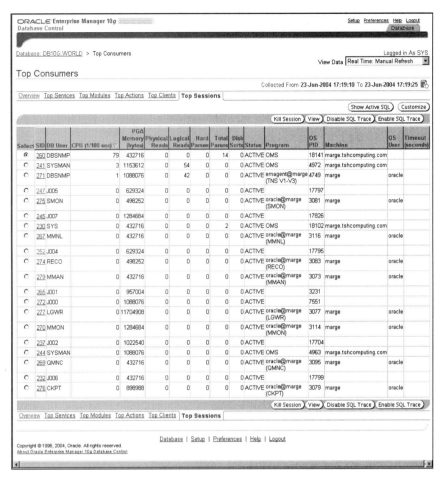

Figure 5.8 – *OEM 10g DB Control: Top Consumers (Top Sessions)*

Clicking on an individual session in the OEM navigator displays session-specific information in the right-hand pane. The 'General' tab, shown in Figure 5.9, displays more session specific information, most of which is retrieved from the *v$session* view.

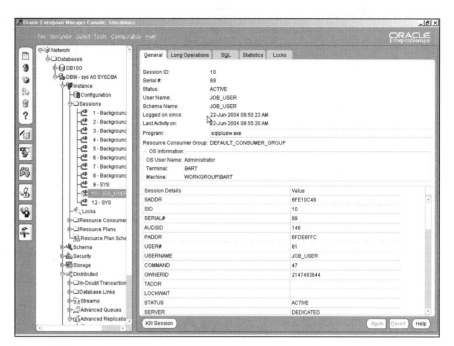

Figure 5.9 – *OEM: Session (General)*

The equivalent of this screen in the OEM 10g DB Control is called the Session Details (General) screen, shown in Figure 5.10.

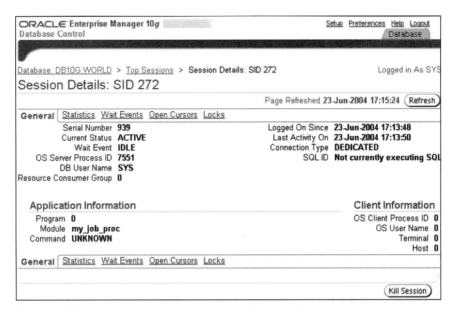

Figure 5.10 – *OEM 10g DB Control: Session Details (General)*

The 'Long Operations' tab in OEM displays information from the *v$session_longops* view. Figure 5.11 shows the progress of a session running the *my_job_proc* procedure.

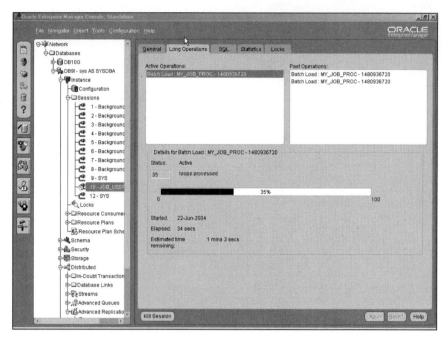

Figure 5.11 – *OEM: Session (Long Operations)*

The *session_open_cursors.sql* script allows the user to display any statements being executed by a specific session. This is accomplished through the use of the *v$open_cursors* view and joins to the *v$sql* view in order to retrieve the full statement.

💾 session_open_cursors.sql

```
--  ******************************************************
--  Copyright © 2005 by Rampant TechPress
--  This script is free for non-commercial purposes
--  with no warranties.  Use at your own risk.
--
--  To license this script for a commercial purpose,
--  contact info@rampant.cc
--  ******************************************************
--  Parameters:
--    1) SID.
--  ******************************************************

set verify off

select
   -- s.sql_id,   -- 10g only
```

```
   s.address,
   s.hash_value,
   s.sql_text
from
   v$sql s,
   v$open_cursor oc
where
   s.address = oc.address
and
   s.hash_value = oc.hash_value
and
   oc.sid = &1
;
```

The output expected from this script is displayed below.

```
SQL> @session_open_cursors 272

ADDRESS   HASH_VALUE
--------  ----------
SQL_TEXT
----------------------------------------------------------------------------------------
----------------------------------------------------------------------------------------
-------------------
59A35624  849200136
DECLARE job BINARY_INTEGER := :job;  next_date TIMESTAMP WITH TIME ZONE := :mydate;  broken
BOOLEAN := FALSE;  job_name VARCHAR2(30) := :job_name;  job_owner VARCHAR2(30) :=
:job_owner;  job_start TIM
ESTAMP WITH TIME ZONE := :job_start;  window_start TIMESTAMP WITH TIME ZONE :=
:window_start;  window_end TIMESTAMP WITH TIME ZONE := :window_end;  BEGIN  BEGIN
my_job_proc('CREATE_PROGRAM (BLOCK)');
END;  :mydate := next_date; IF broken THEN :b := 1; ELSE :b := 0; END IF; END;

1 row selected.
```

Extra code is added automatically to support the functionality of the 10g
scheduler. If this script were run against an Oracle9i instance, one would
expect to just see their original job text.

In OEM, the session SQL tab displays the SQL or PL/SQL statement that is
currently being run by the session. If the current statement is a query, an
execution plan is then displayed. (Figure 5.12)

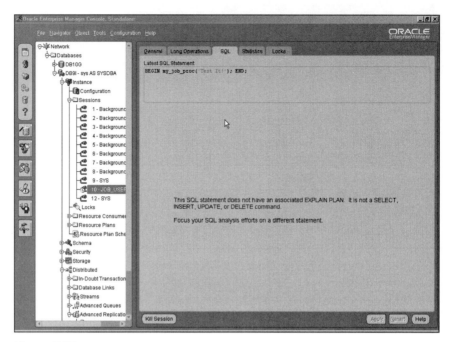

Figure 5.12 – *OEM: Session (SQL)*

The OEM 10g DB Control equivalent of this screen is called the Session Details (Open Cursors) page, shown in Figure 5.13.

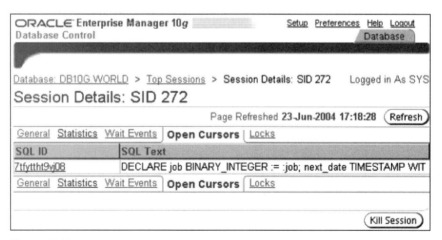

Figure 5.13 – *OEM 10g DB Control: Session Details (Open Cursors)*

The *v$sesstat* view displays session specific statistics, which is already used in the *sessions.sql* script. The *v$statname* view associates a descriptive name for each of the statistics gathered in the *v$sesstat* view. The *session_statistics.sql* script uses both views to display all statistics about a specified session.

🖫 session_statistics.sql

```
-- **************************************************
-- Copyright © 2005 by Rampant TechPress
-- This script is free for non-commercial purposes
-- with no warranties.  Use at your own risk.
--
-- To license this script for a commercial purpose,
-- contact info@rampant.cc
-- **************************************************
-- Parameters:
--    1) SID.
-- ****************************************************************

set verify off

select
   sn.name,
   ss.value,
   decode(sn.class,
         1,  'User',
         2,  'Redo',
         4,  'Enqueue',
         8,  'Cache',
         16, 'OS',
         32, 'RAC',
         64, 'SQL',
         128, 'Debug',
         null) as class
from
   v$sesstat ss,
   v$statname sn
where
   ss.statistic# = sn.statistic#
and
   ss.sid = &1
order by
   sn.name
;
```

A cut-down version of the output from this script is displayed below.

```
SQL> @session_statistics

NAME                                          VALUE CLASS
--------------------------------------------- ----------- -------
CPU used by this session                          0 User
CPU used when call started                        0 Debug
CR blocks created                                 0 Cache
Cached Commit SCN referenced                      0 Debug
Commit SCN cached                                 0 Debug
DB time                                           0 User
DBWR buffers scanned                              0 Cache
DBWR checkpoint buffers written                   0 Cache
DBWR checkpoints                                  0 Cache
DBWR free buffers found                           0 Cache
.
.

332 rows selected.
```

The 'Statistics' tab in OEM displays all statistics that are relevant for the current session as shown in Figure 5.14.

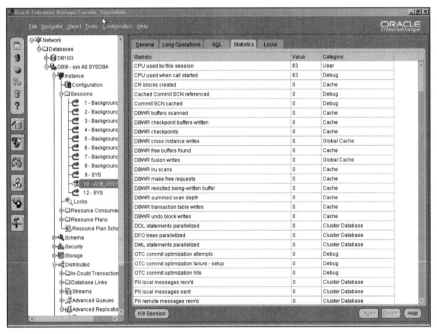

Figure 5.14 – *OEM: Session (Statistics)*

Session statistics are displayed on the Session Details (Statistics) page of OEM 10g DB Control as shown in Figure 5.15.

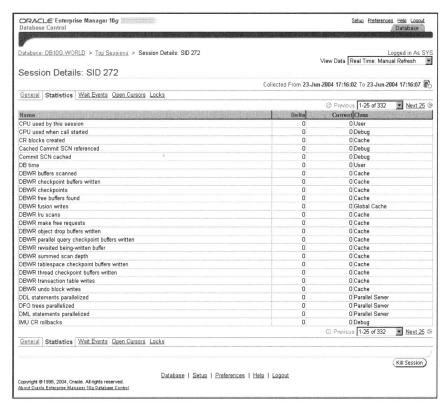

Figure 5.15 – *OEM 10g DB Control: Session Details (Statistics)*

The *session_waits.sql* script uses the *v$session_waits* view to display session specific wait information.

🖫 session_waits.sql

```
--  *****************************************************
--  Copyright © 2005 by Rampant TechPress
--  This script is free for non-commercial purposes
--  with no warranties.  Use at your own risk.
--
--  To license this script for a commercial purpose,
--  contact info@rampant.cc
--  *****************************************************
--  Parameters:
--     1) SID.
--  *****************************************************
```

```
set verify off
set linesize 170

column wait_class format a10
column event format a25
column p1 format 9999999999
column p1text format a15
column p2 format 9999999999
column p2text format a15
column p3 format 9999999999
column p3text format a15

select
   w.event,
   w.p1,
   w.p1text,
   w.p2,
   w.p2text,
   w.p3,
   w.p3text,
   w.seconds_in_wait as wait_time_cs
from
   v$session_wait w
where
   w.sid = &1
order by
   w.seq#
;
```

A typical output from this script is displayed below.

```
SQL> @session_waits 272

EVENT              P1 P1TEXT     P2 P2TEXT     P3 P3TEXT   WAIT_TIME_CS
----------------- ---- --------- ---- --------- ---- --------- ------------
PL/SQL lock timer 100 duration    0               0                     74

1 row selected.
```

Oracle10g also gives access to historical wait information via the *v$session_wait_history* view. The *session_waits_10g.sql* script is a rewrite of the *session_waits.sql* script that uses this view.

💾 session_waits_10g.sql

```
-- ************************************************
-- Copyright © 2005 by Rampant TechPress
-- This script is free for non-commercial purposes
-- with no warranties.  Use at your own risk.
--
-- To license this script for a commercial purpose,
-- contact info@rampant.cc
-- ************************************************
```

```
-- Parameters:
--    1) SID.
-- ****************************************************************

set verify off
set linesize 170

column wait_class format a10
column event format a25
column p1 format 9999999999
column p1text format a15
column p2 format 9999999999
column p2text format a15
column p3 format 9999999999
column p3text format a15

select
   e.wait_class,
   w.event,
   w.p1,
   w.p1text,
   w.p2,
   w.p2text,
   w.p3,
   w.p3text,
   w.wait_time as wait_time_cs
from
   v$session_wait_history w,
   v$event_name e
where
   e.name = w.event
and
   w.sid = &1
order by
   w.seq#
;
```

The output expected from this script is displayed below.

```
SQL> @session_waits_10g 272

WAIT_C EVENT               P1 P1TEXT   P2 P2TEXT   P3 P3TEXT   WAIT_TIME_CS
------ ------------------ --- -------- --- -------- --- -------- ------------
Idle   PL/SQL lock timer  100 duration   0            0              101
Idle   PL/SQL lock timer  100 duration   0            0              101
Idle   PL/SQL lock timer  100 duration   0            0              101
Idle   PL/SQL lock timer  100 duration   0            0              101
Idle   PL/SQL lock timer  100 duration   0            0              101
Idle   PL/SQL lock timer  100 duration   0            0              101
Idle   PL/SQL lock timer  100 duration   0            0              101
Idle   PL/SQL lock timer  100 duration   0            0              101
Idle   PL/SQL lock timer  100 duration   0            0              101
Idle   PL/SQL lock timer  100 duration   0            0              101

10 rows selected.
```

The OEM 10g DB Control displays the same information on the Session Details (Wait Events) screen show in Figure 5.16.

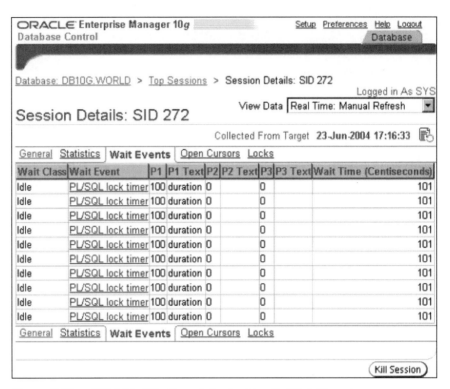

Figure 5.16 – *OEM 10g DB Control: Session Details (Wait Events)*

The *v$lock* view gives access to information about session specific locks. The *session_locks.sql* script combines this view with the *v$session* and *v$process* views to display lock information in a convenient form.

🖫 session_locks.sql

```
-- ******************************************************
-- Copyright © 2005 by Rampant TechPress
-- This script is free for non-commercial purposes
-- with no warranties.  Use at your own risk.
--
-- To license this script for a commercial purpose,
-- contact info@rampant.cc
-- ******************************************************
-- Parameters:
--    1) SID.
-- ******************************************************
```

```
set verify off
set linesize 120

select
    s.program,
    l.block as sessions_blocked,
    l.sid,
    s.serial#,
    p.spid,
    s.sql_hash_value,
    l.type as lock_type,
    l.lmode as mode_held,
    l.request as mode_requested,
    l.ctime as time_in_mode
from
    v$lock l,
    v$session s,
    v$process p
where
    l.sid = s.sid
and
    s.paddr = p.addr
and
    l.sid = &1
;
```

In OEM, the 'Locks' tab (Figure 5.17) displays information about locks that are held by the current session.

Figure 5.17 – *OEM: Session (Locks)*

The Session Details (Locks) screen (Figure 5.18) is the OEM 10g DB Control equivalent of the above screen.

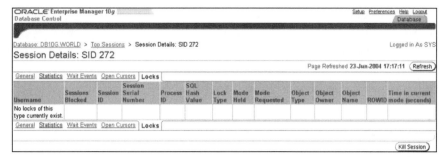

ORACLE Enterprise Manager 10g
Database Control
Setup Preferences Help Logout
Database

Database: DB1DG.WORLD > Top Sessions > Session Details: SID 272
Logged in As SYS
Session Details: SID 272

Figure 5.18 – *OEM 10g DB Control: Session Details (Locks)*

Notice that all the session-specific screens give the option to kill the session.

Now that methods for monitoring sessions for both 10g and previous versions of Oracle database have been introduced, the next section will present information on when and how to kill an Oracle session associated with running jobs.

Killing Oracle Sessions

On occasion, it may be necessary to kill an Oracle session that is associated with a running job. The first step in the process is to identify the session to be killed.

Running jobs that were scheduled using the *dbms_job* package can be identified using the *dba_jobs_running* view. The *jobs_running.sql* script listed below uses this view along with the *v$session* and *v$process* views to gather all information needed about the running jobs.

🖫 **running_job_processes.sql**

```
--  ************************************************
--  Copyright © 2005 by Rampant TechPress
--  This script is free for non-commercial purposes
--  with no warranties.  Use at your own risk.
--
--  To license this script for a commercial purpose,
--  contact info@rampant.cc
--  ************************************************
```

Oracle Job Scheduling

```
set feedback off
alter session set nls_date_format='DD-MON-YYYY HH24:MI:SS';
set feedback on

select
   jr.job,
   s.username,
   s.sid,
   s.serial#,
   p.spid,
   s.lockwait,
   s.logon_time
from
   dba_jobs_running jr,
   v$session s,
   v$process p
where
   jr.sid = s.sid
and
   s.paddr = p.addr
order by
   jr.job
;
```

The type of output expected from this script is listed below.

```
SQL> @running_job_processes

  JOB USERNAME      SID     SERIAL# SPID LOCKWAIT LOGON_TIME
----- ---------- ------ ---------- ---- -------- --------------------
   42 JOB_USER      265          3 3231          23-JUN-2004 08:21:25
   99 JOB_USER      272         77 3199          23-JUN-2004 08:55:35

2 rows selected.
```

Running jobs that were scheduled using the *dbms_scheduler* package can be identified using the *dba_scheduler_running_jobs* view. The *jobs_running_10g.sql* script listed below uses this view along with the *v$session* and *v$process* views to gather all information needed about the running jobs.

💾 running_job_processes_10g.sql

```
select
   rj.job_name,
   s.username,
   s.sid,
   s.serial#,
   p.spid,
   s.lockwait,
   s.logon_time
from
   dba_scheduler_running_jobs rj,
   v$session s,
   v$process p
where
   rj.session_id = s.sid
and
   s.paddr = p.addr
order by
   rj.job_name
;
```

The type of output expected from this script is listed below.

```
SQL> @running_job_processes_10g

JOB_NAME                 USERNAME SID SERIAL# SPID LOCK  LOGON_TIME
------------------------ -------- --- ------- ---- ----- -------------------
TEST_FULL_JOB_DEFINITION SYS      272     125 3199       23-JUN-2004 09:22:12

1 row selected.
```

Regardless of the job scheduling mechanism, the important thing to note is that there are *sid*, *serial#*, and *spid* values associated with the running jobs. The *sid* and *serial#* values are necessary in order to kill the session, while the *spid* value is necessary if the associated operating system process or thread must be killed directly.

To kill the session from within Oracle, the *sid* and *serial#* values of the relevant session can then be substituted into the following statement:

```
alter system kill session 'sid,serial#';
```

With reference to the job listed above by the *jobs_running_10g.sql* script, the statement would look like this.

```
SQL> alter system kill session '272,125';

System altered.
```

This command tells the specified session to rollback any un-committed changes and release any acquired resources before terminating cleanly. In some situations, this cleanup processing may take a considerable amount of time, in which case the session status is set to "marked for kill" until the process is complete.

Under normal circumstance no further actions are needed, but occasionally it may be necessary to bypass this cleanup operation to speed up the release of row and object locks held by the session. Killing the operating system process or thread associated with the session releases the session's locks almost immediately, forcing the PMON process to complete the rollback operation.

 Killing the operating system processes associated with Oracle sessions should be used as a last resort. Killing the wrong process could result in an instance crash and loss of data.

In UNIX and Linux environments, the *kill* command is used to kill specific processes. In order to use this command, the operating system processes *id* must be specified. The *jobs_running.sql* and *jobs_running_10g.sql* scripts list the operating system process *id* associated with each running job in the *spid* column. With this information, the operating system process can be killed by issuing the following command:

```
kill -9 3199
```

The *ps* command can be used to check the process list before or after killing the operating system process.

```
ps -ef | grep ora
```

In Windows environments, Oracle runs as a single multi-threaded process, so a specific process is unable to be killed. Instead, Oracle provides the *orakill.exe* command to allow a specific thread within the Oracle executable to be killed.

```
orakill.exe ORACLE_SID spid
```

The first parameter should not be confused with the *sid* value of the Oracle session. It is in fact the SID associated with the instance. The *spid* value in windows environments identifies the thread within the Oracle executable, rather than an operating system process *id*. With reference to the job listed above by the *jobs_running_10g.sql* script, the command issued would look something like this.

```
C:> orakill.exe DB10G 3199
```

These processes can be used to kill jobs, sessions or processes, as needed. In the next section, the *dbms_application_info* package will be introduce. This package can be used to help monitor jobs and their sessions.

dbms_application_info

Although the *dbms_application_info* package is not directly related to job scheduling, it is valuable for identifying and monitoring the progress of any sessions that support scheduled jobs. The package allows programs to add information to the *v$session* and *v$session_longops* views to make tracking of session activities more simple and more accurate.

When a program initiates, it should register itself using the *set_module* procedure to indicate that it is currently using the session.

```
PROCEDURE set_module (
  module_name  IN  VARCHAR2,
  action_name  IN  VARCHAR2)
```

The *module_name* parameter is used to specify the program name; while the *action_name* parameter is used to indicate what the program is currently doing.

As programs progress, the *set_action* procedure can be used to alter the value of the *action* column of the *v$session* view.

```
PROCEDURE set_action (
  action_name  IN  VARCHAR2)
```

Assuming there was a procedure called *add_order*, which adds an order into an application schema, the following *dbms_application_info* package might be used.

```
BEGIN
  DBMS_APPLICATION_INFO.set_module(
    module_name => 'add_order',
    action_name => 'insert into orders');

  -- Do insert into ORDERS table.
```

```
DBMS_APPLICATION_INFO.set_action(
    action_name => 'insert into order_lines');

-- Do insert into ORDER_LINESS table.

DBMS_APPLICATION_INFO.set_action(
    action_name => 'complete');
END;
/
```

In the above example, the *set_module* procedure sets the value of the *module* column in the *v$session* view to *add_order*, while the ACTION column is set to the value *insert into orders*.

The action is regularly amended using the *set_action* procedure to make sure the ACTION column of the *v$session* view stays accurate.

The *set_client_info* procedure allows information to be stored in the CLIENT_INFO column of the *v$session* view.

```
PROCEDURE set_client_info (
    client_info  IN  VARCHAR2)
```

The following example may be executed to indicate that the procedure is being run as a job.

```
BEGIN
  DBMS_APPLICATION_INFO.set_client_info(
    client_info => 'job');
END;
/
```

The following query shows that the values in the *v$session* view are being set correctly.

```
select
    module,
    action,
    client_info
from
    v$session
where
    username = 'JOB_USER'
;

MODULE              ACTION            CLIENT_INFO
------------------  ----------------  -------------------------
add_order           complete          job

1 row selected.
```

The *set_session_longops* procedure can be used to publish information about the progress of long operations by inserting and updating rows in the *v$session_longops* view.

```
PROCEDURE set_session_longops (
    rindex        IN OUT  PLS_INTEGER,
    slno          IN OUT  PLS_INTEGER,
    op_name       IN      VARCHAR2     DEFAULT NULL,
    target        IN      PLS_INTEGER DEFAULT 0,
    context       IN      PLS_INTEGER DEFAULT 0,
    sofar         IN      NUMBER       DEFAULT 0,
    totalwork     IN      NUMBER       DEFAULT 0,
    target_desc   IN      VARCHAR2     DEFAULT 'unknown target',
    units         IN      VARCHAR2     DEFAULT NULL)
```

This procedure is especially useful when operations contain long running loops such as in the example below.

```
DECLARE
    l_rindex      PLS_INTEGER;
    l_slno        PLS_INTEGER;
    l_totalwork   NUMBER;
    l_sofar       NUMBER;
    l_obj         PLS_INTEGER;
BEGIN
    l_rindex      := DBMS_APPLICATION_INFO.set_session_longops_nohint;
    l_sofar       := 0;
    l_totalwork := 10;

    WHILE l_sofar < 10 LOOP
        -- Do some work
        DBMS_LOCK.sleep(5);
        l_sofar := l_sofar + 1;

        DBMS_APPLICATION_INFO.set_session_longops(
            rindex       => l_rindex,
            slno         => l_slno,
            op_name      => 'BATCH_LOAD',
            target       => l_obj,
            context      => 0,
            sofar        => l_sofar,
            totalwork    => l_totalwork,
            target_desc => 'BATCH_LOAD_TABLE',
            units        => 'rows');
    END LOOP;
END;
/
```

While the above code is running, the contents of the *v$session_longops* view can be queried as follows.

```
column opname format A20
column target_desc format A20
column units format A10

select
   opname,
   target_desc,
   sofar,
   totalwork,
   units
from
   v$session_longops
where
   opname = 'BATCH_LOAD';
```

The resulting output looks something like the one listed below.

```
OPNAME                TARGET_DESC           SOFAR  TOTALWORK UNITS
--------------------  --------------------  -----  --------- --------
BATCH_LOAD            BATCH_LOAD_TABLE          3         10 rows

1 row selected.
```

The *my_job_proc* procedure that is used throughout this book utilizes the *dbms_application_info* package.

In Oracle10g, the *dbms_monitor* package can be used to initiate SQL tracing for sessions based on their *service*, *module* and *action* attributes, making the use of the *dbms_application_info* package even more valuable. A complete introduction to these SQL tracing enhancements is beyond the scope of this book, but the following example shows how the *dbms_monitor* package is used in this context.

```
BEGIN
  DBMS_MONITOR.serv_mod_act_trace_enable (
    service_name   => 'my_service',
    module_name    => 'add_order',
    action_name    => 'insert into order_lines');

  DBMS_MONITOR.serv_mod_act_trace_disable (
    service_name   => 'my_service',
    module_name    => 'add_order',
    action_name    => 'insert into order_lines');
END;
/
```

The same attributes can be used by the new *trcsess* utility to consolidate information from several trace files into a single file, which can then be processed by the TKPROF utility. The following example searches all files with a file extension of ".trc" for trace information related to the specified

dbms_application_info

service, module and action. The resulting information is written to the "client.trc" file.

```
trcsess output=client.trc service=my_service module=add_order
action="insert into order_lines" *.trc
```

This section showed how the *dbms_application_info* package offers valuable tools for identifying and monitoring the progress of any sessions that support scheduled jobs. The next section will present how the *dbms_system* package can be used to write text directly to trace files and alert logs.

dbms_system

The *dbms_system* package is an undocumented and unsupported package that contains a number of useful functions and procedures, including the *ksdwrt* procedure.

```
PROCEDURE ksdwrt (
  dest  IN  BINARY_INTEGER,
  tst   IN  VARCHAR2)
```

The ksdwrt procedure allows the text to be written directly to the alert log and trace files. The *dest* parameter indicates the destination of the message, which can be one of the following.

- A trace file.

- The alert log.

- Both.

The *tst* parameter is used to specify the text that should be written to the destination.

The following command shows how it can be used to write text to the alert log.

```
SQL> exec dbms_system.ksdwrt(2, '*** KSDWRT Test ****');
```

Checking the instances alert log will reveal that a message like the following message has been appended.

```
Wed Jun 23 12:14:46 2004
*** KSDWRT Test ****
```

The *ksdwrt* procedure name is not that memorable in and of itseld, so one may wish to wrap it up in a more obvious procedure as shown in the *write_to_alert_log.sql* below.

 write_to_alert_log.sql

```
-- ****************************************************
-- Copyright © 2005 by Rampant TechPress
-- This script is free for non-commercial purposes
-- with no warranties.  Use at your own risk.
--
-- To license this script for a commercial purpose,
-- contact info@rampant.cc
-- ****************************************************


-- ********************************************************************
-- Parameters:
--    1) Text to be written to the alert log.
-- ********************************************************************

CREATE OR REPLACE PROCEDURE write_to_alert_log (
  p_text  IN  VARCHAR2) AS
BEGIN
  sys.dbms_system.ksdwrt(2, p_text);
END;
/
SHOW ERRORS
```

Now users have an additional tool that can be used capture user defined text in an alert log or trace file. The *my_job_proc* procedure that is used throughout this book as a running example makes used of the *dbms_system* package, so this tool can be added to that procedure, if desired.

💣 **The alert log is a very important file and filling it with lots of extra text may distract attention from important messages. In addition, Oracle support may wish to use alert log contents to diagnose problems, so use this functionality with discretion.**

Conclusion

In this chapter, several important aspects of monitoring running jobs have been covered, including:

- Monitoring legacy jobs using SQL*Plus and Oracle Enterprise Manager (OEM), and identifying their associated sessions.

- Creating a job run history for legacy jobs similar to those provided by the Oracle10g scheduler.

- Monitoring jobs using SQL*Plus and the OEM 10g DB Control, and identifying their associated sessions.

- Monitoring the sessions associated with running jobs.

- Killing the sessions associated with running jobs.

- Using the *dbms_application_info* and the *dbms_system* packages to simplify the monitoring of jobs.

The next chapter will detail some of the more advanced features of the Oracle10g scheduler.

Advanced Scheduling Topics

Time to hit you with some advanced topics!

Introduction

This chapter will present an assortment of advanced topics related to administration of the Oracle10g scheduler. Topics to be covered include setting default scheduler attributes along with object specific attributes, scheduler logging, resource allocation and security.

Setting Scheduler Attributes

There are currently four scheduler attributes:

- *current_open_window* (read-only)

- *default_timezone*

- *log_history*

- *max_job_slave_processes*

Management of the scheduler attributes requires the MANAGE SCHEDULER privilege. To influence the default behavior of the scheduler, three of the attributes can be altered using the *set_scheduler_attribute* procedure. These values can be displayed using the *show_scheduler_attribute.sql* script, which utilizes the *get_scheduler_attribute* procedure.

🖫 show_scheduler_attribute.sql

```
--  ****************************************************
-- Copyright © 2005 by Rampant TechPress
-- This script is free for non-commercial purposes
-- with no warranties.  Use at your own risk.
--
-- To license this script for a commercial purpose,
-- contact info@rampant.cc
--  ****************************************************

set verify off

variable v_value VARCHAR2(1000);

BEGIN
  DBMS_SCHEDULER.get_scheduler_attribute (
    attribute => '&1',
    value     => :v_value);
END;
/

print v_value
```

The following sections will present more detail regarding each of the scheduler attributes starting with the *current_open_window* attribute.

current_open_window

This is a read-only attribute which returns the name of the window that is currently open or active. The *show_scheduler_attribute.sql* script is used to display the value of the *current_open_window* attribute.

```
SQL> @show_scheduler_attribute.sql current_open_window

V_VALUE
------------------------------------------------------------------
WEEKEND_WINDOW
```

default_timezone

As the name implies, this attribute sets the default time zone for the scheduler. When a job is scheduled using the calendar syntax to define a repeat interval, the scheduler needs to know which time zone to apply when calculating the next run date. Since a time zone cannot be specified explicitly by the calendar syntax, it must be derived from the following sources, in the order noted below:

- The time zone of the job's *start_date* attribute.

- The current session's time zone.

- The scheduler's *default_timezone* attribute.

- The time zone returned by the *systimestamp* function.

The following example sets the *default_timezone* attribute to a value of 'US/Eastern' and displays the change.

```
BEGIN
  DBMS_SCHEDULER.set_scheduler_attribute (
    attribute => 'default_timezone',
    value     => 'US/Eastern');
END;
/

SQL> @show_scheduler_attribute.sql default_timezone

V_VALUE
--------------------------------------------------
US/Eastern
```

log_history

This parameter controls the length of time scheduler logs are kept. Each day the scheduler purges any logs that are older than this retention time, specified in days. Any value within the range of one to 999 can be specified, with the default value being 30 days. The following example sets the *log_history* attribute to a value of 60 days and displays the change.

```
BEGIN
  DBMS_SCHEDULER.set_scheduler_attribute (
    attribute => 'log_history',
    value     => 60);
END;
/
```

```
SQL> @show_scheduler_attribute.sql log_history

V_VALUE
------------------------------------------------
60
```

max_job_slave_processes

Unlike the scheduler in Oracle 9i, the Oracle10g scheduler is not constrained by the *job_queue_processes* parameter. Instead, it will start as many job slave processes as needed to cope with the current load. Although limiting the total number of job slave processes should not be necessary under normal circumstances, the *max_job_slave_processes* parameter allows the capability to do so if required. Any value within the range of one to 999 can be specified, with the default value being NULL. The following example sets the *max_job_slave_processes* attribute to a value of 100 and displays the change.

```
BEGIN
  DBMS_SCHEDULER.set_scheduler_attribute (
    attribute => 'max_job_slave_processes',
    value     => 100);
END;
/

SQL> @show_scheduler_attribute.sql max_job_slave_processes

V_VALUE
------------------------------------------------
100
```

To remove this limit simply set the value to NULL.

```
BEGIN
  DBMS_SCHEDULER.set_scheduler_attribute (
    attribute => 'max_job_slave_processes',
    value     => NULL);
END;
/

SQL> @show_scheduler_attribute.sql max_job_slave_processes

V_VALUE
------------------------------------------------
```

With that introduction to how to set scheduler attributes, the next section will present a look at how job priorities can be assigned within a job class.

Job Priorities

When several jobs within the same job class are scheduled to start at the same time, the job coordinator uses the job priority to decide which job to execute first. In the following example, a job is created and its *job_priority* attribute is set to one using the *set_attribute* procedure.

```
BEGIN
  DBMS_SCHEDULER.create_job (
    job_name        => 'test_priority_job',
    job_type        => 'PLSQL_BLOCK',
    job_action      => 'BEGIN DBMS_LOCK.sleep(10); END;',
    start_date      => SYSTIMESTAMP,
    repeat_interval => 'freq=minutely;',
    end_date        => SYSTIMESTAMP + 1/48,
    enabled         => FALSE,
    comments        => 'Job used to test priorities.');

  DBMS_SCHEDULER.set_attribute (
    name      => 'test_priority_job',
    attribute => 'job_priority',
    value     => 1);

  DBMS_SCHEDULER.enable (name => 'test_priority_job');
END;
/
```

The attribute can be set to any value in the range from one to five, in which one is the highest priority. If a priority is not specified during the job creation, it is assigned the default value of three.

The priority of a job can be displayed using the *dba_scheduler_jobs* view, as shown by the following query:

```
select
   job_name,
   job_priority
from
   dba_scheduler_jobs
order by
   job_priority
;

JOB_NAME                      JOB_PRIORITY
----------------------------- ------------
TEST_PRIORITY_JOB                        1
GATHER_STATS_JOB                         3
PURGE_LOG                                3

3 rows selected.
```

This introduction to priorities illustrates that assigning a priority to jobs within a job class is easy. The next section will present information on scheduler logging that is available as part of the Oracle10g scheduler.

Scheduler Logging

The Oracle10g scheduler logs a number of events including job maintenance, job run activity and window activity. It also gives some degree of control over the level of logging performed by the scheduler.

The *log_history* scheduler attribute can be used to control the volume of historical logging information. Yet, if a specific job or job class has a different history requirement, the *set_attribute* procedure can be used to override this value.

```
BEGIN
  -- Alter log history for a specific job.
  DBMS_SCHEDULER.set_attribute (
    name      => 'test_job',
    attribute => 'log_history',
    value     => 30);

  -- Alter log history for a specific job class.
  DBMS_SCHEDULER.set_attribute (
    name      => 'test_job_class',
    attribute => 'log_history',
    value     => 90);
END;
/
```

There are several types of scheduler logs which can be managed separately. In the following sections, information will be presented on each type of logging available, starting with job logs.

Job Logs

There are three levels of logging associated with scheduled jobs. They are noted below, along with the appropriate constants defined in the *dbms_scheduler* package:

- *logging_off* - No logging.

- *logging_runs* - Only run events are logged.

- *logging_full* - All events that happen to a job during its lifetime are logged.

The logging level of a job is typically set by associating it to a job class with the appropriate logging level. Since the default logging level for a job class is *logging_runs* and all jobs are associated with a job class, the default logging level for a job is *logging_runs*.

Alternatively, the *logging_level* parameter of a job can be set directly using the *set_attribute* procedure, as shown below.

```
BEGIN
  DBMS_SCHEDULER.set_attribute (
    name      => 'test_log_job',
    attribute => 'logging_level',
    value     => DBMS_SCHEDULER.logging_off);
END;
/
```

For security reasons, this method cannot change the logging level to a value lower than that of its associated class. For example, if the jobs associated job class has a logging level of *logging_runs*, the *set_attribute* procedure could only be used to switch the jobs logging level to *logging_full* and back to *logging_runs*. By doing so, administrators of the scheduler can dictate a minimum level of auditing for job execution.

The *job_log_lifecycle.sql* script creates, updates, enables and drops a job; effectively producing a full lifecycle of events in the job log.

🖫 job_log_lifecycle.sql

```
-- ************************************************
-- Copyright © 2005 by Rampant TechPress
-- This script is free for non-commercial purposes
-- with no warranties.  Use at your own risk.
--
-- To license this script for a commercial purpose,
-- contact info@rampant.cc
-- ************************************************

BEGIN
  -- Remove all logs for this job.
  DBMS_SCHEDULER.purge_log(job_name => 'test_log_job');

  -- Create job class with full logging.
  DBMS_SCHEDULER.create_job_class (
    job_class_name          => 'test_logging_class',
    resource_consumer_group => 'default_consumer_group',
    logging_level           => DBMS_SCHEDULER.logging_full);

  -- Create job links to previous job class.
  DBMS_SCHEDULER.create_job (
```

```
   job_name          => 'test_log_job',
   job_type          => 'PLSQL_BLOCK',
   job_action        => 'BEGIN NULL; END;',
   job_class         => 'test_logging_class',
   enabled           => FALSE,
   auto_drop         => FALSE,
   comments          => 'Job used to job logs.');

   -- Update the job.
   DBMS_SCHEDULER.set_attribute (
   name        => 'test_log_job',
   attribute => 'start_date',
   value      => SYSTIMESTAMP);

   -- Enable the job.
   DBMS_SCHEDULER.enable (name => 'test_log_job');

   -- Pause to let the job run.
   DBMS_LOCK.sleep(30);

   -- Drop the job.
   DBMS_SCHEDULER.drop_job (job_name => 'test_log_job');

   -- Drop the job class.
   DBMS_SCHEDULER.drop_job_class (job_class_name =>
'test_logging_class');v

END;
/
```

This script clears down any log information associated with the job it creates, allowing it to be run multiple times with the same result.

The *job_logs.sql* script uses the *dba_scheduler_job_log* view to display log information for a specific job or all jobs.

🖫 job_logs.sql

```
-- ************************************************
-- Copyright © 2005 by Rampant TechPress
-- This script is free for non-commercial purposes
-- with no warranties.  Use at your own risk.
--
-- To license this script for a commercial purpose,
-- contact info@rampant.cc
-- ************************************************
-- Parameters:
--    1) Specific job name or 'all' jobs.
-- ********************************************************************

set feedback off
alter session set nls_timestamp_tz_format='DD-MON-YYYY
HH24:MI:SS.ff';
```

```
set feedback on

column owner format a10
column job_name format a30
column operation format a10
column status format a10
column log_date format a27

select
    owner,
    job_name,
    operation,
    status,
    log_date
from
    dba_scheduler_job_log
where
    job_name = decode(upper('&1'), 'ALL', job_name, upper('&1'))
order by
    log_date
;
```

Using the previous two scripts, the sort of logging one would expect for a job with full logging enabled can be seen.

```
SQL> @ job_log_lifecycle.sql

PL/SQL procedure successfully completed.

SQL> @ job_logs.sql test_log_job

OWNER       JOB_NAME        OPERATION   STATUS      LOG_DATE
----------  --------------- ----------  ----------  ---------------------------
JOB_USER    TEST_LOG_JOB    CREATE                  21-AUG-2004 15:21:23.795000
JOB_USER    TEST_LOG_JOB    UPDATE                  21-AUG-2004 15:21:23.811000
JOB_USER    TEST_LOG_JOB    ENABLE                  21-AUG-2004 15:21:23.827000
JOB_USER    TEST_LOG_JOB    RUN         SUCCEEDED   21-AUG-2004 15:21:23.874000
JOB_USER    TEST_LOG_JOB    SUCCEEDED               21-AUG-2004 15:21:23.874000
JOB_USER    TEST_LOG_JOB    DROP                    21-AUG-2004 15:21:54.577000

6 rows selected.
```

The job logs provide only top-level information about the jobs. Further details are logged in the job run details log which is covered in the next section.

Job Run Details

Every row in the *dba_scheduler_job_log* view for a run event has an associated row in the *dba_scheduler_job_run_details* view. This view provides more details about the job run including requested start date, actual start date, duration and CPU usage etc.

The *scheduled_job_details.sql* and *job_run_history.sql* scripts from Chapter 5 use the *dba_scheduler_job_run_details* view to display the run history for a specific job.

```
SQL> @job_run_history all 5

JOB_NAME                     OWNER     STATUS     COMPLETION_DATE      RUN_DURATION
------------------------     --------  ---------  --------------------  ------------
TEST_FULL_JOB_DEFINITION JOB_USER SUCCEEDED 21-AUG-2004 15:31:43            1
TEST_FULL_JOB_DEFINITION JOB_USER SUCCEEDED 21-AUG-2004 15:29:43            1
TEST_FULL_JOB_DEFINITION JOB_USER SUCCEEDED 21-AUG-2004 15:27:43            1
TEST_FULL_JOB_DEFINITION JOB_USER SUCCEEDED 21-AUG-2004 15:25:43            1
TEST_FULL_JOB_DEFINITION JOB_USER SUCCEEDED 21-AUG-2004 15:23:43            1

5 rows selected.
```

The job logs and job run detail logs allow the tracking of all job activity but do not reveal what the active resource plan was during the job runs. This information is provided by the window logs, which is covered in the next section.

Window Logs

There is no logging level associated with window logs. A window log entry is created whenever a window is created, dropped, opened, closed, overlapped, disabled or enabled. The *window_logs.sql* script uses the *dba_scheduler_window_log* view to display window log information about a specific window, or all windows.

💾 window_logs.sql

```
-- *****************************************************
-- Copyright © 2005 by Rampant TechPress
-- This script is free for non-commercial purposes
-- with no warranties.  Use at your own risk.
--
-- To license this script for a commercial purpose,
-- contact info@rampant.cc
-- *****************************************************
-- Parameters:
--    1) Specific window name or 'all' windows.
-- *********************************************************************

set feedback off
alter session set nls_timestamp_tz_format='DD-MON-YYYY HH24:MI:SS';
set feedback on

column window_name format a30
```

```
column operation format a10
column status format a10
column log_date format a27

select
   window_name,
   operation,
   status,
   log_date
from
   dba_scheduler_window_log
where
   window_name = decode(upper('&1'), 'ALL', window_name,
upper('&1'))
order by
   log_date
;
```

An example of the output produced by this script is shown below.

```
SQL> @window_logs.sql all

WINDOW_NAME                     OPERATION  STATUS     LOG_DATE
------------------------------  ---------- ---------- --------------------
WEEKNIGHT_WINDOW                OPEN                  20-AUG-2004 07:00:01
WEEKNIGHT_WINDOW                CLOSE                 20-AUG-2004 15:00:01
WEEKNIGHT_WINDOW                OPEN                  21-AUG-2004 07:00:00
WEEKNIGHT_WINDOW                CLOSE                 21-AUG-2004 15:00:00
WEEKEND_WINDOW                  OPEN                  21-AUG-2004 15:00:02

5 rows selected.
```

Each entry in the *dba_scheduler_window_log* view for a close operation has an associated entry in the *dba_scheduler_window_details* view. This view provides additional information including the requested start date, actual start date and window duration. The *window_details.sql* script makes use of this view.

💾 window_details.sql

```
-- ****************************************************
-- Copyright © 2005 by Rampant TechPress
-- This script is free for non-commercial purposes
-- with no warranties.  Use at your own risk.
--
-- To license this script for a commercial purpose,
-- contact info@rampant.cc
-- ****************************************************
-- Parameters:
--    1) Specific window name or 'all' windows.
-- ********************************************************************
set feedback off
alter session set nls_timestamp_tz_format='DD-MON-YYYY HH24:MI:SS';
```

```
set feedback on

set linesize 120

column window_name format a30
column log_date format a27
column actual_start_date format a27
column actual_duration format 99999

select
   window_name,
   log_date,
   actual_start_date,
   extract(minute from actual_duration) as actual_duration
from
   dba_scheduler_window_details
where
   window_name = decode(upper('&1'), 'ALL', window_name,
upper('&1'))
order by
   log_date
;
```

An example of the output produced by this script is shown below.

```
SQL> @window_details.sql all

WINDOW_NAME                       LOG_DATE
ACTUAL_START_DATE                 ACTUAL_DURATION
------------------------------    ---------------------------  ---------
------------------   ---------------
WEEKNIGHT_WINDOW                  20-AUG-2004 15:00:01            19-AUG-
2004 22:00:01                     0
WEEKNIGHT_WINDOW                  21-AUG-2004 15:00:00            20-AUG-
2004 22:00:00                     0

2 rows selected.
```

Now that the various types of scheduler logs have been introduced, it makes sense to examine their management. It has been shown that the contents of the scheduler logs are managed automatically, but the next section will illustrate how to manually purge the scheduler logs.

Purging Logs

On occasion, it may be necessary to manually purge the scheduler logs prior to any regularly scheduled automatic purge. This can be accomplished using the *purge_log* procedure.

```
PROCEDURE purge_log(
  log_history        IN PLS_INTEGER DEFAULT 0,
  which_log          IN VARCHAR2    DEFAULT 'JOB_AND_WINDOW_LOG',
  job_name           IN VARCHAR2    DEFAULT NULL)
```

The parameters and usages associated with this procedure are listed below:

- *log_history* - This determines the age of the logs that should be kept. Valid values range between zero and 999 with the default being zero.

- *which_log* - This indicates which log or logs should be purged. The possible parameters are *job_log*, *window_log* and *job_and_window_log*, with the latter being the default value.

- *job_name* - This limits the purge operation of a specific job, job class or comma separated list. By default, this parameter is set to NULL, which indicates logs for all jobs should be purged.

The following example shows how the procedure can be used:

```
BEGIN
  DBMS_SCHEDULER.purge_log (
    log_history => 5,
    which_log   => 'JOB_AND_WINDOW_LOG',
    job_name    => 'my_text_job');

  DBMS_SCHEDULER.purge_log (
    log_history => 15,
    which_log   => 'JOB_LOG',
    job_name    => 'my_text_job_class');

  DBMS_SCHEDULER.purge_log (
    log_history => 0,
    which_log   => 'WINDOW_LOG',
    job_name    => 'my_text_job');
END;
/
```

To purge all entries for both the job and window logs, simply call the procedure with no parameters.

```
SQL> EXECUTE DBMS_SCHEDULER.purge_log;
```

The *auto_purge* procedure uses the *log_history* values defined at the scheduler, job class and job *log_history* level to determine which logs should be purged. This procedure runs as part of the scheduled purge process, but can also be run manually.

```
SQL> EXECUTE DBMS_SCHEDULER.auto_purge;
```

Depending on the circumstances, it is possible to manage the purging of logs manually as well as automatically. Moving on to the management of resources, it was mentioned previously that windows are involved in the link between the scheduler and the resource manager. In the following section, the link between these two functional areas will be examined.

Resource Manager

Job classes, windows and window groups provide a link between the scheduler and the resource manager. The syntax for creating these scheduler objects was presented in Chapter 2, so this section will illustrate how they should be used. Since a complete investigation of the resource manager is beyond the scope of this book, this section will focus on the basic elements needed to start integrating resource management into job schedules.

The *dbms_resource_manager* package is an API which provides a means of controlling the allocation of system resources between Oracle sessions. Information about resource allocation can be displayed using the *dba_rsrc_%* views, which can be listed using the *table_comments.sql* script from Chapter 2, as shown below.

```
SQL> @table_comments.sql sys dba_rsrc

TABLE_NAME                           COMMENTS
------------------------------------ ------------------------------------
DBA_RSRC_CONSUMER_GROUPS             all the resource consumer groups
DBA_RSRC_CONSUMER_GROUP_PRIVS        Switch privileges for consumer groups
DBA_RSRC_GROUP_MAPPINGS              all the consumer group mappings
DBA_RSRC_MANAGER_SYSTEM_PRIVS        system privileges for the resource
                                     manager
DBA_RSRC_MAPPING_PRIORITY            the consumer group mapping attribute
                                     priorities
DBA_RSRC_PLANS                       All the resource plans
DBA_RSRC_PLAN_DIRECTIVES             all the resource plan directives

7 rows selected.
```

Modifications to resource management must be complete and valid before they are applied to the system. For this reason, most operations using the *dbms_resource_manager* package are performed in a pending area where they are validated before being applied. The following code shows the procedure calls which must enclose any modifications:

```
BEGIN
  DBMS_RESOURCE_MANAGER.clear_pending_area;
  DBMS_RESOURCE_MANAGER.create_pending_area;

  -- Do something

  DBMS_RESOURCE_MANAGER.validate_pending_area;
  DBMS_RESOURCE_MANAGER.submit_pending_area;
END;
/
```

To illustrate the use of the resource manager, assume there is a system in which OLTP operations must take priority over batch operations during the day. At night, the situation is reversed such that batch operations take priority over OLTP operations.

To model this scenario, create two new consumer groups for the OLTP and batch tasks using the *create_consumer_group* procedure.

```
PROCEDURE create_consumer_group(
   consumer_group   IN   VARCHAR2,
   comment          IN   VARCHAR2,
   cpu_mth          IN   VARCHAR2 DEFAULT 'ROUND-ROBIN')
```

The *create_consumer_groups.sql* script uses this procedure to create the OLTP and batch consumer groups.

🖫 create_consumer_groups.sql

```
-- *****************************************************
-- Copyright © 2005 by Rampant TechPress
-- This script is free for non-commercial purposes
-- with no warranties.  Use at your own risk.
--
-- To license this script for a commercial purpose,
-- contact info@rampant.cc
-- *****************************************************

CONN sys/password AS SYSDBA
BEGIN
  DBMS_RESOURCE_MANAGER.clear_pending_area;
  DBMS_RESOURCE_MANAGER.create_pending_area;

  -- Create the consumer groups
  DBMS_RESOURCE_MANAGER.create_consumer_group(
    consumer_group => 'oltp_consumer_group',
    comment        => 'OLTP process consumer group.');

  DBMS_RESOURCE_MANAGER.create_consumer_group(
    consumer_group => 'batch_consumer_group',
    comment        => 'Batch process consumer group.');
```

```
  DBMS_RESOURCE_MANAGER.validate_pending_area;
  DBMS_RESOURCE_MANAGER.submit_pending_area;
END;
/
```

The *consumer_groups.sql* script listed below uses the *dba_rsrc_consumer_groups* view to display information about the consumer groups that have been created.

🖫 consumer_groups.sql

```
-- ***************************************************
-- Copyright © 2005 by Rampant TechPress
-- This script is free for non-commercial purposes
-- with no warranties.  Use at your own risk.
--
-- To license this script for a commercial purpose,
-- contact info@rampant.cc
-- ***************************************************

column comments format a60

select
   consumer_group,
   comments
from
   dba_rsrc_consumer_groups
order by
   consumer_group
;
```

The output from this script is displayed below.

```
SQL> @consumer_groups.sql

CONSUMER_GROUP                   COMMENTS
------------------------------   -------------------------------------------------
-
AUTO_TASK_CONSUMER_GROUP         System maintenance task consumer group
BATCH_CONSUMER_GROUP             Batch process consumer group.
DEFAULT_CONSUMER_GROUP           consumer group for users not assigned to any
                                 group
LOW_GROUP                        Group of low priority sessions
OLTP_CONSUMER_GROUP              OLTP process consumer group.
OTHER_GROUPS                     consumer group for users not included in any
                                 group in the active top-plan
SYS_GROUP                        Group of system sessions

7 rows selected.
```

The *delete_consumer_groups.sql* script uses the *delete_consumer_group* procedure to clean up the consumer groups created for the example. The consumer groups can only be removed if they have no dependant plan directives.

💾 delete_consumer_groups.sql

```
-- ***************************************************
-- Copyright © 2005 by Rampant TechPress
-- This script is free for non-commercial purposes
-- with no warranties.  Use at your own risk.
--
-- To license this script for a commercial purpose,
-- contact info@rampant.cc
-- ***************************************************

BEGIN
  DBMS_RESOURCE_MANAGER.clear_pending_area();
  DBMS_RESOURCE_MANAGER.create_pending_area();

  -- Delete consumer groups.
  DBMS_RESOURCE_MANAGER.delete_consumer_group (
    consumer_group => 'oltp_consumer_group');

  DBMS_RESOURCE_MANAGER.delete_consumer_group (
    consumer_group => 'batch_consumer_group');

  DBMS_RESOURCE_MANAGER.validate_pending_area;
  DBMS_RESOURCE_MANAGER.submit_pending_area();
END;
/
```

With the consumer groups present, a resource plan can be created using the *create_plan* procedure, and it can be associated to the consumer groups using the *create_plan_directive* procedure.

```
PROCEDURE create_plan (
  plan                     IN  VARCHAR2,
  comment                  IN  VARCHAR2,
  cpu_mth                  IN  VARCHAR2 DEFAULT 'EMPHASIS',
  active_sess_pool_mth     IN  VARCHAR2 DEFAULT
'ACTIVE_SESS_POOL_ABSOLUTE',
  parallel_degree_limit_mth IN  VARCHAR2 DEFAULT
'PARALLEL_DEGREE_LIMIT_ABSOLUTE',
  queueing_mth             IN  VARCHAR2 DEFAULT 'FIFO_TIMEOUT')

PROCEDURE create_plan_directive (
  plan                     IN  VARCHAR2,
  group_or_subplan         IN  VARCHAR2,
  comment                  IN  VARCHAR2,
  cpu_p1                   IN  NUMBER DEFAULT NULL,
  cpu_p2                   IN  NUMBER DEFAULT NULL,
  cpu_p3                   IN  NUMBER DEFAULT NULL,
```

```
cpu_p4                        IN   NUMBER DEFAULT NULL,
cpu_p5                        IN   NUMBER DEFAULT NULL,
cpu_p6                        IN   NUMBER DEFAULT NULL,
cpu_p7                        IN   NUMBER DEFAULT NULL,
cpu_p8                        IN   NUMBER DEFAULT NULL,
active_sess_pool_p1           IN   NUMBER DEFAULT NULL,
queueing_p1                   IN   NUMBER DEFAULT NULL,
parallel_degree_limit_p1      IN   NUMBER DEFAULT NULL,
switch_group                  IN   VARCHAR2 DEFAULT NULL,
switch_time                   IN   NUMBER DEFAULT NULL,
switch_estimate               IN   BOOLEAN DEFAULT FALSE,
max_est_exec_time             IN   NUMBER DEFAULT NULL,
undo_pool                     IN   NUMBER DEFAULT NULL,
max_idle_time                 IN   NUMBER DEFAULT NULL,
max_idle_blocker_time         IN   NUMBER DEFAULT NULL,
switch_time_in_call           IN   NUMBER DEFAULT NULL)
```

The *day_plan.sql* script uses these procedures to create a resource plan suitable for daytime processing. The OLTP operations are associated 80% of the CPU on level one; while batch operations receive 100% of the remaining CPU at level two. The *switch_group* and *switch_time* parameters are used in the OLTP plan directive to specify that OLTP processes lasting more than 60 seconds should be switched to the batch consumer group. The *other_groups* consumer group must be included in any valid plan as it provides resource allocation information for any processes that are not explicitly associated with the consumer groups.

🖫 day_plan.sql

```
-- **************************************************
-- Copyright © 2005 by Rampant TechPress
-- This script is free for non-commercial purposes
-- with no warranties.  Use at your own risk.
--
-- To license this script for a commercial purpose,
-- contact info@rampant.cc
-- **************************************************

BEGIN
  DBMS_RESOURCE_MANAGER.clear_pending_area;
  DBMS_RESOURCE_MANAGER.create_pending_area;

  -- Create a new plan
  DBMS_RESOURCE_MANAGER.create_plan(
    plan    => 'day_plan',
    comment => 'Plan suitable for daytime processing.');

  -- Assign consumer groups to plan and define priorities
  DBMS_RESOURCE_MANAGER.create_plan_directive (
    plan            => 'day_plan',
    group_or_subplan => 'oltp_consumer_group',
```

```
      comment            => 'Give OLTP processes higher priority - level
1',
    cpu_p1              => 80,
    switch_group        => 'batch_consumer_group',
    switch_time         => 60);

  DBMS_RESOURCE_MANAGER.create_plan_directive (
    plan                => 'day_plan',
    group_or_subplan => 'batch_consumer_group',
    comment            => 'Give batch processes lower priority - level
2',
    cpu_p2              => 100);

  DBMS_RESOURCE_MANAGER.create_plan_directive(
    plan                => 'day_plan',
    group_or_subplan => 'OTHER_GROUPS',
    comment            => 'all other users - level 3',
    cpu_p3              => 100);

  DBMS_RESOURCE_MANAGER.validate_pending_area;
  DBMS_RESOURCE_MANAGER.submit_pending_area;
END;
/
```

The *night_plan.sql* script creates a resource plan suitable for nighttime processing in which the resource allocation is the reverse of the daytime processing, such that batch processes receive 80% of the CPU at level one, and OLTP operations receive 100% of the remaining CPU at level two. Once again, the *other_groups* consumer group is specified as a catch-all.

🖫 night_plan.sql

```
-- *****************************************************
-- Copyright © 2005 by Rampant TechPress
-- This script is free for non-commercial purposes
-- with no warranties.  Use at your own risk.
--
-- To license this script for a commercial purpose,
-- contact info@rampant.cc
-- *****************************************************

BEGIN
  DBMS_RESOURCE_MANAGER.clear_pending_area;
  DBMS_RESOURCE_MANAGER.create_pending_area;

  -- Create a new plan
  DBMS_RESOURCE_MANAGER.create_plan(
    plan    => 'night_plan',
    comment => 'Plan suitable for daytime processing.');

  -- Assign consumer groups to plan and define priorities
  DBMS_RESOURCE_MANAGER.create_plan_directive (
    plan                => 'night_plan',
```

```
     group_or_subplan => 'batch_consumer_group',
     comment          => 'Give batch processes lower priority - level
2',
     cpu_p1           => 80);

   DBMS_RESOURCE_MANAGER.create_plan_directive (
     plan             => 'night_plan',
     group_or_subplan => 'oltp_consumer_group',
     comment          => 'Give OLTP processes higher priority - level
1',
     cpu_p2           => 100);

   DBMS_RESOURCE_MANAGER.create_plan_directive(
     plan             => 'night_plan',
     group_or_subplan => 'OTHER_GROUPS',
     comment          => 'all other users - level 3',
     cpu_p3           => 100);

   DBMS_RESOURCE_MANAGER.validate_pending_area;
   DBMS_RESOURCE_MANAGER.submit_pending_area;
END;
/
```

The *resource_plan_directives.sql* script uses the *dba_rsrc_plan_directives* view to display information about the resource plans currently defined on the system.

🖫 resource_plan_directives.sql

```
-- ****************************************************
-- Copyright © 2005 by Rampant TechPress
-- This script is free for non-commercial purposes
-- with no warranties.  Use at your own risk.
--
-- To license this script for a commercial purpose,
-- contact info@rampant.cc
-- ****************************************************

select
   plan,
   group_or_subplan,
   status
from
   dba_rsrc_plan_directives
order by
   plan,
   group_or_subplan
;
```

The output from the *resource_plan_directives.sql* script is displayed below.

```
SQL> @resource_plan_directives.sql

PLAN                          GROUP_OR_SUBPLAN                STATUS
----------------------------  ------------------------------  ------
DAY_PLAN                      BATCH_CONSUMER_GROUP            ACTIVE
DAY_PLAN                      OLTP_CONSUMER_GROUP             ACTIVE
DAY_PLAN                      OTHER_GROUPS                    ACTIVE
INTERNAL_PLAN                 OTHER_GROUPS                    ACTIVE
INTERNAL_QUIESCE              OTHER_GROUPS                    ACTIVE
INTERNAL_QUIESCE              SYS_GROUP                       ACTIVE
NIGHT_PLAN                    BATCH_CONSUMER_GROUP            ACTIVE
NIGHT_PLAN                    OLTP_CONSUMER_GROUP             ACTIVE
NIGHT_PLAN                    OTHER_GROUPS                    ACTIVE
SYSTEM_PLAN                   LOW_GROUP                       ACTIVE
SYSTEM_PLAN                   OTHER_GROUPS                    ACTIVE
SYSTEM_PLAN                   SYS_GROUP                       ACTIVE

12 rows selected.
```

The resource manager is only activated when a default resource plan is assigned. Only one resource plan can be active at any given time. Resource plan switches can be automated using scheduler windows or performed manually by setting the *resource_manager_plan* parameter using the *alter system* command as shown below.

```
alter system set resource_manager_plan = day_plan;
```

The currently active resource plan can be identified by querying the *v$rsrc_plan* view as shown in the *active_plan.sql* script listed below.

🖫 active_plan.sql

```
-- ***************************************************
-- Copyright © 2005 by Rampant TechPress
-- This script is free for non-commercial purposes
-- with no warranties.  Use at your own risk.
--
-- To license this script for a commercial purpose,
-- contact info@rampant.cc
-- ***************************************************

select
    *
from
    v$rsrc_plan
;
```

The output from the *active_plan.sql* script is displayed below.

```
SQL> @active_plan.sql

NAME                             IS_TO
-------------------------------  -----
DAY_PLAN                         TRUE

1 row selected.
```

The *delete_plans.sql* script uses the *delete_plan* procedure to remove the resource plans defined in this example. The *resource_manager_plan* parameter is unset before the plans are deleted, which deactivates the resource manager.

🖫 delete_plans.sql

```
-- ***************************************************
-- Copyright © 2005 by Rampant TechPress
-- This script is free for non-commercial purposes
-- with no warranties.  Use at your own risk.
--
-- To license this script for a commercial purpose,
-- contact info@rampant.cc
-- ***************************************************

alter system set resource_manager_plan = '';

BEGIN
  DBMS_RESOURCE_MANAGER.clear_pending_area();
  DBMS_RESOURCE_MANAGER.create_pending_area();

  -- Delete plans.
  DBMS_RESOURCE_MANAGER.delete_plan (
    plan => 'day_plan');

  DBMS_RESOURCE_MANAGER.delete_plan (
    plan => 'night_plan');

  DBMS_RESOURCE_MANAGER.validate_pending_area;
  DBMS_RESOURCE_MANAGER.submit_pending_area();
END;
/
```

With the plans present, the *create_job_classes.sql* script can be used to create job classes that are associated with the OLTP and batch consumer groups.

🖫 create_job_classes.sql

```
-- ***************************************************
-- Copyright © 2005 by Rampant TechPress
-- This script is free for non-commercial purposes
-- with no warranties.  Use at your own risk.
--
```

```
-- To license this script for a commercial purpose,
-- contact info@rampant.cc
-- ***************************************************

BEGIN
   DBMS_SCHEDULER.create_job_class(
      job_class_name          => 'oltp_job_class',
      resource_consumer_group => 'oltp_consumer_group',
      comments                => 'OLTP process job class.');

   DBMS_SCHEDULER.create_job_class(
      job_class_name          => 'batch_job_class',
      resource_consumer_group => 'batch_consumer_group',
      comments                => 'Batch process job class.');
END;
/
```

Using the *job_classes.sql* script from Chapter 2, it can be noted that the job classes were created correctly.

```
SQL> job_classes.sql

JOB_CLASS_NAME                  RESOURCE_CONSUMER_GROUP
------------------------------  ------------------------------
DEFAULT_JOB_CLASS
AUTO_TASKS_JOB_CLASS            AUTO_TASK_CONSUMER_GROUP
BATCH_JOB_CLASS                 BATCH_CONSUMER_GROUP
OLTP_JOB_CLASS                  OLTP_CONSUMER_GROUP

4 rows selected.
```

The *drop_job_classes.sql* script uses the *drop_job_class* procedure to remove the job classes used in this example.

🖫 drop_job_classes.sql

```
-- ***************************************************
-- Copyright © 2005 by Rampant TechPress
-- This script is free for non-commercial purposes
-- with no warranties.  Use at your own risk.
--
-- To license this script for a commercial purpose,
-- contact info@rampant.cc
-- ***************************************************
BEGIN
   DBMS_SCHEDULER.drop_job_class (
      job_class_name          => 'oltp_job_class');

   DBMS_SCHEDULER.drop_job_class (
      job_class_name          => 'batch_job_class');
END;
/
```

The consumer groups and job classes that have been created will work properly for jobs scheduled by the SYS user, but extra privileges must be granted before they can be used by other users. First, grant the EXECUTE privilege on both job classes, and then make sure the user can switch consumer groups properly by calling the *grant_switch_consumer_group* procedure from the *dbms_resource_manager_privs* package. The *job_class_resource_privileges.sql* script performs both tasks, granting the necessary privileges to a user called *job_user*.

🖫 job_class_resource_privileges.sql

```
-- **************************************************
-- Copyright © 2005 by Rampant TechPress
-- This script is free for non-commercial purposes
-- with no warranties.  Use at your own risk.
--
-- To license this script for a commercial purpose,
-- contact info@rampant.cc
-- **************************************************

grant execute on oltp_job_class to job_user;
grant execute on batch_job_class to job_user;

BEGIN
  DBMS_RESOURCE_MANAGER_PRIVS.grant_switch_consumer_group (
    grantee_name   => 'JOB_USER',
    consumer_group => 'OLTP_CONSUMER_GROUP',
    grant_option   => TRUE);

  DBMS_RESOURCE_MANAGER_PRIVS.grant_switch_consumer_group (
    grantee_name   => 'JOB_USER',
    consumer_group => 'BATCH_CONSUMER_GROUP',
    grant_option   => TRUE);
END;
/
```

With the job classes and privileges in place, create a job to test the resource manager. The *test_resource_manager_job_1.sql* script connects to a user called, job_user, and creates a job associated with the *oltp_job_class* job class.

🖫 test_resource_manager_job_1.sql

```
-- **************************************************
-- Copyright © 2005 by Rampant TechPress
-- This script is free for non-commercial purposes
-- with no warranties.  Use at your own risk.
--
-- To license this script for a commercial purpose,
```

```
-- contact info@rampant.cc
-- *************************************************

conn job_user/job_user
BEGIN
  DBMS_SCHEDULER.create_job (
    job_name        => 'test_resource_manager_job_1',
    job_type        => 'PLSQL_BLOCK',
    job_action      => 'BEGIN DBMS_LOCK.sleep(60); END;',
    job_class       => 'oltp_job_class',
    start_date      => SYSTIMESTAMP,
    end_date        => NULL,
    enabled         => TRUE,
    comments        => 'Job to test a job classes use of the
resource manager.');
END;
/
```

The *running_job_consumer_groups.sql* script uses the *dba_scheduler_running_jobs* view to display the consumer groups associated with each running job.

🖫 running_job_consumer_groups.sql

```
-- *************************************************
-- Copyright © 2005 by Rampant TechPress
-- This script is free for non-commercial purposes
-- with no warranties.  Use at your own risk.
--
-- To license this script for a commercial purpose,
-- contact info@rampant.cc
-- *************************************************

select
   job_name,
   resource_consumer_group
from
   dba_scheduler_running_jobs
order by
   job_name
;
```

The output from the *running_job_consumer_groups.sql* script is displayed below.

```
SQL> @running_job_consumer_groups.sql

JOB_NAME                         RESOURCE_CONSUMER_GROUP
-------------------------------  -------------------------------
TEST_RESOURCE_MANAGER_JOB_1      OLTP_CONSUMER_GROUP

1 row selected.
```

The *consumer_group_usage.sql* script uses the *v$rsrc_consumer_group* view to monitor the relative usage of each consumer group.

🖫 consumer_group_usage.sql

```
-- ***************************************************
-- Copyright © 2005 by Rampant TechPress
-- This script is free for non-commercial purposes
-- with no warranties.  Use at your own risk.
--
-- To license this script for a commercial purpose,
-- contact info@rampant.cc
-- ***************************************************

select
   name,
   consumed_cpu_time
from
   v$rsrc_consumer_group
;
```

The output from this script is listed below.

```
SQL> @consumer_group_usage.sql

NAME                              CONSUMED_CPU_TIME
--------------------------------- -----------------
BATCH_CONSUMER_GROUP                              0
OTHER_GROUPS                                   2502
OLTP_CONSUMER_GROUP                              49

3 rows selected.
```

With the resource allocations and job classes defined, all that is left to do is to define windows to automatically switch between the day and night processing plans. The *create_windows.sql* script creates a 10-hour window associated with daytime processing and a 14-hour window associated with nighttime processing, with both windows added to a newly created window group.

🖫 create_windows.sql

```
-- ***************************************************
-- Copyright © 2005 by Rampant TechPress
-- This script is free for non-commercial purposes
-- with no warranties.  Use at your own risk.
--
-- To license this script for a commercial purpose,
-- contact info@rampant.cc
-- ***************************************************
```

```
BEGIN
  DBMS_SCHEDULER.create_window (
    window_name      => 'day_window',
    resource_plan    => 'day_plan',
    start_date       => SYSTIMESTAMP,
    repeat_interval  => 'freq=daily; byhour=8; byminute=0;
bysecond=0;',
    end_date         => NULL,
    duration         => INTERVAL '10' HOUR,
    window_priority  => 'HIGH',
    comments         => 'Day time processing window.');

  DBMS_SCHEDULER.create_window (
    window_name      => 'night_window',
    resource_plan    => 'night_plan',
    start_date       => SYSTIMESTAMP,
    repeat_interval  => 'freq=daily; byhour=18; byminute=0;
bysecond=0;',
    end_date         => NULL,
    duration         => INTERVAL '14' HOUR,
    window_priority  => 'HIGH',
    comments         => 'Night time processing window.');

  DBMS_SCHEDULER.create_window_group (
    group_name   => 'processing_window_group',
    window_list  => 'day_window, night_window',
    comments     => '24 hour processing window group');
END;
/
```

Using the *windows.sql* script defined in Chapter 2, it can be seen that the windows were created successfully.

```
SQL> @windows.sql

WINDOW_NAME              RESOURCE_PLAN                    ENABL ACTIV
----------------------- ------------------------------- ----- -----
DAY_WINDOW              DAY_PLAN                         TRUE  FALSE
NIGHT_WINDOW           NIGHT_PLAN                       TRUE  FALSE
WEEKEND_WINDOW                                          TRUE  TRUE
WEEKNIGHT_WINDOW                                        TRUE  FALSE

4 rows selected.
```

Rather than waiting for the windows to open automatically, they can be forced to open, and the effects on the active resource plan can be monitored. To do this, open the nighttime window using the *open_window* procedure, and then use the *active_plan.sql* script to display the resource plan currently active on the system.

```
BEGIN
  DBMS_SCHEDULER.open_window (
    window_name => 'night_window',
    duration    => INTERVAL '30' MINUTE,
    force       => TRUE);
END;
/

SQL> @active_plan.sql

NAME                             IS_TO
-------------------------------- -----
NIGHT_PLAN                       TRUE

1 row selected.
```

The output from the *active_plan.sql* script shows that opening the nighttime window has activated the nighttime resource plan, as expected. Now, open the daytime window.

```
BEGIN
  DBMS_SCHEDULER.open_window (
    window_name => 'day_window',
    duration    => INTERVAL '30' MINUTE,
    force       => TRUE);
END;
/

SQL> @active_plan.sql

NAME                             IS_TO
-------------------------------- -----
DAY_PLAN                         TRUE

1 row selected.
```

As expected, opening the daytime window has activated the daytime resource plan.

Windows can overlap, but it is not recommended since only one window can be open at any given time. When windows overlap, Oracle decides which one should open by using the following rules:

- If overlapping windows have the same priority, the currently open window will remain open.

- If overlapping windows have different priorities, the window with the highest priority will open and the lower priority window will be closed.

- When a window closes, the overlapping window with the highest percentage time remaining will open.

- When an open window is dropped, it is automatically closed.

The *drop_windows.sql* script uses the *drop_window* and *drop_window_group* procedures to remove the windows and window group defined in this example.

🖫 *drop_windows.sql*

```
-- *************************************************
-- Copyright © 2005 by Rampant TechPress
-- This script is free for non-commercial purposes
-- with no warranties.  Use at your own risk.
--
-- To license this script for a commercial purpose,
-- contact info@rampant.cc
-- *************************************************

BEGIN
  DBMS_SCHEDULER.drop_window (
    window_name      => 'day_window',
    force            => TRUE);

  DBMS_SCHEDULER.drop_window (
    window_name      => 'night_window',
    force            => TRUE);

  DBMS_SCHEDULER.drop_window_group (
    group_name  => 'processing_window_group',
    force            => TRUE);
END;
/
```

This section has shown how resource plans are created, linked to job classes and switched by windows. Armed with this information, it should be quite simple to create resource allocation schemes to suit various scheduling needs.

Now that information on how to manage the allocation of resources between jobs has been presented, the next section will detail how scheduler objects can be transferred between databases.

Export/Import and the Scheduler

Jobs defined using the *dbms_jobs* package can be exported and imported using the *exp* and *imp* utilities at both schema and full database level.

The import and export of scheduler objects defined using the *dbms_scheduler* package is only supported via the new *datapump* utilities (*expdp* and *impdp*), which are also capable of transferring legacy job definitions. The export process generates Data Definition Language (DDL) which is used to recreate the scheduler objects as they were originally defined, including time zone information. The following simple example shows how these utilities work.

First, a directory object for the *expdp* and *impdp* utilities to work with must be created.

```
conn system/password
create or replace directory export_dir AS '/tmp/';
grant read, write on directory export_dir to job_user;
```

Then, a basic job to be exported by the *expdp* utility is created.

```
conn job_user/job_user
BEGIN
  DBMS_SCHEDULER.create_job (
    job_name        => 'test_expdp_job_1',
    job_type        => 'PLSQL_BLOCK',
    job_action      => 'BEGIN DBMS_LOCK.sleep(10); END;',
    start_date      => SYSTIMESTAMP,
    repeat_interval => 'freq=hourly;',
    end_date        => SYSTIMESTAMP + 1,
    enabled         => TRUE,
    comments        => 'Job to test expdp.');
END;
/
```

From the operating system prompt, run the *expdp* utility to export the *job_user* schema. The following listing shows both the export command and the export log output:

```
expdp system/password schemas=JOB_USER directory=EXPORT_DIR
dumpfile=JOB_USER.dmp
 logfile=expdpJOB_USER.log

Export: Release 10.1.0.2.0 - Production on Saturday, 11 September,
2004 17:47

Copyright (c) 2003, Oracle.  All rights reserved.

Connected to: Oracle Database 10g Enterprise Edition Release
10.1.0.2.0 - Production
With the Partitioning, OLAP and Data Mining options
FLASHBACK automatically enabled to preserve database integrity.
Starting "SYSTEM"."SYS_EXPORT_SCHEMA_01":  system/********
schemas=JOB_USER dire
ctory=EXPORT_DIR dumpfile=JOB_USER.dmp logfile=expdpJOB_USER.log
Estimate in progress using BLOCKS method...
Total estimation using BLOCKS method: 0 KB
Processing object type SCHEMA_EXPORT/USER
```

```
Processing object type SCHEMA_EXPORT/SYSTEM_GRANT
Processing object type SCHEMA_EXPORT/ROLE_GRANT
Processing object type SCHEMA_EXPORT/DEFAULT_ROLE
Processing object type SCHEMA_EXPORT/TABLESPACE_QUOTA
Processing object type
SCHEMA_EXPORT/SE_PRE_SCHEMA_PROCOBJACT/PROCACT_SCHEMA
Processing object type SCHEMA_EXPORT/PROCEDURE/PROCEDURE
Processing object type SCHEMA_EXPORT/PROCEDURE/ALTER_PROCEDURE
Processing object type
SCHEMA_EXPORT/SE_POST_SCHEMA_PROCOBJACT/PROCOBJ
Master table "SYSTEM"."SYS_EXPORT_SCHEMA_01" successfully
loaded/unloaded
**********************************************************************
Dump file set for SYSTEM.SYS_EXPORT_SCHEMA_01 is:
  /tmp/JOB_USER.DMP
Job "SYSTEM"."SYS_EXPORT_SCHEMA_01" successfully completed at 17:48
```

On completion of the export, the *impdp* utility can be run with the *sqlfile* parameter set to create a DDL script containing all the object creation code. The following listing shows both the import command and the import log output:

```
impdp system/password sqlfile=JOBS.sql directory=EXPORT_DIR
dumpfile=JOB_USER.dmp
 logfile=impdpJOB_USER.log

Import: Release 10.1.0.2.0 - Production on Saturday, 11 September,
2004 17:48

Copyright (c) 2003, Oracle.  All rights reserved.

Connected to: Oracle Database 10g Enterprise Edition Release
10.1.0.2.0 - Produc
tion
With the Partitioning, OLAP and Data Mining options
Master table "SYSTEM"."SYS_SQL_FILE_FULL_01" successfully
loaded/unloaded
Starting "SYSTEM"."SYS_SQL_FILE_FULL_01":  system/********
sqlfile=JOBS.sql dire
ctory=EXPORT_DIR dumpfile=JOB_USER.dmp logfile=impdpJOB_USER.log
Processing object type SCHEMA_EXPORT/USER
Processing object type SCHEMA_EXPORT/SYSTEM_GRANT
Processing object type SCHEMA_EXPORT/ROLE_GRANT
Processing object type SCHEMA_EXPORT/DEFAULT_ROLE
Processing object type SCHEMA_EXPORT/TABLESPACE_QUOTA
Processing object type
SCHEMA_EXPORT/SE_PRE_SCHEMA_PROCOBJACT/PROCACT_SCHEMA
Processing object type SCHEMA_EXPORT/PROCEDURE/PROCEDURE
Processing object type SCHEMA_EXPORT/PROCEDURE/ALTER_PROCEDURE
Processing object type
SCHEMA_EXPORT/SE_POST_SCHEMA_PROCOBJACT/PROCOBJ
Job "SYSTEM"."SYS_SQL_FILE_FULL_01" successfully completed at 17:48
```

The resulting *sqlfile* (JOBS.sql) contains creation DDL for all the *job_user* schema objects, including the following job creation script code.

```
BEGIN
dbms_scheduler.create_job ('"TEST_EXPDP_JOB_1"',
job_type=>'PLSQL_BLOCK', job_action=>
'BEGIN DBMS_LOCK.sleep(10); END;'
, number_of_arguments=>0,
start_date=>'11-SEP-04 17.43.18.552000 +01:00', repeat_interval=>
'freq=hourly;'
, end_date=>'12-SEP-04 17.43.18.000000 +01:00',
job_class=>'"DEFAULT_JOB_CLASS"', enabled=>FALSE,
auto_drop=>TRUE,comments=>
'Job to test expdp.'
);
dbms_scheduler.enable('"TEST_EXPDP_JOB_1"');
COMMIT;
END;
/
```

It can be helpful to keep scheduler object definitions as text files in a source control system. As a result, the object definitions would be loaded using the original text files rather than transferring them between databases.

Now that methods for importing and exporting jobs to and from the scheduler have been introduced, the focus of the following section will shift to information on the use of services and instance stickiness in Real Application Cluster (RAC) environments.

Services and Instance Stickiness

Services allow the classification or grouping of applications within a database. This allows application priorities and resource allocation to be managed more effectively. Services can be defined and utilized in both single-node and Real Application Cluster (RAC) environments. The RAC is where they are most useful as they facilitate the coordination of grid computing.

A job class can be assigned to a service, which affects how jobs associated with the job class are executed. When using RAC, jobs belonging to a job class will only run in a RAC instance that is assigned to the specific service. The following rules apply to job classes in relation to services:

- All job classes are assigned to a service. If a service is not explicitly specified, the job class is assigned to the default service, meaning it can run on any RAC instance in the cluster.

- Dropping a service will cause any dependant job classes to be reassigned to the default service.

- Specifying a non-existent service will cause the job class creation to fail.

Services can be configured using the Database Configuration Assistant (*dbca*), *srvctl* utility or the *dbms_service* package. The *dbms_service* package is limited to service administration on a single node; while the *dbca* and *srvctl* utilities can perform cluster-wide configuration and administration. Examples of administering services with the *dbms_service* package are show below.

```
BEGIN
  -- Create a new service associated with the specified TSN service
name.
  DBMS_SERVICE.create_service (
    service_name => 'test_service',
    network_name => 'DB10G.MYDOMAIN.COM');

  -- Start the specified service.
  DBMS_SERVICE.start_service (
    service_name => ' test_service');

  -- Disconnects all sessions associated with the specified service.
  DBMS_SERVICE.disconnect_session (
    service_name => 'test_service');

  -- Stop the specified service.
  DBMS_SERVICE.stop_service (
    service_name => 'test_service');

  -- Delete the specified service.
  DBMS_SERVICE.delete_service (
    service_name => 'test_service');
END;
/
```

Some examples of using the *srvctl* utility to do similar actions are listed below.

```
# Create the service on two nodes.
srvctl add service -d DB10G -s TEST_SERVICE -r DB10G1,DB10G2

# Stop and start the service on a single or multiple nodes.
srvctl stop service -d DB10G -s TEST_SERVICE -i DB10G1,DB10G2
srvctl start service -d DB10G -s TEST_SERVICE -i DB10G1
```

```
# Disable and enable the service on a single or multiple nodes.
srvctl disable service -d DB10G -s TEST_SERVICE -i DB10G1,DB10G2
srvctl enable service -d DB10G -s TEST_SERVICE -i DB10G1

# Display the current status of the service.
srvctl status service -d DB10G -s TEST_SERVICE -v

# Remove the service from both nodes.
srvctl remove service -d DB10G -s TEST_SERVICE -i DB10G1,DB10G2
```

Once a service is present, it can be assigned to a job class during creation or subsequently using the *set_attribute* procedure, as shown below.

```
BEGIN
  DBMS_SCHEDULER.create_job_class (
    job_class_name => 'test_job_class',
    service        => 'test_service');

  DBMS_SCHEDULER.set_attribute (
    name      => 'test_job_class',
    attribute => 'service',
    value     => 'admin_service');
END;
/
```

The following scenario will explain more specifically how services can be used to partition applications in a three node RAC environment.

For services to function correctly, the Global Services Daemon (GSD) must be running on each node in the cluster. The GSD's are started using the *gsdctl* utility, which is part of the Cluster Ready Services (CRS) installation, so they must be started from that environment.

```
# Set environment.
export ORACLE_HOME=/u01/app/oracle/product/10.1.0/crs
export PATH=$ORACLE_HOME/bin:$PATH

# Start GSD daemon.
gsdctl start
```

Once the GSD's are running, the user must check that the cluster configuration is correct. The following command and output show the expected configuration for a three node database called ORCL.

```
srvctl config database -d ORCL
server01 ORCL1 /u01/app/oracle/product/10.1.0/db_1
server02 ORCL2 /u01/app/oracle/product/10.1.0/db_1
server03 ORCL3 /u01/app/oracle/product/10.1.0/db_1
```

This configuration is typically performed during the cluster database creation, but it can be performed subsequently using the following commands.

```
srvctl add database -d ORCL -o /u01/app/oracle/product/10.1.0/db_1
srvctl add instance -d ORCL -i ORCL1 -n server01
srvctl add instance -d ORCL -i ORCL2 -n server02
srvctl add instance -d ORCL -i ORCL3 -n server03
```

Assume that two applications should run in the following way:

- OLTP - Should run on nodes one and two of the RAC, but is able to run on node three if nodes one and two are not available.

- BATCH - Should run on node three, but is able to run on nodes one and two if node three is not available.

To meet this requirement, the following services can be created:

```
# Set environment.
export ORACLE_HOME=/u01/app/oracle/product/10.1.0/db_1
export PATH=$ORACLE_HOME/bin:$PATH

# Create services.
srvctl add service -d ORCL -s OLTP_SERVICE -r ORCL1,ORCL2 -a
ORCL1,ORCL2,ORCL3
srvctl add service -d ORCL -s BATCH_SERVICE -r ORCL3 -a
ORCL1,ORCL2,ORCL3
```

The OLTP_SERVICE is able to run on all RAC nodes, indicated by the -a option, but will run in preference on nodes one and two, indicated by the -r option. The BATCH_SERVICE is able to run on all RAC nodes, indicated by the -a option, but will run in preference on node three, indicated by the -r option.

The services can be started and stopped using the following commands.

```
srvctl start service -d ORCL -s OLTP_SERVICE
srvctl start service -d ORCL -s BATCH_SERVICE

srvctl stop service -d ORCL -s OLTP_SERVICE
srvctl stop service -d ORCL -s BATCH_SERVICE
```

The Oracle10g scheduler allows jobs to be linked with job classes, which in turn can be linked to services to allow jobs to run on specific nodes in a RAC environment. To support the requirements for the job, two job classes might have to be created as follows.

```
-- Create OLTP and BATCH job classes.
BEGIN
  DBMS_SCHEDULER.create_job_class(
    job_class_name => 'OLTP_JOB_CLASS',
    service        => 'OLTP_SERVICE');

  DBMS_SCHEDULER.create_job_class(
    job_class_name => 'BATCH_JOB_CLASS',
    service        => 'BATCH_SERVICE');
END;
/

-- Make sure the relevant users have access to the job classes.
GRANT EXECUTE ON sys.oltp_job_class TO job_user;
GRANT EXECUTE ON sys.batch_job_class TO job_user;
```

These job classes can then be assigned to existing jobs or during job creation.

```
-- Create a job associated with a job class.
BEGIN
  DBMS_SCHEDULER.create_job (
    job_name        => 'my_user.oltp_job_test',
    job_type        => 'PLSQL_BLOCK',
    job_action      => 'BEGIN NULL; END;',
    start_date      => SYSTIMESTAMP,
    repeat_interval => 'FREQ=DAILY;',
    job_class       => 'SYS.OLTP_JOB_CLASS',
    end_date        => NULL,
    enabled         => TRUE,
    comments        => 'Job linked to the OLTP_JOB_CLASS.');
END;
/

-- Assign a job class to an existing job.
EXEC DBMS_SCHEDULER.set_attribute ('MY_BATCH_JOB', 'JOB_CLASS',
'BATCH_JOB_CLASS');
```

The use of services is not restricted to scheduled jobs. These services can be used in the tnsnames.ora file to influence which nodes are used for each applications. An example of the tnsnames.ora file entries are displayed below.

```
OLTP =
  (DESCRIPTION =
    (LOAD_BALANCE = ON)
    (FAILOVER = ON)
    (ADDRESS = (PROTOCOL = TCP)(HOST = server01)(PORT = 1521))
    (ADDRESS = (PROTOCOL = TCP)(HOST = server02)(PORT = 1521))
    (ADDRESS = (PROTOCOL = TCP)(HOST = server03)(PORT = 1521))
    (CONNECT_DATA =
      (SERVICE_NAME = OLTP_SERVICE)
      (FAILOVER_MODE =
        (TYPE = SELECT)
```

```
        (METHOD = BASIC)
        (RETRIES = 20)
        (DELAY = 1)
      )
    )
  )

BATCH =
  (DESCRIPTION =
    (LOAD_BALANCE = ON)
    (FAILOVER = ON)
    (ADDRESS = (PROTOCOL = TCP)(HOST = server01)(PORT = 1521))
    (ADDRESS = (PROTOCOL = TCP)(HOST = server02)(PORT = 1521))
    (ADDRESS = (PROTOCOL = TCP)(HOST = server03)(PORT = 1521))
    (CONNECT_DATA =
      (SERVICE_NAME = BATCH_SERVICE)
      (FAILOVER_MODE =
        (TYPE = SELECT)
        (METHOD = BASIC)
        (RETRIES = 20)
        (DELAY = 1)
      )
    )
  )
```

Provided applications use the appropriate connection identifier, they should only connect to the nodes associated to the service.

Although not directly related to services, it is sensible to discuss the concept of instance stickiness at this point. It has been shown that services can be used to associate jobs to one or more RAC instances in the cluster, but having a job run on a different instance each time can result in performance issues. For example, a job on the first node of the cluster may be executed, during which time all the data necessary to perform the job is read from disk into the buffer cache. On the second execution the job runs on the second node.

As most of the data necessary to perform the job is already in the cache of the first node, the data must be passed across the clusters interconnect before the second job can proceed. If the job had executed on the first node again, this network transfer would not have been necessary. This is the reason for instance stickiness.

The *instance_stickiness* parameter for an individual job defaults to TRUE, meaning that the job will run repeatedly on the same node, assuming it is available and not severely overloaded. The default value can be modified using the *set_attribute* procedure as shown below.

```
BEGIN
  DBMS_SCHEDULER.set_attribute (
    name      => 'test_stickiness_job',
    attribute => 'instance_stickiness',
    value     => FALSE);
END;
/
```

With the *instance_stickiness* parameter set to FALSE, the job can run on any available node in the cluster.

Now that information has been presented on how services can be used in a RAC environment, it would be prudent to move on to the subject of the security issues related to the scheduler.

Security

Chapter 2 of this text outlined roles and privileges associated with the scheduler, which form the basis of the security mechanism. All users that need to schedule jobs should be granted the CREATE JOB privilege, while users that need to administer the scheduler should be granted the MANAGE SCHEDULER privilege. Granting excessive privileges can be dangerous, in terms of security risks, as users may be able to run code as different users. Granting the CREATE ANY JOB privilege enables a user to schedule a job as the SYSTEM user, which effectively gives them unlimited privileges. In addition to running commands, the user could grant to themself any extra privileges using a method like the one listed below.

```
-- Check the current roles assigned to JOB_USER.
conn sys/password as sysdba
select
   granted_role
from
   user_role_privs
where
   username = 'JOB_USER';

GRANTED_ROLE
------------------------------
CONNECT
SELECT_CATALOG_ROLE

2 rows selected.
```

```
-- Grant excessive privileges to JOB_USER by accident.
grant create any job to job_user;

-- JOB_USER exploits the extra privileges by creating a job
-- as the SYSTEM user to grant the DBA role to JOB_USER.
conn job_user/job_user

BEGIN
  DBMS_SCHEDULER.create_job (
    job_name        => 'system.dangerous_job',
    job_type        => 'PLSQL_BLOCK',
    job_action      => 'BEGIN EXECUTE IMMEDIATE ''GRANT DBA TO
job_user''; END;',
    start_date      => SYSTIMESTAMP,
    enabled         => TRUE);
END;
/

-- Check the current roles assigned to JOB_USER.
-- Notice that the DBA role is present.
select
  granted_role
from
  user_role_privs
where
  username = 'JOB_USER';

GRANTED_ROLE
------------------------------
CONNECT
DBA
SELECT_CATALOG_ROLE

3 rows selected.
```

The scheduler allows external jobs to be run using the executable *program_type* or *job_type*, which may introduce a whole set of security issues. If a privileged operating system user runs external jobs, any database user with the CREATE JOB privilege has the ability to run operating system commands and scripts as that privileged user. Needless to say, this can quickly become a security nightmare.

Depending on the operating system, there may be some extra post installation steps required to configure jobs to run as a low-privileged guest user.

The safest option is not to allow any users except the DBAs to create jobs. Not only does this limit any potential security holes, but it also prevents users from scheduling resource intensive and inefficient jobs without understanding the consequences.

Over the last few years, the number of security flaws identified in software packages has risen dramatically to the point where the identification of new flaws is almost a daily occurrence. Unfortunately, Oracle software is not immune to this problem, so every effort should be made to keep on top of the latest security advisories and patches. This approach should dramatically reduce the amount of security holes in the system.

With security issues addressed, the following section will introduce the methods available for setting scheduler object-specific attributes.

Setting Scheduler Object Attributes

Many scheduler object attributes can be amended after object creation using the *set_attribute* overloaded procedures. Enabled objects are typically disabled, amended and then re-enabled. Problems during this process result in the object being left in a disabled state, which results in the generation of an error. Objects that are already disabled remain disabled after they are altered.

Using the *set_attribute* procedure against job classes, windows and window groups requires the MANAGE SCHEDULER privilege.

In most cases, alterations to objects do not affect the currently running instance of that object. For example, altering a window definition will not affect the currently open window, but its effect will be seen the next time that window opens.

The following tables show which attributes can be altered for each object type. Many of the attributes can be set during object creation, but some can only be altered subsequently.

Table 6.1 below lists the associated job attributes and their descriptions.

ATTRIBUTE	DESCRIPTION
logging_level	The amount of logging that should be done for this job, specified by the constants *logging_off*, *logging_runs* and *logging_full*.
restartable	Specifies whether a job can be restarted in the event of a failure. If set to TRUE, a failure will result in the job being retried up to six times. The run and failure counts are not incremented as part of failure retries. The scheduler waits for one second after a failure before a retry. After each successive failure, the delay is increased by a factor of 10. The retries end when a retry is successful, the sixth retry fails or the run date of the next retry is later than the next scheduled "proper" run date.
max_failures	Specifies the number of consecutive failures after which the job is disabled. Valid values range from one to 1,000,000 with the default value being NULL, which implies no limit.
max_runs	Specifies the maximum number of times the job can run, after which it is disabled and its status is set to COMPLETED.
job_weight	Specifies the degree of parallelism with valid values ranging from one to 100, with the default value being one.
instance_stickiness	Specifies if the job should attempt to run on the same instance in a RAC environment. Typically, the server with the lightest load will run a job. If this parameter is set to TRUE, all subsequent runs will occur on the same RAC node unless it is unavailable or extremely overloaded.
stop_on_window_close	Specifies whether the job should be forced to stop when the open window which specifies its schedule closes. If set to FALSE, the job will continue to run after the window closes, but its resource allocation may change.
job_priority	Specifies the priority in which the jobs should be executed by the scheduler if multiple jobs share the same run date. The default value is three, with valid values ranging from one to five.
schedule_limit	Specifies the maximum delay allowable between the proposed run date and the actual run date, after which the scheduled run will be skipped. On a heavily loaded system there may be some delay before a job is executed. This parameter allows an

ATTRIBUTE	DESCRIPTION
	upper limit to be set, between one minute and 99 days, after which the job run is deemed not desirable and can skipped until the next scheduled job run. A value of NULL implies the job cab be run regardless of any delay. When a job run is skipped, it has no effect on the run or failure counts, but the event is logged.
program_name	The name of the program which defines the action of the job. This parameter and the inline program definition attributes (job_action, job_type and number_of_arguments) are mutually exclusive.
job_action	The actual work that is done by the job.
job_type	The type of action associated with this job (plsql_block, stored_procedure or executable).
number_of_arguments	The number of arguments required by this job. Programs that use arguments, must have their arguments defines before they can be enabled.
schedule_name	The name of the schedule, window or window group used to define the job schedule. This parameter and the inline schedule attributes (start_date, end_date and repeat_interval) are mutually exclusive.
repeat_interval	The definition of how often the job should execute. A value of NULL indicates that the job should only run once. The repeat interval is defined using a PL/SQL expression or the calendaring syntax, which is new to Oracle10g.
start_date	The date when this schedule will take effect. This may be in the future scheduled jobs are being set up in advance.
end_date	The date when this schedule will stop. This combined with the start_date parameter enables a job to be scheduled for a finite period of time.
job_class	The job class associated with this job. If no job_class is defined, the default_job_class is assigned.
auto_drop	Indicates if the job should be dropped once it has run for the last time.
comments	Free text, allowing additional information to be recorded.

Table 6.1 – *Job attributes and descriptions*

Table 6.2 below lists the associated program attributes and their descriptions.

ATTRIBUTE	DESCRIPTION
program_action	The actual work that is done by the program.
program_type	The type of action associated with this program (plsql_block, stored_procedure or executable).
number_of_arguments	The number of arguments required by this program. Programs using arguments must have their arguments defined before they can be enabled.
comments	Free text, allowing additional information to be recorded.

Table 6.2 – *Program attributes and descriptions*

Table 6.3 below lists the associated schedule attributes and their descriptions.

ATTRIBUTE	DESCRIPTION
repeat_interval	The definition of how often the job should execute. A value of NULL indicates that the job should only run once. The repeat interval is defined using a calendaring syntax, which is new to Oracle10g.
start_date	The date when this schedule will take effect. This may be in the future if scheduled jobs are being set up in advance.
end_date	The date when this schedule will stop. This combined with the start_date parameter enables a job to be scheduled for a finite period of time.
comments	Free text, allowing additional information to be recorded.

Table 6.3 – *Schedule attributes and descriptions*

Table 6.4 below lists the associated job class attributes and their descriptions.

ATTRIBUTE	DESCRIPTION
resource_consumer_group	The resource consumer group associated with the job class.
service	The service database object the job belongs to, not the tnsnames.ora service.
logging_level	The amount of logging that should be done for this job, specified by the constants logging_off, logging_runs and logging_full.
log_history	The number of days the logging information is kept before purging.
comments	Free text, allowing additional information to be recorded.

Table 6.4 – *Job class attributes and descriptions*

Table 6.5 below lists the associated window attributes and their descriptions.

ATTRIBUTE	DESCRIPTION
resource_plan	The resource plan associated with the window. When the window opens, the system switches to use the associated resource plan. When the window closes, the system switches back to the previous resource plan.
window_priority	The priority ('LOW' or 'HIGH') of the window. In the even of multiple windows opening at the same time windows with a high priority take precedence over windows with a low priority, which is the default.
duration	The length of time in minutes the window should remain open.
schedule_name	The date after which the scheduler starts to return valid run dates.
repeat_interval	The date after which the scheduler starts to return valid run dates.
start_date	The date when this window will take effect. This may be in the future, if you are setting up window in advance.
end_date	The date when this window will stop. This combined with the start_date parameter enables a window to be scheduled for a finite period of time.
comments	Free text, allowing additional information to be recorded.

Table 6.5 – *Window attributes and descriptions*

Table 6.6 below lists the associated window group attributes and their descriptions.

ATTRIBUTE	DESCRIPTION
Comments	Free text, allowing additional information to be recorded.

Table 6.6 – *Window group attributes and descriptions*

Familiarity with these attributes and their descriptions will assist the properly authorized user in amending object attributes using the *set_attribute* overloaded procedures.

Conclusion

This chapter has introduced a wide variety of advanced scheduler topics including:

- Setting scheduler attributes to affect the default actions of the scheduler.

- Assigning job priorities to affect the order of execution of jobs within classes.

- Controlling the volumes and types of logs produced by the scheduler.

- Use of the links between the scheduler and the resource manager to control resource allocation for scheduled tasks.

- Transferring scheduler objects between databases.

- Use of services in Real Application Cluster (RAC) databases.

- Security considerations for the scheduler.

- Setting scheduler object specific attributes.

Book Conclusion

In the past the Oracle scheduler has been relegated to scheduling simple database tasks, but in my opinion the Oracle 10g scheduler provides the first real alternative to operating system schedulers.

This book is intended to give the reader an in-depth knowledge of the Oracle scheduling mechanisms available in both Oracle 10g and previous Oracle versions, along with an overview of operating system schedulers. Armed with this information you can create complex scheduling patterns along with simple run-only-once jobs.

As an author it is great to get feedback about your work. If you have any comments or suggestions feel free to post them on my forum at **http://www.oracle-base.com/forums/** or e-mail me at **info@rampant.cc**

For up to date articles, scripts and tips on a wide variety of Oracle topics visit my website **http://www.oracle-base.com**.

Regards

Tim...

Dr. Timothy S Hall

Index

About Dr. Timothy Hall

Dr. Tim Hall is an Oracle Certified Professional DBA (7.3, 8, 8i, 9i, 10g) and has been involved in DBA, design and development work with Oracle databases since graduating from university in 1994 with a PhD in Molecular Genetics.

Tim Hall has vast knowledge of the Oracle software stack and has worked as a consultant for several multi-national companies on projects ranging from real-time control systems to OLTP web applications. Since 2000 he has published over 200 articles on his website <u>www.oracle-base.com</u> covering a wide range of Oracle features.

Tim has been a Karate black belt since 1993 and is a practitioner and qualified teacher of Hatha and Ashtanga yoga. In addition he enjoys running, having completed 2002 London Marathon.

About Mike Reed

When he first started drawing, Mike Reed drew just to amuse himself. It wasn't long, though, before he knew he wanted to be an artist. Today he does illustrations for children's books, magazines, catalogs, and ads.

He also teaches illustration at the College of Visual Art in St. Paul, Minnesota. Mike Reed says, "Making pictures is like acting — you can paint yourself into the action." He often paints on the computer, but he also draws in pen and ink and paints in acrylics. He feels that learning to draw well is the key to being a successful artist.

Mike is regarded as one of the nation's premier illustrators and is the creator of the popular "Flame Warriors" illustrations at www.flamewarriors.com, a website devoted to Internet insults. "To enter his Flame Warriors site is sort of like entering a hellish Sesame Street populated by Oscar the Grouch and 83 of his relatives." – Los Angeles Times. (http://redwing.hutman.net/%7Emreed/warriorshtm/lat.htm)

Mike Reed has always enjoyed reading. As a young child, he liked the Dr. Seuss books. Later, he started reading biographies and war stories. One reason why he feels lucky to be an illustrator is because he can listen to books on tape while he works. Mike is available to provide custom illustrations for all manner of publications at reasonable prices. Mike can be reached at www.mikereedillustration.com.